VENICE & VERONA FOR THE SHAMELESS HEDONIST

ARIELA BANKIER

2015

Front Cover Photo: canadastock/Shutteretock.com.
Back Cover Photo: canadastock/Shutterstock.com

Series Manager: Ariela Bankier

Editor: Emma Tracey

Technical Editor: Lorna Simmons

General note: Travel information tends to change quickly. Shops may close without notice, and some sites and restaurants may change or reduce their opening hours unexpectedly. For this reason, we recommend confirming the details in this guide before your departure, just to be on the safe side.

Venice & Verona *for the* Shameless Hedonist

The difference between a good trip, and an incredible one

ARIELA BANKIER

Table of contents

There is a difference between a good trip and an incredible one.

And while planning a reasonably enjoyable vacation in Venice, Verona and their surroundings isn't too much of a challenge, designing a unique and memorable journey is an entirely different story.

Venice & Verona for the Shameless Hedonist was written for travelers who, much like us, want more. This book is for those who aren't interested in settling for the usual round of restaurants, touristy shops and attractions that are listed in most guides and online. Rather, this guide was written for fellow travelers who seek to discover and experience the very best that Venice and Verona have to offer—from the finest places to enjoy a good meal with a mesmerizing view to first-rate hotels overlooking the Grand Canal; from personalized rowing lessons that will turn you into a real *gondoliere* to cooking classes held in grand historic mansions; from tiny but delicious neighborhood eateries only the locals know about to the most scenic wine tours; from pampering spas to private after-hours tours in the city's best museums; from the hottest events and most sought-after carnival parties to the best *cicheti* bars and best-value shops that hide just off Piazza San Marco.

While the main focus of the guide is the city of Venice itself, we couldn't ignore the temptations hidden in the environs. We have toured the highways and byways of Veneto to bring you the best of the best, including restaurants with panoramic views in Verona, must-visit wineries in the hills of Prosecco and Valpolicella, the top thermal spring spas of Abano Terme, the best outlet shopping villages, and even tips on where you can rent a Ferrari and take it out for a spin. All of these attractions are located within an hour's drive of Venice, making them the perfect destination for a day trip outside the city.

This guide is the result of years of research, and includes suggestions and ideas that will speak to different travelers. It was composed with passion and, naturally, reflects our taste. But we have taken into account the opinions of many others. We have trusted the experiences of friends, family, and local connoisseurs, in the hope of offering a comprehensive and balanced list. For this reason, we recommend using this guide as a reference book, alongside your standard travel guide. Read through it, choose the suggestions that interest you most, and incorporate them into your trip. Even if you use no more than five to ten of our recommendations, we are confident those will be some of the most memorable moments of your vacation.

There is something for everyone in the guide. Foodies will discover dozens of recommendations to help them navigate Venice's many restaurants, *cicheti* bars and specialty food shops. We make suggestions about where to taste the best traditional Venetian delicacies, where to enjoy an authentic and delicious *aperitivo*, and where you might find the finest local gastronomy. We list both Michelin-starred restaurants and small neighborhood eateries that serve up the freshest seafood straight from the lagoon, expertly prepared risotto, creamy polenta, tender steaks, and imaginative *antipasti*.

Wine lovers will be pleased to discover several tips dedicated to the world-famous wines of Veneto. We explain the regional wine tradition; where to buy the best bottles of Valpolicella, Amarone, Prosecco and Soave; which centuries-old estates sell the most delicious reds and whites; which *enoteche* are perfect for enjoying a merry drink with the locals; and which wine tours and tastings simply shouldn't be missed.

Shopping enthusiasts will enjoy our tips. For bargain hunters, we know all about discount Armani and Roberto Cavalli in Venice and Verona's leading outlet villages and hidden outlet shops. We also list all the must-visit streets and alleys that offer the absolutely best shops for clothing, leather gloves, jewelry and shoes in Venice, and even an exclusive shop selling handcrafted items made by the inmates at Venice's women's prison.

We offer top tips on the most authentic Venetian mask ateliers; exclusive décor boutiques; antique shops and markets; and old-world shops stocking traditional and handmade paper goods. Naturally, we dedicate an entire section to Venice's famous glass industry, and recommend several family-run Murano glass shops where savvy buyers will find stunning artifacts that aren't available anywhere else.

Nature buffs and experience-seekers will appreciate our tips about guided hikes and excursions, rowing lessons in the Venetian lagoon, kayak lessons, exciting helicopter rides above Venice and Verona, adrenalin-filled quad tours of the dolomites, and horseback rides across the Veneto countryside. We also list some of the best panoramic spots in Venice, Verona and Veneto, and reveal several hidden corners of beauty, perfect for a memorable picnic or a relaxing walk.

History and art lovers will revel in our suggestions about colorful medieval parades, opulent 18th century villas that once entertained the most prominent noble families and world leaders, and tours of charming historical gardens that are famous across Europe. We also review some of the most important festivals and cultural events that take place in Venice, everything from the Carnival, the art Biennale and the Redentore celebration to the world-famous Venice Film Festival and the city's most popular rowing competitions.

Even though Venice is an expensive city, we make a point of recommending activities that are suitable for various budgets. And while we do propose a number of high-end resorts and pricey restaurants, we also believe that a shameless hedonist doesn't necessarily have to be a big spender. Years of traveling in Italy have proven to us that price is not always a reflection of quality; in fact, many of the most delicious and unique discoveries we've made are surprisingly affordable, and we consistently try to bring them to the attention of our readers.

Lastly, we do our best to make our readers' traveling experiences as easy and hassle-free as possible, leaving them time and energy to focus on the beauty and magic of Venice itself. For this reason, we have included valuable information in our detailed introduction that will help you bypass the most common tourist pitfalls. We have also included an index at the end of the book, listing the featured attractions and recommendations by category. To read more of our reviews and updates, visit us at: www.travel-italy.guru.

We hope you have a wonderful adventure in Venice and Verona and discover the charms of this region, just as we have been doing for the past decade.

Buon Viaggio!

Ariela Bankier

Planning Your Trip

Choosing When to Travel

Venice and Verona are busy year-round, but the busiest months are July through August. There are pros and cons to summer travel in Venice. The pros are obvious—most of the cultural events and festivities (not just in Venice but in the Veneto region) take place in the summer. The days are longer, which means you can get more done. And the fine weather permits you to explore every angle without worrying about storms or the "*acqua alta*" (the periodic rising of the water level in Venice, which leads to extensive flooding in the city). Additionally, hours of operation for attractions are longer, as they are adapted for the influx of tourists. The cons, on the other hand, are also quite clear. During the summer months, everything is extremely crowded, especially the public transport system and the popular sights. There are hordes of people in every canal and piazza, and there are long lines for every major attraction. Hotel prices are also higher; a well-located apartment or room in a popular hotel can cost 35% to 40% more during the summer months.

The loveliest times of the year to visit Venice, in our opinion, are May through June and September. Though you may come across occasional bad weather, for the most part the weather is pleasant, most shops and attractions are open, and the city is relatively calmer and less crowded. From November to March, rain tends to spoil most of the fun.

Documents You'll Need Before Leaving

If you are an EU citizen, you will just need your ID card. We also recommend bringing your national health certificate with you; it allows you to receive free emergency medical treatment if needed. If you are from outside the EU, you will need to bring a passport. Passports must be valid for at least six more months from the date of your entry into Italy. We also recommend making photocopies and virtual copies of all your important documents in case anything gets lost or stolen. Scan the documents and e-mail them to yourself, or save them onto a USB drive, or both.

If you plan on renting a car, you will need a driver's license and a credit card. Most companies require at least two years of driving experience, and the credit card must be under the same name as the driver's license.

You may also want to print out driving or walking directions to your hotels. If you plan on sleeping in Venice, be sure to find out in advance which *vaporetto* (public water bus) stop is closest to your hotel, and print out precise walking instructions.

If you've booked any e-tickets or rented your car online, print out the confirmation letter. Some companies require just the code you were sent; others require the actual printed ticket/voucher, especially if there is a barcode on it.

If you are flying with low-cost companies like Ryanair or EasyJet, carefully read about their online check-in process and luggage limitations, which can be very strict, and print out any required documentation.

Local Money and Credit Cards

Like the rest of the EU, prices in Italy are in euro. As of July 2015, €1 was worth about $1.14 or £0.74, though you should check the rates yourself before traveling. Venice is a city of tourists, and it is quite easy to find a place to exchange money; there are exchange offices (*Cambio*, in Italian) in the train station, the airport, and the city center. In Verona you can exchange money in the airport, at the central train station, and in the city center. When exchanging money, in Italy or in your home country, ask for bills no bigger than €50. €100 bills are hard to break, and €500 bills, which are very rare, will arouse suspicion.

If you have an international credit card (a very useful item; contact your bank for more information.) you can also simply withdraw money in the local currency from ATMs across Italy. This has become an increasingly popular solution for tourists, as most exchange places offer poor exchange rates and charge a high additional handling fee. Withdrawing cash from the ATM also saves visitors from the need to travel with large amounts of cash. Though these cards do save a great deal of hassle, they are also notorious for the high commissions charged by the banks, both for the withdrawals and for the conversion from dollars/pounds to euro, so do check in advance what those might be. We also recommend notifying your bank before you leave the country that you will be using your card abroad. Some travelers forget to do so, and their cards get blocked, because the bank thinks the card was stolen and is being used fraudulently.

If you are planning to use your US credit card in Italy (not just for withdrawing money but also for paying in hotels and restaurants), you should know that many businesses only accept Visa and MasterCard. American Express and Diners are far less common in Italy, and some small restaurants and shops don't accept them at all.

Lastly, note that US credit cards and European credit cards have different security systems. While the new standard in Europe is cards with microchips (and a PIN code), many cards in the US still rely on magnetic strips. Though most machines in Italy can read both types of cards, some machines, especially automatic machines (such as ticket selling machines in train stations and gas machines at gas stations), might not be able to read your card. If you have a PIN for your card that consists of numbers and letters, contact your bank and replace it. ATM machines in Italy can only read cards with four- or five-digit PINs.

Fraud

Two of the most common frauds involve counterfeit bills or coins and identity theft. The probability that you will be given a counterfeit €20, or even €100, bill is extremely low. This trick is mostly used in stores when trying to scam the owners. Counterfeit coins, however, can sometimes be found in markets; check the €2 coin you're given as change to make sure it really is a €2 coin and not an old 500-lire coin. The two look very similar, but the lire is obviously now worth nothing. Identity theft happens when thieves attach small cameras to ATMs to steal PINs. Simply cover your hand with your other hand, your wallet, or a scarf while entering the PIN to avoid any problems.

Another thing to watch out for is people who stop you on the street and ask you to sign various petitions, usually "against drugs," "against poverty," or "for the children." These are obviously not real campaigns, and even though they may be quite persistent, we highly recommend you avoid giving them your signature.

Crime

Both Venice and are Verona are very calm cities, and even though there is, naturally, some criminal activity, tourists rarely feel unsafe. The biggest hassle is pickpockets, and the items most at risk are your wallet, your camera and your smartphone. A little common sense will go a long way toward avoiding unpleasant events. Never leave your phone or camera unattended or in a half-open bag, especially when you are on the *vaporetto* (in Venice), on the bus (in Verona), or at a crowded tourist sight. Don't carry all of your money in one bag, so that even if you do get targeted, you won't lose $600. If your hotel has a reliable safe, leave some of your money there. Always keep your hand on your bag, and never put your wallet in your pocket or in the outer or side pockets of your backpack or purse, where it can be pulled out without you even noticing. We promise you that the pickpockets in Venice could teach Fagin, Oliver Twist and the rest of the crew a trick or two.

Even more importantly, don't put your documents and your cash in the same wallet; that way, if your wallet does happen to get stolen, you will still have your passport and tickets, and your vacation won't be ruined. Write down the emergency number of your credit card company so you can call immediately if your credit card is stolen. For obvious reasons, don't keep that piece of paper in your wallet. Instead, hide it, together with an emergency 100-euro bill, in some unlikely place. If you do get robbed, you will need to file a complaint at the police station, so they can help you get new documents and for insurance purposes. Try to do this as quickly as possible, as some banks and insurance companies insist that you lodge a complaint within the first twenty-four hours of the robbery.

Insurance

Consider taking out some kind of travel and luggage insurance. There are several options available, and a quick search online will yield affordable results. If you plan on taking part in any physical activities while on vacation, or if you suffer from any medical problems, good travel insurance becomes an even better idea.

Emergency Numbers and Medical Emergencies

Call 113 or 112 from any phone to reach the police.

Call 118 for an ambulance.

If you need a pharmacy, hospital or any other shop or service, call 1254. This will put you in touch with an information service, where an operator will help you find whatever you are looking for. Alternatively, use the Italian yellow pages website: www.paginegialle.it

Medical Assistance

There are a number of private clinics in Venice, but finding an English-speaking doctor can be difficult. If there is an emergency, go directly to the hospital. Venice's main hospital is SS. Giovanni e Paolo Hospital (Castello 6777, Campo Santi Giovanni e Paolo. *Vaporetto* stop: Ospedale. Tel: 041.529.4111). You won't be turned away even if you don't have insurance, and it may even cost less than a private doctor. Alternatively, take a cab from Piazzale Roma straight to the hospital in Mestre (10 minutes from Venice). The Mestre Hospital can be found in Via Paccagnella 11. Tel: 041.9657111.

In Verona, go to the AOUI Hospital in Piazzale Aristide Stefani 1. Tel: 045.812.1111, www.ospedaleuniverona.it.

If you have travel insurance, don't forget to contact your insurance company before going to any hospital or clinic. Most insurance companies will provide you with the name of a specific English-speaking doctor they work with, and won't necessarily cover the expenses at other clinics.

Additionally, we highly recommend bringing some basic medicines with you—ear and eye drops, pain killers, antacid, vitamins, and, of course, whatever prescription drugs you require. (Bring extra, just in case.) There are numerous pharmacies in Venice, but they won't necessarily carry the specific medicines you are used to, and trying to translate the name, or finding out the local equivalent of the medicine you need when you are ill, can be quite a hassle.

Calling Home and Using the Internet While in Italy

Aside from the well-known apps you can use on your computer or smartphone to call home, such as Skype or WhatsApp, you can also buy a local SIM card to use during your travels. This is an especially good idea if you plan on staying for a week or more in Italy. Keep the SIM after you return home, and use it for your next trip to Italy. It should remain functional for two to five years.

A local SIM card will work with your phone as long as you have a GSM-compatible, unlocked phone—which means it will work in Europe—and your phone allows the use of SIM cards other than the original one. If you don't have such a phone, you can get one in Italy for a very reasonable fee. An Italian SIM card costs €5 to €10 and is already charged with that amount. You can add more money and activate an Internet service that will allow you to use your phone and the Internet during your entire trip in Italy for a very low fee. You will need an ID or passport to buy a SIM card, as the shop must make a photocopy for legal reasons. Normally, your phone will be activated within 24 hours or less. You can buy a SIM card at the airport, at the Santa Lucia train station in Venice, or at any of the main cell phone operators' shops (try WIND, TIM or VEDODAFONE). These can be found on the main streets in both Venice and Verona. Make sure you buy a SIM card from an authorized shop only.

Ask for *ricaricabile*, which means pay-as-you-go, and ask the shop to activate the cheapest Internet offer they have, which usually works out at around €9 per month. Don't forget to deactivate the service when you leave Italy.

If you are using your own non-Italian SIM card, make sure you deactivate international data roaming, which can be very costly.

Getting into Italian Mode

Hours of operation

As time goes by, more shops and museums are adopting what is known as *orario continuato*, which means they are open all day long, but this is not yet the norm for Italian businesses. Many shops, especially in smaller towns but also in Venice and Verona, still operate according to traditional business hours.

Shops: Tuesday–Saturday, 10:00 a.m. –1:00 p.m. and 3:00/4:00 p.m.–6:30/7:00/7:30 p.m.; Sunday, most shops are either closed or open during the morning hours only; Monday, many shops are open in the afternoon only (especially in Verona).

Banks: Monday–Friday: 8:30 a.m.–12:30/1:00/1:30 p.m. and 2:00/2:30 p.m.–3:30/4:00/4:30 p.m. Closed weekends.

Trains: There are very few trains after 10:00 p.m. and virtually no trains between midnight and 5:00 a.m., except for a few night trains.

Restaurants: Most restaurants are closed one day a week, and the closing day changes from restaurant to restaurant. The most common closing days are Monday and Tuesday. Additionally, many restaurants close for vacation in January, February, and a couple of weeks in August.

Museums: In Venice, most (but not all) museums are open daily. If you are traveling to other parts of Italy, know that many museums are closed on Monday. To be on the safe side, check the museum's website before visiting.

National Holidays

Everything, including museums, attractions, and most shops and restaurants, will be closed on:

January 1	New Year's Day
January 6	Epiphany
Monday after Easter	Easter Monday
April 25	Liberation Day
May 1	International Workers' Day
June 2	Republic Day
August 15	Assumption Day
November 1	All Saints' Day
December 8	Immaculate Conception Day
December 25	Christmas
December 26	St. Stephen's Day

Traveling Off-Season and in August

August, though part of the high season, is a month when many Italians go on vacation. Although they often don't bother to mention it on their websites, some restaurants, markets, and shops may close for a week or two for what is known as *ferie*, or vacation holiday. This is most common during the second and third weeks of August. If you are traveling during that period, it might be a good idea to double-check whether a place is open before making your way there.

When traveling off-season, from November to April, you run the risk of finding quite a few places, especially restaurants, but in some cases even attractions and museums, closed or with reduced hours of operation. Additionally, many shops close down for the winter break, which lasts from the third week of December until January 7. Certain tourist attractions may also close down in January and February and reopen in March. Double-check everything to be on the safe side. This is yet another advantage of having a local SIM; you can always call before driving somewhere, avoiding the disappointment of finding closed doors.

Understanding Italian Phone Numbers

Italian home and office telephone numbers have an area code, followed by the number. Rome's area code, for example, is 06, Milan's is 02, and Venice's is 041. Whether you call a number from within Italy or from abroad, you have to dial the full area code, including the zero at the beginning (unlike area codes in other countries, where you must remove the zero when calling from abroad).

Cell phone numbers begin with 3. For example: 338.2222222 or 329.4444444, etc. Calling a cell phone is more expensive than calling a landline.

Understanding Addresses in Venice

The address system in Venice is different from other cities in Italy, and has to do with the city's unique structure. It is also very hard to navigate, and even if you are given the most precise address possible, it is still very likely that you will get lost. Venice is built like a crazy maze, and navigating it is a skill that has to be honed during one lifetime, at least.

The most basic thing you should know is that Venice is divided into six wards, or neighborhoods (*sestieri* in Italian). There are three wards on one side of the Grand Canal, and three on the other side. The six wards are: San Marco, Cannaregio, Dorsoduro, Santa Croce, Castello and San Polo.

A typical address in Venice includes the name of the ward followed by the house number. For example: Hotel Ciao, San Marco 3427. This indicates that Hotel Ciao is located within the San Marco ward, at number 3427. However, unless you are using a GPS, there is no way of knowing exactly where number 3427 is located within the large perimeter of San Marco ward. For this reason, most locals add a second piece of information, indicating the specific *calle* (street, in Venetian lingo) on which the hotel is located, or at least the nearest *campo* (town square). With that extra piece of information, the address is: Hotel Ciao, Calle dei Genti, San Marco 3427. This means that you have to locate Calle dei Genti within the San Marco ward, and somewhere along that street you will find the hotel you are looking for.

Since Venetians are aware of just how impossible their system is, they usually add some more information when possible, and tell you the nearest *vaporetto* stop and the nearest church (both serve as an anchor point for starting your navigation).

As you can imagine, navigating the streets of Venice without a very good map or GPS is somewhat of an impossible mission. The map provided by the tourist information office isn't enough. It can only give you a general indication of the layout of the city and the main *calli* (streets) and *campi* (town squares). This is actually sufficient for finding the largest sights in town (Piazza San Marco, the Rialto Bridge, the Accademia, etc.), but isn't enough if you want to locate any specific restaurants or hotels. We usually use the GPS on our phone (and bring an extra battery, since the GPS will leave your phone empty in no time), but there are traditional paper maps, too. If you want to invest in a serious road map, then buy a book called *Calli, Campielli e Canali*. It lists all the streets, the tiniest alleys, and all the canals and bridges in an easy-to-follow manner, and is very useful. Alternatively, pick up a good map of the city (such as the one published by the Italian Touring Club) at a newsstand. This should be enough for standard navigation. It is also worth mentioning that throughout the historic center you will find brass signs indicating the way to Piazza San Marco, the Rialto Bridge or the Santa Lucia train station. That, together with the constant stream of people making their way to these focal points, will help you know in which general direction to proceed.

One last piece of information has to do with the peculiar nomenclature in Venice. While everywhere else in Italy a street is called *via*, and a town square is called a *piazza*, in Venice the locals have come up with very different terminology, which is useful to learn in advance:

Ca': The Venetian term for *palazzo* (building, in Italian. Usually indicates an important building, not just any house).

Calle: the Venetian word for *via*, meaning street.

Campo: the local name for *piazza*. Remember, in Venice there is only one piazza and that's Piazza San Marco. All the other town squares are known as *campo* (or *campiello*—a little town square). Most *campi* (the plural form of *campo*) are named after the church around which they are built, and are an important focal point in your attempts to navigate the city.

Canale: a large canal

Fondamenta: a road along the water

Ramo: a street branching from a larger street

Riva: the roads along the Grand Canal.

Salizzada: a wider street

Ponte: bridge

Understanding Addresses in Verona and the Rest of Italy

Venice aside, addresses in Italy always include the name of the street (*via* in Italian), the name of the town, and the province in which the town is located. For example: Hotel Ciao, Via Marconi 4, Negrar (Verona). In this case, Hotel Ciao is located on Marconi Street, in the town of Negrar, which is in the province of Verona. The reason the province is added to the address is that there are many towns with the same name all over Italy, and without specifying the province there will be confusion. This is also helpful to remember when you are setting your GPS. Note that the province is named after its largest town, but that doesn't mean that everything will be close to that town. The province of Verona, for example, consists of the city of Verona and 97 other towns and villages, some of which are quite far from Verona itself. If booking a hotel, never rely exclusively on the address provided to determine whether the hotel is close enough to the city center; we recommend always consulting Google maps, too.

Most addresses are similar to the example reported above, but in some cases, especially when looking for hotels and restaurants that are located in the countryside, you will find addresses like this:

Hotel Buongiorno
Via Puccini 14
Loc. San Terme
Verona

Loc. stands for *località*, and it simply means a suburb or small village that technically is part of the town but is physically located outside the town itself. If you don't have a car, you will have a very difficult time reaching these places. Another type of address you may encounter is:

Agriturismo Ciao Bella
Pod. Marche
Verona

Pod. stands for *podere*, which means a farm, and in this example, the farm is located near Verona (but not actually in Verona). A *podere* will always be in the countryside. Typically this address belongs to a horseback riding ranch, an *agriturismo* (a B&B on a farm) or even a remote restaurant. If you book an *agriturismo* or dinner in such a place, see if they can give you their GPS coordinates, which will make navigation much easier.

Driving, Parking, and Renting a Car

Driving in Italy

Though you don't need a car in Venice (or Verona, for that matter, as it is quite small), you might decide to rent a car to visit other parts of northern Italy. If you are an EU citizen, your driver's license is valid in Italy, and you need no other documentation. If you are traveling from outside the

EU, you need to obtain an International Driving Permit before leaving for Italy. Driving in Italy is just like driving in any other country. Don't be intimidated by stories of horrifying and insane Italian drivers; for the most part, they are not true.

The Italian road system is fairly easy to navigate. There are two kinds of highways in Italy: free and toll. Those with a toll are called *autostrada*, and they are marked with green road signs. The free roads have different names (SP, SR, SS, etc.) but are always marked with blue road signs. When traveling in northern Italy, it is likely that you will choose to use the *autostrada* most of the time. Traveling on the small country roads takes a lot more time, and what you save on tolls you spend on gas. Ideally, take the *autostrada* when traveling between large cities, but choose the smaller and far more scenic country roads when you tour the province itself.

Drinking and driving: The maximum amount of alcohol permitted in your blood while driving is 0.5 mg/ml. This is especially relevant if you plan on doing any wine tasting in the many delightful little vineyards of the Valpolicella and Prosecco hills during your trip.

What are ZTLs and Why Should They Be Avoided?

Limited traffic zones (in Italian, *zona traffico limitato* – ZTLs) are an issue that many tourists aren't aware of. They should be, however, as ZTLs are the main reason tourists are fined when traveling in Italy. Most towns in Italy protect their historical centers, which is where most of the attractions are, by defining them as ZTLs where only residents can drive or park. There is a security camera at the entrance to any ZTL that registers your vehicle number and sends you or your rental company notification of a fine, which, together with the handling fees charged by the rental company, is about €100.

Stories about tourists getting confused, entering the same ZTL three times in less than 10 minutes, and being fined each time are more common than you'd think. Our best advice is to simply avoid driving in the city center (*centro storico*, in Italian). Most town centers, including Verona, are so small that you don't really need a car anyway. If arriving by car, park in a car park outside the *centro storico* and walk or take a bus from there. You will usually find very accessible car parks, especially in touristy towns.

What does a ZTL sign look like? A white circle surrounded by a red ring and next to it another sign saying ZTL (or *zona traffico limitato*).

Renting a Car in Italy

The major rental companies in Italy are Avis, Europcar, Sixt, and Hertz. In Venice, they all have offices at the airport, and a number of companies keep offices at Piazzale Roma, too. In Verona, all the major rental companies keep an office at the airport and some have a smaller office near the train station, too. We suggest looking into all four before booking a car.

You can rent a car in Italy if you are over 21 and have had a license for more than two years. Some companies require only one year of experience. When renting a car, you have to present personal identification (a passport or an ID card for EU citizens) and a credit card, though not a debit card. The name of the person renting the car must be on both; for example, you can't rent a car with Mr. Smith's license and pay with Mrs. Smith's credit card. There are a number of insurance options, but we recommend taking the most comprehensive. Regardless of the type of insurance you have, mark every scratch and bump on the car. Some insurance deals claim to be all-inclusive, but the small print can reveal that damage to things like mirrors, the underside of the car, the wheels or even the car upholstery is not covered.

You should know that most cars in Italy have a manual transmission (stick). If you don't feel comfortable driving such a car, make sure you specifically order a model you are comfortable with. Most cars in Italy run on gas (*benzina*, in Italian) but some run on diesel. Cars that run on diesel will save you money.

Always fill the gas tank when returning the car; you will be charged extra if the company has to fill it for you. You will also be charged extra for returning the car dirty; you don't have to take it to the car wash; just make sure it's acceptably clean. Charges can also be incurred for returning the car at a different office than the one where you picked it up, handling any fines or tickets you receive, and renting accessories such as a GPS, snow chains, or baby seats.

GPS units are very useful and we highly recommend using them with this guide for a number of reasons. First, they are far more convenient to use than maps (phone apps like Waze are excellent, but will use up your battery very quickly, leaving you lost with a dead phone). Second, signs in Italy are often hard to understand or follow. It is not unusual to find a tiny sign indicating the exit to the town you need just a few meters before the exit itself. Signs on regular country roads (i.e., not *autotstrada*) are often quite small and can't be easily seen from afar. On rural roads, which are also very poorly illuminated, it is highly unlikely that you will be able to see any of the signs if driving after dark. A GPS will save you the hassle of having to play detective and indicate when and where to turn. If you plan on renting a car with a GPS for a week or more, it's probably cheaper to buy your own GPS, as long as it has recently updated European maps on it. You can walk into any of the three largest chain stores for electronics in Italy—Mediaworld, Euronics, or Unieuro—and buy a GPS that includes all world maps for about €100 and then take it back home with you. You can also buy a GPS at home and bring it with you.

Snow chains are required by law if traveling between mid-November and mid-April. Rental companies never seem to mention this, but if you are stopped by the police and don't have snow chains or snow tires, you are the one who will have to pay a hefty fine, not the rental company.

One last thing: Try not to fill your car with gas on Sunday. There is usually no one manning gas stations on Sunday, so you will have to use the automatic machine; it isn't complicated at all, but may be a problem if you don't have exact change.

Parking

Parking spaces marked with white lines or no lines at all mean parking is free. That is, of course, unless there is a sign prohibiting parking in that area. Blue lines mean you have to pay for parking: Look for the parking meters around the parking lot or on the street, decide how long you will stay, and put the appropriate amount of change in the machine. (Note that these machines only accept coins, not bills.) Take the receipt the machine prints out and put it facing out, on the dashboard of your car, near the steering wheel. Yellow lines mean you can't park there; these spaces are reserved for those with permits.

To find out more about parking in Venice and Verona, consult our "Parking in Venice" and "Parking in Verona" sections below.

Moving around on Public Transportation

Trains

Trains are an excellent way to move around and reach the main towns. Venice's main train station is **Venezia Santa Lucia**, and Verona's is **Verona Porta Nuova.**

The two main train companies that operate from Venezia Santa Lucia are **Trenitalia** and **Italo**. Trenitalia is Italy's national train company, and as such it covers the entire country, going to every province and small town. Italo, on the other hand, is a relatively new and privately owned company that connects only the major cities in Italy, such as Rome, Florence, Venice, and Napoli. Verona, for example, isn't currently serviced by the Italo lines.

Buying a Ticket for a Trenitalia Train

The Trenitalia trains can be divided into two categories: regular trains, known as regional or IC trains, and high-speed trains, which are collectively known as Freccia trains. The high-speed Freccia trains connect major cities—like Rome, Milan, or Florence—but not small towns (those can only be reached on the IC or regional trains). Freccia tickets are more expensive and they have a specific time and place for boarding. If you miss your train, you'll have to go to the ticket office and change your ticket. Regional trains, on the other hand, have no specific seating or boarding restrictions.

To buy a ticket in the train station, go to the ticket office (*Biglietteria* in Italian) or use the self-service machines. The self-service machines are easy to use, and you can select a menu in English, too. But before you start, take a look at the pictures at the top of the machine; some only have a picture of a credit card, which means they don't accept cash.

When purchasing a ticket from the self-service machines, you will be given the option to purchase either first-class or second-class tickets. It is worth noting that on regional trains (unlike Freccia trains) first class is no different from second class, and sometimes is even unmarked. So, on regional trains, it makes sense to choose the second-class option and save the money.

Lastly, a useful tip: If you are traveling a short distance, usually under 80 km, say from Venice to Mestre or Treviso, you can buy a generic "up to X km" ticket at a newspaper stand, instead of waiting in line at the ticket office. Just make sure this ticket covers the right distance. Ask the vendor, "Va bene per X?" meaning, "Is this ticket okay for reaching X?" In the Venice train station there is a newsstand next to Track 3, and two more stands outside the station itself.

Whichever ticket you buy, always validate it in one of the little white-and-green machines near the tracks before getting on the train. A ticket is valid for six hours from the time it is validated. A non-validated ticket can lead to a hefty fine.

Buying a Ticket for an Italo Train

Italo offers only one kind of train, the standard Italo train, but the cars are divided into various categories, offering various seating plans—there are "smart tickets" that can be bought in advance for a considerable discount, XL seats, seats with a cinema service, and more. To find out about the various seating options and to review Italo's many offers, consult their website: www.italotreno.it. Italo tickets can be bought online, or at the Italo ticket office (which is usually located near the Trenitalia ticket office).

Finding Your Way in the Train Station

With the exception of Venice and Verona, most train stations in Veneto are rather small and easy to navigate. Tracks are called *binari* (singular *binario*), and in every station you will find screens or electronic boards listing the departing trains (*partenze*) and the arriving trains (*arrivi*).

It can happen that when you go to look for your train on the departures board, the board lists a different destination than what is on your ticket. Let's say, for example, that you've just bought a ticket to go to from Venice to Treviso. Your ticket says "Treviso" and you were told at the ticket office that the train will leave at 4:00 p.m. Yet, when you check the departures (*partenze*) board to find out which track (*binario*) your train is leaving from, you don't see a train leaving for Treviso at 4:00, there's only a train to Udine. Don't be alarmed. The station that appears on the departures board is the final destination, and most regional trains (and some high speed Freccia trains) make several stops along the way. It is very likely that the stop you need to reach isn't the final destination of the train, which is why it doesn't appear on the board. Simply walk to the track and check the more detailed board on the track itself. It will list all the stops along the route. If you are still unsure, simply ask one of the station staff.

Getting to Venice

By airplane

Venice has its own airport, the Marco Polo Airport, which is located about seven kilometers from the city center. It isn't a very large airport, but it is convenient, and many national and international flights land here. The airport has a detailed website where you can read more about the various airlines that fly here, as well as parking in the airport and other services: www.veniceairport.it.

To get from the airport to Venice city center, you will need to take a water taxi (about €120) or use the services of the Alilaguna company, which operates a private *vaporetto* (water bus) that connects the airport with Venice. The public *vaporetto* system does not cover the airport. The Alilaguna tickets cost €14 one-way and €27 for a round trip, and you may board with one suitcase and one handbag. Extra luggage will be charged separately (about €3 per bag). Alternatively, if you don't want to arrive by water, take a bus or a regular taxi from the airport to Piazzale Roma (a taxi will cost €40 to €50). Then, from Piazzale Roma, proceed on the public *vaporetto* (water bus) lines.

By train

Trains from all over Italy arrive at Venice's main train station, Venezia Santa Lucia. The station has been expanded in recent years, and today you will find, among other things, the ticket office for Trenitalia trains, the ticket office for Italo trains, a small tourist information office, a number of shops, and a luggage deposit room where you can leave your bags (both the tourist information office and the luggage room are located by Track 1). Right outside the train station you will find the stop for many of the *vaporetto* lines; almost every *vaporetto* line in town makes a stop at Santa Lucia (the train station *vaporetto* stop is called: Ferrovia).

By car

Venice is built on the water, so driving is obviously out of the question. The farthest point you can get to with your car is one of parking lots offered to visitors. From that point on, you can walk, take a private water taxi, or use the public *vaporetto* system.

The two best-known parking lots in Venice are located in **Piazzale Roma** (www.avmspa.it) and in **Tronchetto** (www.veniceparking.it). Both are very large and well-connected to Venice itself (by the public *vaporetto* system), which means you can get directly to town from the parking lot without having to get a water taxi; both are fairly expensive—about €25 per day (depending on the size of your vehicle and the time of your arrival). Note that most parking lots calculate a day from the time of your arrival until midnight, not 24 full hours). You can usually book a spot in advance and save up to 50% on the cost.

Other parking options are available. If you don't necessarily want to park in Venice itself, you can park in the large parking lot in front of the **Mestre** train station (in Viale Stazione 10, right next to the Best Western Hotel Bologna). If you come on a weekday, you might pay as little as €10 a day, though prices change in high season and on weekends. Consult their website to find out more and book in advance: www.sabait.it. To reach Venice from this parking lot, simply cross the street, enter the Mestre train station, and take the regional train to Venezia Santa Lucia.

Another option is parking at the **Venice Airport Parking Lot**. Prices at the airport are much more reasonable than the lots in Piazzale Roma and Tronchetto, and you can pay as little as €4.50 a day if you book a spot in advance, online. The main issue, however, is getting from the airport to the city center, which can be fairly expensive. If you plan on parking for just one day, then choosing the airport parking lot doesn't make much sense. But if you plan on spending a number of days in town, or even a week, then the airport lot is absolutely worth considering. Find out more here: www.veniceairport.it.

Getting to Verona

By train

If you are planning a day trip to Verona from Venice, you will most likely take the train. Trains leave every 15 to 45 minutes (depending on the hour of the day. Note that there are very few trains between 10:00 a.m. and 11:50 a.m. and after 9:00 p.m.). With the Freccia trains, you will be in Verona within 80 minutes. With the regional trains, your trip will take about 2.5 hours.

By plane

Verona is major city in Veneto, and as such, it prides itself on its own airport (Verona Villafranca Airport, sometimes referred to as "Valerio Catullo Airport"). When searching for a convenient flight to Italy, it is worth considering flying to Verona instead of Venice, if you find a good deal. Verona's airport is located right outside the city, and is connected to the main train station via shuttle bus, which runs every 20 minutes (between 5:30 a.m. and 11:30 p.m.).

By car

The easiest way to reach Verona is by car. The reason is that Verona's train station, unlike in most other towns in Italy, is quite far away from the town center and has to be reached by bus. With a car, on the other hand, you can park at one of the centrally located parking lots, which are just two minutes (on foot) away from the main sights. Use your GPS to navigate your way to the town center (take care not to go into any ZTLs) and park at **Parcheggio Cittadella** (located in Piazza Cittadella, just 200 meters from the Arena), where you will find a small street-level parking lot and a very large underground parking lot; or at the **Arena Parcheggio** (Via M. Bentegodi 8), which is also quite conveniently located and close to the Arena. Note that parking in Verona is rather expensive (about €16 for 24 hours).

Moving around in Venice

The two most common ways to move around in Venice are by foot and by the public *vaporetto* system (which is operated by ACTV – www.actv.it). The *vaporetti* are basically water buses, and they connect various points in the city as well as some of the main islands in the lagoon (Lido, Murano and Burano, etc.). A single fare on the *vaporetto* is quite expensive (currently a ticket costs €7.50), which means that buying a 24-, 36- or 72-hour pass, or a weekly pass, instead of a few single tickets, makes much more sense. If you plan on staying in town for four or five days, buy the weekly ticket, it's a better deal than buying two three-day tickets. Discounts for senior citizens, children, and people under 28 are also available. Note that children under 6 usually don't have to pay at all, but these terms tend to change, and must be verified at the ticket office.

If you plan on visiting various sights and places of interest in Venice, the best option is to buy the **Venezia Unica** city pass. This gives you access to the entire *vaporetto* system (excluding the private Alilaguna vaporetto to the airport) and entry to most of the attractions and museums in Venice. If you book online in advance, you can get even better discounts. We highly recommend consulting their website before your visit: www.veneziaunica.it. Whichever ticket you choose, keep it close at hand—you'll have to validate it with the electronic machines by the vaporetto piers every time you board a *vaporetto*.

The *vaporetto* system may seem complicated at first, but it is actually quite easy to navigate, especially if you are used to metro, tube and underground railway systems. The *vaporetti* leave from small piers. The *vaporetto* line is clearly marked on top, and often the pier is divided into two separate sections—one for each direction.

The two most important lines for tourists are *vaporetto* lines 1 and 2. These cross the Grand Canal and stop at the top tourist sights (Line 1 is the slowest, because it makes more stops en route). You can pick up a map of all the lines and their timetables at the ticket office, including the night *vaporetti*. Note that *vaporetti* have different timetables during the year (in high season and off-season) to match the influx of tourists.

Aside from the *vaporetti*, you will quickly discover that walking is the most common way to get around. And it's a great way to discover the city's hidden corners. If you need to cross from one side of the Grand Canal to the other, you can do so by using the ***traghetti***. This is a secret that locals would like to keep to themselves. Basically, there are only four bridges that connect the two sides of the Grand Canal, so if you want to get from one side to the other, you have to walk quite a distance. The solution? *Traghetti*—gondolas that will help you cross from one side to the other for a modest fee (€1.50). There are a number of *traghetti* crossings; the main ones are: from San Stefano to San Tomà; from the Ferrovia to San Simeon; from Riva del Carbon to Riva del Vin; from San Samuele to Ca' Rezzonico, and from Santa Sofia to Pescheria. Note that these are meant for locals so they have limited operating hours, usually from 8:00 a.m. to 1:00 p.m.

Staying in Venice

Types of lodging in Venice

One of the most difficult tasks for tourists visiting Venice is choosing a place to stay. And as you might expect in a city visited by over 20 million tourists a year, Venice offers quite a selection of lodging options – there are literally hundreds of hotels, bed and breakfasts (B&Bs), apartments and resorts to choose from.

Hotels are one of the most popular choices. Many are located in renovated medieval or Renaissance town houses that have been remodeled to accommodate guests. This means that on the one hand, you will enjoy a truly authentic sojourn, in a *palazzo* (Ca', in Venetian dialect) that was probably erected 200 or 300 or even 500 years ago, and often still boasts original fixtures. On the other hand, this means that modern amenities might be lacking, elevators will be a rare sight, and in many cases the Wi-Fi will be weak, because medieval walls are very thick.

If you are interested in a specific hotel, we highly recommend you book in advance, since many of the better hotels in town are booked solid months in advance. Booking can be done directly through the hotel, or through websites such as www.booking.com, www.expedia.com, www.venere.com, www.skyscanner.com, www.hotel.com, and www.hotelpricebot.com (a website that compares the prices on various websites and helps you choose the best one). These websites often offer very competitive deals, even lower than the prices offered by the hotel websites, but if you need to modify your booking, it might be difficult—read their terms. Whichever hotel you choose, we highly recommend checking the reviews of other travelers on websites such as TripAdvisor and Booking.com before you book.

B&Bs are another popular choice. They offer the comfort of a simple hotel, but in a much more accessible price range. We have recommended a number of B&Bs in this guide, and you can find additional choices on the aforementioned websites, and on specific bed and breakfast websites such as www.bed-and-breakfast.it.

Renting a small apartment can be very convenient, especially if you are traveling as a family. We would recommend consulting websites such as www.homeaway.com, www.homeinitaly.com, www.housetrip.com, www.flipkey.com, www.viewsonevenice.com and www.venicerentapartments.com to find the best options.

If renting an apartment, be sure to ask what the price includes to avoid unpleasant surprises. Is there a minimum number of nights? Does the price include all cleaning charges? Will you be charged separately for electricity, gas, or heating? Does the price include a weekly change of linen and use of the laundry room and Wi-Fi? Is the apartment properly furnished and adequate for daily cooking and living? This last question is especially important if you plan on shopping in local markets and cooking for yourself most nights.

Where to stay

Picking a location to stay in Venice requires a basic understanding of how the city is built and how to move around it. This issue seems important enough for us to review in detail, to help you make the most informed decision.

In or outside Venice?

The first decision you should make is whether you are going to stay in or outside Venice. Many travelers on a budget choose to stay outside of Venice, because in high season hotel prices in town can be very high. These travelers usually end up booking a room in Mestre, which is technically a different city, but from a practical point of view – it's like a suburb of Venice. Other travelers might book a room in a different town altogether (such as Treviso, 30 minutes away). So before we discuss staying in Venice itself, let's discuss the alternatives:

Outside Venice: Mestre

Mestre is the last stop on land before Venice, and is only 15 minutes away from the Venezia Santa Lucia train station. There are some cheap lodging options in Mestre, and some not-so-cheap options (hotels such as the Best Western and the Trieste are priced similarly to hotels in Venice). Personally, we don't recommend booking your stay in Mestre, for a number of reasons. The first and most important reason is ambiance. Venice is an incredibly beautiful city. Certain parts of it, and we don't use this word lightly, are awe-inspiring. Mestre, on the other hand, is industrial and very unappealing. Certain sections, especially those around the train station, are unpleasant, to say the least. It's important to note this, because if you've been dreaming of a Venetian getaway or a special romantic holiday, then spending your days in a hotel in Mestre is going to be a very big letdown. We wouldn't come here unless we found a very good deal that made up for the location and the commute, which brings us to our second point.

Getting from Mestre to Venice is easy enough, but you should know that if you are planning any late nights (after 11:00 p.m.), you won't be able to return to your hotel in Mestre using public transportation. Instead, you'll need to get a taxi from Piazzale Roma, and not only are these expensive, but there are also not that many of them.

If you do decide to book a room or an apartment in Mestre, we recommend choosing one of the many hotels in the area around the train station (the Best Western, located right in front of the Mestre station, is a good choice), and avoiding the hotels that tout themselves as being "just five minutes from Venice by bus." The reason is simple—it is very easy to reach Venice from Mestre by train. The bus, on the other hand, is incredibly crowded and messy.

Outside Venice: Surrounding towns

Some travelers choose to stay in other towns in the area and travel to Venice every morning and evening. The most popular choices are the towns located along the railway line, such as Treviso. In our opinion, this is a reasonable option only if you've found a very good deal on a hotel that is: a) in a town that is no more than 30 minutes from Venice, and b) the hotel is within a five-minute walk from the train station in said town. The Continental Hotel in Treviso is a good example: Treviso is 30 minutes from Venice, and the hotel itself is no more than 200 meters from the Treviso train station. Anything farther won't be as convenient, and won't justify the time you'll have to spend commuting back and forth and the money you'll have to spend on train tickets.

Another option is staying in a resort or a bed and breakfast in the countryside and driving daily to Venice with your rental car (parking each morning in Piazzale Roma or Tronchetto). We would only recommend this option if you are in Venice as part of a longer trip, and you plan on spending just a couple of days in town with your kids and then moving on to other destinations in northern Italy. In that case, a family-friendly resort with a pool would justify the hassle of the daily drive to Venice and the expensive parking.

In Venice

Staying in Venice itself is the best option, in our opinion. With so many hotels, B&Bs and apartments in town, it is very likely that you will find something to your taste and within your budget.

Staying in Venice lets you enjoy and really get to know the town. There's something truly magical about wandering the streets of Venice at night after a romantic meal, walking along the canals, crossing the little bridges lit only by moonlight and the occasional street lamp, and seeing the city at play. At night, when the hustle and bustle of the tourist-flooded town calms down, you really can see another face of Venice. Not having to leave to commute to Mestre or some other town means you can enjoy your evening without needing to constantly check your watch. Dinner can be followed by drinks in a little *campo*, and then just walking around, enjoying yourselves and forgetting the rest of the world exists.

If you decide to stay in Venice itself, choose your hotel based on three main factors: **location, closeness to the vaporetto stops**, and **ambiance**.

While ambiance is a subjective matter and depends on your personal taste, location and closeness to the *vaporetti* are two much more technical details.

As mentioned previously, mainland Venice is divided into six wards: San Marco, Cannaregio and Castello on one side of the canal, and San Polo, Santa Croce and Dorsoduro on the other side of the canal. Giudecca Island is across the lagoon, just minutes from Piazza San Marco, and farther away (between 15 minutes and an hour) are the famous islands of Lido, Murano, Burano, and Torcello. Additionally, a number of hotels are located on private islands of their own in the lagoon (these can be reached by water taxi or using the hotel's shuttle).

Each of these locations offers a different kind of stay. If you want to be in the very heart of Venice, where most shops, events and museums are concentrated, choose a hotel in the San Marco neighborhood. If you want an area that is quieter than San Marco, but still lively, choose Dorsoduro. San Polo, though slightly off the beaten track, is another reasonable choice.

The other wards – Cannaregio, Castello and Santa Croce – are a little too far away from the main sights to be considered a first choice, but they do feature some very good surprises here and there. Choose one of these neighborhoods if you are hunting for a bargain hotel and don't mind spending 20 minutes on the *vaporetto* to reach the city center each day. It's worth remembering that moving around in Venice is a very slow business. Because of the way the city is built, expect everything to take about double the time it would take if you were traveling by land in another city.

Choosing a hotel on one of the islands off the mainland, such as Murano, Burano, and Lido, is not the best idea, as you will be far from the sights and spend a great deal of time commuting (Burano is more than an hour from Venice). If you do specifically want one of the islands, we would suggest Lido; it's only about 20 minutes by public *vaporetto* from the mainland, and offers many beaches to enjoy and a pleasant laid back atmosphere. For a more residential, slightly quirky experience, consider Giudecca. It offers a surprising range of B&Bs that are usually very low-key (apart from the Belmond Cipriani Hotel and the Bauer Hotel, two of the most exclusive addresses in the city). The Giudecca is also home to Venice's only youth hostel.

Lastly, the area around the Santa Lucia train station isn't recommended, unless you are looking for a cheap one- or two-star hotel.

Staying in Verona

Choosing a place to stay in Verona is very simple. Anything within a reasonable walking distance of Piazza Bra and Piazza Erbe—the town's two main squares—is a good choice. To simplify things further, we've listed some delightful B&Bs and romantic *agriturismi* in the guide.

Eating and Drinking in Venice

Food is one of the greatest joys Italy has to offer, and this guide does its best to introduce visitors to the many gastronomic delights available in and around Venice.

Eating in Venice can and should be a series of happy culinary discoveries. However, it is also true that the city is chockablock with mediocre and expensive restaurants that leave visitors hungry and frustrated. To help avoid such disappointments, we have listed not only specific recommendations of some of the best restaurants in town, everything from small family-run *trattorie* to Michelin-starred restaurants, but also several tips and recommendations about what to order and where. Additionally, to really make the most of your dining experiences, it is useful to understand some background on the Italian culinary tradition.

Venice's kitchen is influenced by its position, right on the sea. Fish and seafood are hugely important ingredients, while meat takes a secondary position on the menu (and in some restaurants it disappears altogether). Pasta dishes are very popular, but since this is northern Italy, risotto and polenta dishes can be found almost everywhere. As far as cooking techniques go, it's interesting to remember that Venice was an international power for many centuries; Venetian merchants traveled the world and bought back knowledge, new tastes and trends, and especially spices and cooking techniques, which have blended into local fare.

Verona's kitchen is similar in many ways to the Venetian kitchen, with some modifications. Seafood is less dominant, and far more meat dishes can be found on the menu. The Veronese love their meat, and it is very common to find large platters of cold cuts for *antipasto*, and various grilled meats for your *secondo*. The Veronese aren't shy about eating less-common meats, either, such as horse meat. In fact, you'd be surprised by the number of restaurants that serve *carne di cavallo* (horse meat), especially the famous *pastissada de caval*, a slow-cooked horse stew enriched with Valpolicella wine and spices.

Breakfast, Lunch and Dinner

The three main meals in Italy are *colazione*, *pranzo*, and *cena*. *Colazione*, or breakfast, is usually eaten in a bar. In Italy, that isn't a place that serves alcohol, but rather a venue that serves coffee and snacks in the morning and sandwiches later in the day. Italian breakfast is very limited, and unless you are staying at a good hotel that is accustomed to working with American or German tourists and serves a full breakfast buffet, you might be surprised to find that the traditional Italian *colazione* consists of nothing more than a cappuccino, a brioche, and some marmalade or Nutella to spread on a piece of toast.

Pranzo, or lunch, is usually served between 12:30 p.m. and 2:00 p.m. You will find very few, if any, restaurants that serve lunch later than 2:30 p.m. *Cena*, or dinner, is served between 7:30 p.m. and 9:30 p.m. With the exception of pizzerias, most places won't seat you at a table after 9:30, unless they run two dinner turns (one at 7:30 p.m. and one at 9:00 p.m.).

Unless you buy a sandwich to go or sit down for a light lunch in a bar, you will usually eat in a *ristorante*, a *trattoria*, or an osteria. The *ristorante* is the more high-end, serious dining option; it's stylish and reserved, with prices to match. *Osterie* and *trattorie* are more homey; they cost less and have a more casual atmosphere, but they can also be huge discoveries, as they often offer excellent, authentic Venetian food. To enjoy the best that Venice has to offer, we suggest mixing things up, and trying out both homey *trattorie* and upscale, sophisticated *ristoranti*.

Whichever restaurant you choose, whether it is a neighborhood diner or a 3-star extravaganza, remember that most restaurants are closed one day a week, even in high season. Whenever possible, we have inserted the relevant info in the guide, but for other places not mentioned in this book we recommend you call to see when they are closed.

What should we order?

Breakfast

If you ask for *un caffè*, you'll get an espresso. Alternatively, ask for a *cappuccino* or a *caffè latte*, which is closer to the Starbucks version of coffee, with a lot of milk. Note that if you ask for a *latte* (the popular American term), you will simply get a glass of milk and a perplexed look! You can also try a *macchiato*, which is an espresso with a touch of milk foam. Our personal recommendation for the hot summer months is to ask for a *shakerato* (pronounced "shekerato"), a refreshing cold coffee shaken with ice cubes. If you want it sweetened, make sure you ask for it *con zucchero*. Accompany that with a brioche or *cornetto* (the Italian version of a croissant); there are plenty to choose from, and they will all be on display, together with a small selection of savory sandwiches. If you eat standing up by the bar, as most Italians do, you will be charged less than if you sit down at a table and order. If it's been a long day of sightseeing and you need an afternoon pick-me-up, you can always ask for *un caffè corretto*, which is an espresso "corrected" with a shot of grappa, sambuca or some other liqueur.

Lunch and Dinner

A traditional Italian meal starts with an *antipasto*, which is a selection of meats, seafood dishes, cheeses, and other little bites that will awaken your appetite. The *primo*, or first dish, usually follows and is most typically pasta, soup, or a *risotto*. Next is the *secondo*, or main dish, which usually consists of meat or fish. The *secondo* can be served with a *contorno*, or side dish, usually vegetables, roasted potatoes, or French fries, and is followed by a *dolce*, or dessert and a coffee (*espresso* or a *macchiato*, an Italian will never order a cappuccino after a meal). At dinnertime, this is occasionally followed by an *ammazzacaffè*, also known as *digestivo*. This is a liqueur, like limoncello, to help you digest. Of course, each course is accompanied by wine, whether it's the house wine or your choice of a bottle, and water.

Clearly, you won't be able to order this much food every time you sit down to eat. What most Italians do is choose a *primo* or a *secondo* and add something small that can be shared, like an *antipasto*, a *contorno*, or even just a dessert. Whatever your order, bread and water will be brought to the table. Bread is free, included in the price of the *coperto* (see below), while water is charged separately. You can ask for still water (*naturale*) or fizzy water (*frizzante*). We have yet to see an Italian restaurant that serves tap water.

Naturally, when eating in a *trattoria* or *osteria*, you will be asked if you want the house wine to go with your food. Though the house wine is often perfectly tasty, in recent years we've started ordering a bottle from the menu. The reason is simple: If you are planning to drink more than a glass each, it is worth it to pay a little extra and get a bottle of something better to complement your meal, rather than settling for whatever the restaurant has on hand at the moment.

Antipasti

Venice is famous for its seafood, and one of the best ways to discover the full selection is by trying various *antipasti*. Unlike the restaurants in Milan,

Florence, Rome, or even Verona, where the *antipasti* will often be a plate of cold cuts and cheeses, most Venetian restaurants pride themselves on a wide selection of seafood-based *antipasti* (vegetarian and meat-based options are far more limited).

The two most popular *antipasti* are *sarde in saor* (sweet and sour sardines) and *baccala mantecato* (creamed cod, usually served with polenta). Mixed antipasti plates of steamed or raw seafood are also very popular. These might include everything from tuna carpaccio to raw langoustines (*scampi crudi*), a selection of *gamberi* (shrimp), *cozze* (mussels), *vongole* (clams), grilled or boiled tiny octopuses (*moscardini*), *granseola* (spider crab, typical of Venice), and other seasonal seafood. *Peppata di cozze* (sautéed mussels in tomato sauce), *cappesante gratinate* (creamed scallops), and *moleche fritte* (fried crabs), are also popular.

Primo

On the menu for the *primo* (the first dish) you will usually find either pasta with a seafood based sauce, or a risotto. The stars of the Venetian *primi* are *pasta e fagioli* (a traditional Veneto style stew, made with a meaty broth, pasta and beans, which is quite popular in Verona, too), *spaghetti alle vongole* (spaghetti with clams), *spaghetti alle seppie* (black spaghetti, prepared with cuttlefish ink), *spaghetti allo scoglio* (spaghetti with a mix of clams and shrimp and tomato sauce), *bigoli in salsa* (a thick maccheroni-like pasta typical of Venice, served with a traditional anchovy and sautéed onion sauce), *risotto ai frutti di mare* (seafood risotto), and *risotto agli asparagi* (available in season only—a delightful risotto made with fresh asparagus). You will usually (but not always) find a selection of non-seafood options, too, such as ravioli, gnocchi, lasagna, pasta with tomato sauce, and more.

In Verona the choice also includes many meat-based *primi*. Some of the better-known dishes are *risi e bisi* (a rice and pea dish), gnocchi served with various condiments, pumpkin-filled tortellini, anything with polenta, and the famous *risotto all'amarone* (a classic risotto cooked with the rich-tasting Amarone wine).

Secondo

For the main dish, the *secondo*, you will normally be given a choice of fish- or meat-based dishes. (Once again, the fish-based selection is much wider in most restaurants in Venice. Check the menu before sitting down for your meal, to make sure there is something that matches your preferences.)

Meat lovers will want to try the most famous Venetian dish, *fegato alla Veneziana* (veal liver cooked in sauce and served with polenta). Other popular options are *spezzatino* (beef stew), *ossobuco* (braised veal shank) steaks and grilled meats. Those who are ready to sample more delicacies of the sea will enjoy an abundant selection of fresh grilled fish and seafood, such as *coda di rospo* (monk fish), *anguilla* (eel), *branzino* (sea bass), *orata* (seabream), or *scampi* (langoustines). *Seppia alla Veneziana*, also known as *seppie al nero* (cuttlefish in black ink sauce, served with polenta) is a very popular option, as is *frittura mista*, a mixed deep-fried platter (which usually consists of calamari, shrimp and *scampi*, often still in their shells). *Baccala matecato*, mentioned earlier in the *antipasti* section, is also eaten as a *secondo* (the size of the portion is simply larger).

In Verona, try the aforementioned *pastissada de caval* (horse stew), *bollito con la peara* (veal cooked with spices, bread, cheese, and bone marrow), and grilled meats.

Contorno

For the side dish, the *contorno*, you will often find *patate al forno* (oven-baked potatoes), *patatine fritte* (French fries), *fagioli* (white beans), *spinaci* (spinach), *ceci* (chickpeas), *verdure alla brace/alla griglia* (roasted/grilled vegetables), *insalata mista/insalata verde* (a simple salad, though you should know that the Italian definition of a salad is very limited, usually involving little more than lettuce, a few other green leaves, and a couple of lonesome cherry tomatoes).

Pizza

Pizza is, of course, a hugely popular choice for many Italians. A meal in a pizzeria is much cheaper than a dinner in a trattoria, and can be just as enjoyable. We recommend choosing a pizzeria that advertises itself with the magic words *forno a legna* (real wood-burning stove). In Venice there is no shortage of popular venues. For an authentic flavor, try Pier Dickens pizzeria in the lively Campo Santa Margherita. For a pizza with a view, try Ristorante-Pizzeria Alvise, right next to the Fondamente Nuove *vaporetto* stop.

Vegetarian

If you are a vegetarian, there are a few precautions you should take when visiting restaurants in Venice, or Italy, for that matter. First, you should know that most (but not all) soups are made with meat or chicken stock. If you are unsure about the contents of a dish, just ask: *"Sono vegetariano, c'e' carne o pesce?"* (Pronounced, "Sono vegettariano, che carne o peshe?"). The Italian idea of vegetarianism can be difficult, however, and while most waiters have no trouble telling you if there's meat in the dish, they often don't think it's a problem if there's chicken broth in it, or lard, or gelatine, or any other animal by-products. More than once we asked whether a certain dish was vegetarian, and were told that it was. On further investigation we found small pieces of salami in the sauce, or noticed that the broth had a distinct meaty flavor. When we confronted the waiter with our findings, he simply answered, slightly offended, "There's just a little bit—only for the taste!"

You should also know that most hard cheeses are produced with *caglio* (rennet, produced from cows). Some cheesemakers offer a cheese made with *caglio vegetale*, suitable for vegetarians. Vegetarians should also avoid anything containing *strutto* and *lardo*, both of which mean lard. It might seem strange, but *strutto* is sometimes found in breads, *focacce*, and pastries. The safest choices for vegetarians are pizzas, pasta dishes (risottos tend to be trickier, because of the stock used in preparing them) and, naturally, salads. While there aren't many restaurants in Venice that cater specifically to vegetarians, almost any self respecting *trattoria* should be able to muster up a vegetarian dish to accommodate guests. If you are looking for a wider selection we would recommend trying **La Zucca** (Calle del Tintor, Santa Croce 1762, near the San Stae *vaporetto* stop, open Monday-Saturday, 12:30 p.m.-2:30 p.m. & 7:00 p.m.-10:30 p.m.), a fun and zero-frills neighborhood eatery that offers plenty of vegetarian options.

Desserts

Italians have a talent for salty baked goods. Their *focaccia* and *schiacciata* are famous the world over. Italian desserts, on the other hand, tend to be a little disappointing, suffer from lack of imagination, and are often rather heavy. With the exception of a real *ristorante*, desserts are typically not homemade. If a restaurant does make its desserts in-house, it will usually make a point of explicitly stating *dolci fatti in casa* (homemade dessert) on the menu. Look around and check out the desserts served to others in the restaurant. If they don't seem that tempting, skip them and head for a *gelato* or *granita* instead.

Aperitivo

An *aperitivo* is a light snack and cocktail consumed before dinner, much like the Spanish tapas or the French aperitif. The *aperitivo* is popular all over Italy, but in Venice it is a culture unto itself. Here, taverns and restaurants open early and offer a large selection of snacks and canapés (all on display at the counter), together with various local wines and popular cocktails. To make the most of your *aperitivo*, do as the locals do: Order a Spritz (the most popular cocktail on the menu, made with bubbly Prosecco and a shot of slightly bitter Aperol or Campari), add two to five cicheti from the selection at the bar (a cicheto typically costs between €1.5 and €2.5) and then sip and munch away, standing up, with the rest of the merry Italians.

Your *aperitivo* can consist of just a short visit at one *bacaro* (a tavern that serves the traditional Venetian *aperitivo*) before dinner, or can be expanded into a tour of a number of popular *bacari* (a *bacaro* crawl), sampling various local delicacies in tiny portions in each tavern, and enjoying an inexpensive and diverse meal on the go.

The selection on offer changes from *bacaro* to *bacaro*, but most include the following staples in their *aperitivo* buffet: *baccala mantecato*; *sarde in saor*; *polpette* (meatballs, usually deep-fried); tiny sandwiches; canapès; slices of cheese or ham; mozzarella in *carozza* (coated and deep-fried mozzarella); and a selection of tiny *crostini* with inventive toppings, everything from Gorgonzola and nuts to ricotta, pumpkin and pistachios to salmon, mustard and sautéed artichokes.

Since the Venetian *aperitivo* is such a big part of local culture, and because it really is great fun, we have dedicated a number of tips in this guide to the subject, listing the best *bacari* in different parts of Venice. The *aperitivo* is also extremely popular in Verona, which was under Venetian occupation for hundreds of years, and has historically been influenced by Venice in more ways than one.

Tipping and the *Coperto*

To request the bill at the end of your meal simply ask the waiter for "*il conto per favore*," pronounced as it is written. Once this is done, the issue of tipping arises. Restaurants in Italy charge what is called *coperto*, which means a fixed fee for "opening the table." Contrary to what many tourists believe, it has nothing to do with how much bread you eat or whether you ask for water. In Venice the *coperto* is often higher than in other cities in Italy and ranges between €1 and €3 per person. Michelin-starred restaurants and other famous venues will easily double that fee. Water is charged separately.

Since restaurants charge a *coperto*, tipping isn't mandatory. You may want to leave a 10% tip at the end of a dinner, but only do this if you were especially pleased with the service, as it is not obligatory. Tipping in taxis, hotels, etc. is up to you. Doing so will be appreciated, but it really isn't considered a major faux pas if you don't do it. The one case in which tipping may be a good idea is when someone goes out of their way to help you, in which case a tip is the best way to show your appreciation.

Wine

There are many books dedicated to the complex and fascinating subject of Italian wines, so it goes without saying that any introduction we give here is only meant as a very general primer. However, seeing as there are several recommendations in this guide for wine-tasting tours and activities, and since you will surely sample a number of Vento's fine wines during your travels, it would be foolish not to provide a general summary of the local wine industry.

Venice and Verona are located in the Veneto region, which is one of the most important wine-producing regions in Italy. The best-known wines produced in this area are Valpolicella, Amarone, Prosecco, Soave, and Bardolino.

Amarone di Valpolicella (often simply referred to as Amarone) is a rich and powerful red. It is considered the most prestigious wine produced in Veneto and one of the most prestigious (and expensive) in all of Italy. It is full-bodied and complex, has a light bitter undertone, and is made with a mix of Corvina, Rondinella and other permitted grape varieties.

Bardolino is a light red wine produced around the town of Bardolino, on the eastern shores of Lake Garda, in the province of Verona. It is a much simpler wine, but also very drinkable.

Soave is a very well-known and loved white wine. It is fresh, smooth, straw-colored, and fruity. It is produced in the province of Verona using a blend of Garganega, Trebbiano di Soave and Chardonnay grapes. Since there is such a huge selection of Soave wines available, we recommend you stick to tasting and buying Soave DOCG wines, to a guarantee a good level of quality.

Valpolicella is a fruity and perfumed red wine. It is one of the best and most popular choices in the region, and an excellent go-to wine when touring Veneto. It goes especially well with meat-based dishes. There are different categories and classes to Valpolicella, including Valpolicella Classico DOC, Valpolicella Classico Superiore, and Valpolicella Ripasso, each of which is made following different techniques that confer a somewhat different taste.

Prosecco is the best-known sparkling wine in Italy. It is prepared with Glera grapes, and since 2009 it has been regulated, which means that today you can find Prosecco DOC wines with guaranteed quality. Prosecco wines differ based on their level of foaminess and sweetness. The drier version is known as Brut, while the sweet is referred to as Dolce. A good in-between choice is Extra-Dry Prosecco. In Venice, you will often enjoy a glass of bubbly Prosecco on its own, or as one of the two main ingredients of the famous Bellini cocktail or the Spritz cocktail.

Wine Classification

All Italian wines adhere to a classification system set by the government. This system protects local production, so that a wine from the North of Italy, for example, won't be able to advertise itself as a Chianti, and a wine produced near Florence won't be marketed as a Valpolicella. This system ensures that certain quality standards are followed, and divides wines into four major categories:

> **Vino da Tavola,** or table wine, is the simplest wine available. Don't waste your time with it.
>
> **IGT** stands for *indicazione geografica tipica*, and defines wine that comes from a specific geographic location. Though it's not the highest classification, there are some very good wines in this category. Ironically, in recent years many important producers who refused to adapt their wine-making recipes to the government guidelines could no longer call their wine DOC and were forced to define it IGT.
>
> **DOC,** *denominazione d'origine controllata,* means you are guaranteed a product of a certain quality, from a specific area, made according to specific guidelines.
>
> **DOCG,** *denominazione d'origine controllata e garantita*, marks the highest-quality wines.

The best way to learn more about Italian wines is, quite simply, to drink them. In Italy, wine isn't considered a snooty hobby reserved for the rich; it's a way of life and a popular traditional passion. Most Italians grow up with wine on their family dinner tables, and develop a palate from an early age. Many, and not necessarily just foodies, are well-informed about good products.

Choosing the "right" wine is, in many cases, simply a question of taste. We have recommended several award-winning and excellent-value wines in this guide, but there are many other fine wines to enjoy.

Top marks and high prices are often used as proof of a wine's quality, but both factors can be misleading. Your taste may be different from that of a noted wine critic, and some excellent wines simply go unnoticed, which doesn't mean you should exclude them from your tasting list. Prices, too, can be misleading, and while they can offer guidance, they are not an automatic guarantee of quality and taste. You will be surprised at the reasonably priced, quality finds you might come across in the local *enoteca*, or at one of the large supermarkets, which usually have a respectable selection of excellent wines priced under €25. But it actually shouldn't be surprising that the selection is so appealing here; this is, after all, where most Italians go to do their shopping and pick up a bottle or two for their party or family dinner.

Booking in Advance

If there is a specific restaurant you want to try, we highly recommend booking a day or two in advance. With hotels, the situation is much trickier. Venice is busy almost year-round, but during the summer months it is packed to the rafters, and the most popular hotels are booked solid months in advance. Start your research early to guarantee the room you want.

Verona isn't as busy as Venice, but in high season it can be hard to find openings at good B&Bs and hotels. Advance reservations are recommended here, too.

Italian Manners

Italians take manners very seriously. They pride themselves on their *buona educazione* (proper education), and appreciate it when others play by the same rules. It's considered rude, for instance, to ask for something without first saying "Excuse me" (*scusi*, pronounced "skuzi"). Starting a conversation with scusi and ending it with *grazie tante* ("Thank you very much"; note that the word is pronounced graziE, not graziA, as many tourists mistakenly say) will leave a good impression and help you get better service at hotels, restaurants, and attractions. The polite way to say "Goodbye" is *arrivederci*, while the polite way to say "Hello" when arriving somewhere is *buongiorno* or *buonasera*, depending on whether it's day (*giorno*) or night (*sera*). Of course, like anywhere, a smile goes a long way.

That said, we have to admit that no matter how polite a tourist may be, service in Italy can be lacking at times. Though the majority of Italians are friendly and welcoming, be prepared for the occasional annoyed waiter or shopkeeper. If it makes any difference, know that it's usually not personal; salesmen and waiters are often short with locals as well as foreigners (to many of the local businesses, a foreigner is anyone that didn't grow up on the same street and go to the same kindergarten as them). Sometimes you may get the feeling that Italians get better service, and occasionally you'll be right. Often, however, it's not because you are being discriminated against, it's simply due to the language barrier. Most Italians don't speak English very well and keep their sentences as short as possible to avoid embarrassment.

Lastly, it is worth mentioning that Italians are very attentive to fashion and style, and usually prefer to dress up rather than down. Take a look around any given centrally located *piazza* on a Saturday night, and you will immediately understand what we are talking about. The women are all in skimpy dresses, 6-inch heels and perfectly done hair, and the men walk around in chic jackets and pricey shoes. This means that even though most Italian restaurants have a far more relaxed dress code than that of their French counterparts, they do welcome slightly more elegant attire. You will probably feel more welcome (and get better service) if you dress the part.

Venice

01 **Book a Hotel Right on the Grand Canal** for a Memorable Stay

Staying in a hotel right on Venice's famous main canal, the Grand Canal, is a dream for many. It is as impressive and memorable a sojourn as you will find.

There are many exclusive and dazzling hotels along the Grand Canal, from the Gritti to the Bauer to the Aman and Hotel Londra; they offer extraordinary stays, provided, that is, you are willing to spend a very hefty sum for the pleasure. Finding a hotel in a reasonable price range, on the other hand, can be harder. But not impossible!

The **Hotel Canal Grande** is the embodiment of the classic romantic Venetian hotel. Perfectly located across the water from the Basilica della Salute and just minutes from Piazza San Marco, this four-star hotel is one of the most romantic and elegant choices in the city.

It is housed in a historic mansion—Ca' Polacco—and the rooms and communal spaces, which are strewn with 18th century Rococo antique furniture and art, beautifully reflect the hotel's past.

The best rooms here are, naturally, those with a view of the Grand Canal (some of the double rooms offer a view of Campo San Simeon, instead. Make sure you book the right one). Breakfast can be enjoyed outside, on the terrace by the water.

Equally perfect is **Hotel Palazzo Stern.** Set in a handsome 15th century Moorish *palazzo* right on the Grand Canal, this family-run hotel offers a reasonably priced stay (considering the location) and plenty of charisma.

The *palazzo* was bought and handsomely restored by the Sterns,

a family of art lovers, and their dedication to style and architecture explains the meticulous renovation job. The hotel retains a lot of antique décor, which gives it a distinct personality, including hand-carved medieval marble columns, a gilded ceiling in the lobby, ornate sculptures, original Fortuny lights, and even stone staircases (modern amenities, such as satellite TV and espresso makers, are also available). Service is friendly and helpful, and hotel reception will usually try to upgrade you to a better room if there happens to be an opening when you come (there are far better chances of that happening if you visit off-season).

The standard rooms are comfortable, but the deluxe double rooms are more elegant and detailed. The finest choice is, of course, the beautiful suites, which overlook the Grand Canal (book well in advance, as they fill up quickly).

But rest assured that whatever room you choose, you will still be able to enjoy the view; breakfast for all guests is served on a marble terrace overlooking the Grand Canal. Is there any better way to start the day?

Palazzo Sant'Angelo is yet another fine choice. This luxury 4-star hotel is located in a beautiful historic converted mansion within walking distance of the Rialto Bridge. In addition to the regular rooms, the hotel offers junior and deluxe suites (which cost over €500 a night in high season) that provide a particularly enchanting view of the Grand Canal. The suites are opulently decorated in rich reds and golds, and feature luxurious cotton sheets, dark wood furniture and wonderfully dramatic drapes. The hotel can be easily reached, and the *vaporetto* is just a few meters away from the main entrance. The staff is friendly, and minor imperfections, such as the smallish breakfast buffet and occasional outdated fixtures, do little to diminish this special experience.

Lastly, the **Hotel Savoia & Jolanda** is worth considering.

Not all the rooms will live up to the expectations of demanding travelers, but the deluxe junior suite with a canal view surely will, and at certain times of the year it may very well cost less than a standard room in some of Venice's top hotels (If you prefer even greater luxury, head straight to the **Londra Hotel**, next door. It is much more expensive, but quite spectacular).

The Savoia & Jolanda boasts an enviable location just 200 meters from Piazza San Marco, on Riva degli Schiavoni, near the Danieli Hotel; it overlooks not just the Grand Canal, but also parts of the lagoon. The fixtures and fittings are quintessentially Venetian, with antique furniture and handmade Murano glass lamps and chandeliers, which ooze old-world charm. The hotel is divided into two wings; the Savoia wing faces the waterfront (recommended), while the Jolanda wing faces Campo san Zaccaria. Like so many of the hotels in Venice that are located in restored historic mansions, the Savoia & Jolanda suffers from some outdated amenities, but the location and charm make up for that, in our opinion.

Hotel Canal Grande,
Campo San Simeon Grande, San Marco 932 (right off the San Marco Vallaresso *vaporetto* stop). Tel: 041.244.0148, www.hotelcanalgrande.it. ★★★★★

Hotel Palazzo Stern,
Dorsoduro 2792/A (right off the Ca' Rezzonico *vaporetto* stop).
Tel: 041.277.0869,
www.palazzostern.it. ★★★★★

Palazzo Sant'Angelo,
San Marco, 3878/b (right off the Sant'Angelo *vaporetto* stop).
Tel: 041.241.145,
www.palazzosantangelo.com. ★★★★

Hotel Savoia & Jolanda,
Riva degli Schiavoni 4187 (near the Arsenale *vaporetto* stop).
Tel: 041.520.6644,
www.hotelsavoiajolanda.com ★★★★

02 Stop for a Simple and Tasty Lunch off Piazza San Marco

When tummies start to rumble in the tourist-packed streets of Venice, finding a tasty and reasonably priced nibble can be tricky. And at lunchtime, that challenge quadruples. Luckily for our readers, we have found ourselves starving and stranded on more occasions than we care to remember, and have compiled a list of go-to favorites in the vicinity of Piazza San Marco that are perfect for a quick lunch.

Sestante Bar and Restaurant is a friendly little spot, nestled in a tiny alley behind Riva degli Schiavoni and the Bridge of Sighs (Ponte dei Sospiri). During the day it's an accessible eatery that will ease those midday hunger pangs. At night, the setting changes, and new cocktails are constantly added to the list, drawing in quite a crowd. Sestante serves a couple of daily pasta dishes, some of which aren't bad at all, but your best bet is their *cicheti* and small sandwiches, which are actually not so small, quite delicious, and very reasonably priced. Sit down with a *tramezzino* with salmon and egg filling and one or two of their prosciutto *panini*, and you will be more than pleased.

Alternatively, try **Birreria Forst**. This is a friendly, zero-frills, lively tavern, packed with locals and hungry *gondolieri*, all looking for a good-value lunch on the go. The best items on the menu are, without a doubt, the sandwiches and the excellent platters of cold cuts (which they call "chopping boards," presumably because of some sort of Google Translate mishap). One of the platters, paired with a couple of sandwiches or a salad and a Spritz (or beer) will result in a very satisfying lunch.

Lastly, if you are looking for a more refined dining experience, and don't mind a bit of a splurge, Osteria Ai Do Gobbi and Le Chat qui Rit are well worth considering. **Osteria Ai Do Gobbi** is located about 5 minutes from Piazza San Marco; walk along Riva degli Schiavoni, turn left onto Calle Peschiera (behind Ristorante Gabbiano) and continue onto Calle Crosera. While the food here is slightly over-priced, in our opinion, it is also very tasty, the portions are generous, and everything is well-prepared. And because Ai Do Gobbi's kitchen is (usually) open during the afternoon, too, you can have your lunch as late as you wish. The menu is seasonal, but some popular dishes can be found year-round. The *primi* are the restaurants' forte, so try the *pappardelle con scampi, zucca e porcini* (pappardelle with langoustines, pumpkin and porcini mushrooms), the *polipetti in umido con polenta* (cuttlefish with polenta), or the *bigoli con ragu di anatra* (traditional Venetian spaghetti-like pasta served with duck ragout), all of which are very good.

Le Chat Qui Rit is more expensive, but the food is very tasty; it's the kind of friendly and sophisticated gourmet wine bar that foodies can't resist. Come here for an easygoing lunch made with the finest *materie prime* (ingredients), and relax in their chic dining room with a glass from the extensive wine selection that Giovanni Mozzato, the owner and sommelier, keeps on hand. The pasta is quite good, but overpriced. We particularly enjoy their lighter antipasti, such as the delicious cold cuts and cheese platters. Vegetarians and vegans will find a number of dishes to order, too.

Sestante Venezia,
Castello 4687 (in front of Campo San Zaccaria). Tel: 041.476.4210, sestantevenezia.com.
Open Wednesday-Monday, 10:30 a.m.-midnight. Closed Tuesday. ★★★

Birreria Forst,
San Marco 4540 (Calle de le Rasse), behind the Danieli Hotel.
Tel: 041.523.0557. Open Monday-Thursday, 10:00 a.m.-11:00 p.m.; Friday-Saturday, 10:00 a.m.-1:00 p.m.; Sunday, 12:00 p.m.-3:30 p.m. & 6:30 p.m.-11:00 p.m. ★★★★

Osteria ai Do Gobbi,
San Marco 3958 (Calle Crosera).
Tel: 041.241.3608. Open daily, 12:00 p.m.-10:00 p.m. ★★★★

Le Chat Qui Rit,
San Marco 1131 (Calle Tron, right next to Frezzaria). Tel: 041.522.9086, www.chatquirit.it.
Open Monday-Saturday, 12:00 p.m.-10.30 p.m. (the kitchen is open between 12:30 p.m. and 9:30 p.m.). ★★★

03 **Enjoy a Classic *Aperitivo*** at one of Venice's Traditional *bacari* by the Rialto Bridge

In Venice, the *aperitivo* is a culture unto itself. Every evening, the town squares fill with locals and tourists, out to enjoy a pre-dinner cocktail and an array of delicious snacks in one of the city's many *bacari* (a traditional tavern that serves an *aperitivo*). This hallowed tradition was established by Venetian merchants; when they didn't have enough time for lunch, they would grab a small snack and a glass of wine before moving on to their next destination. Today, the *aperitivo* is a popular way for the locals to keep in touch with friends, catch up on gossip and meet for informal drinks.

While quite close to the Spanish custom of tapas, Venetians have formulated their own lingo to describe the *aperitivo* culture. A glass of wine, for example, is known as *ombre*, derived from the Italian word for shadow, *ombra*, a reminder of the days when hard-working merchants would leave their wooden barrels of wine in the cool shade of Piazza San Marco's bell tower. The little snacks are known as *cicheti*, and the neighborhood tavern itself is called a *bacaro* (after the Greek god of wine, Bacchus).

A typical Venetian *aperitivo* consists of about four or five *cicheti* and a drink (or two, or three...). Though white wine is a popular choice, traditional cocktails such as the Spritz (prepared with Prosecco, a bitter base such as Aperol or Campari, and soda water) or the Negroni (prepared with gin, Campari and vermouth) are the Venetians' go-to drinks. Unless, of course, it's peach season, in which case many opt for a fine Bellini cocktail made with the flesh of white peaches and Prosecco. (Be

warned: The more sophisticated bars in town will react with dramatic shock if you ask for a Bellini off-season.)

Whatever your cocktail of choice, it will be accompanied by a tempting selection of the aforementioned *cicheti*, typically priced at €1 to €2 per piece. Each *bacaro* crafts its own original selection, but the most popular *cicheti* are, without a doubt, the *polpette* (small meatballs) and tiny sandwiches or canapés with toppings such as roasted vegetables, shrimp, cured meats, or creamed *baccala* (salted cod). The more sophisticated places have a larger selection of *cicheti*, and might offer other favorites, such as boiled eggs served with *acciughe* (anchovies), slices of cheese, squid in various forms, sausages, and sardines.

Just like the debate over which *gelateria* serves the best ice cream in Florence, or where you can get the best *arancini* in Sicily, the battle for Venice's best *bacaro* and *cicheti* is endless. Over a dozen *bacari* in town claim the title of the most authentic and respected establishment, and at least a dozen more present themselves as the hottest new spots. In our humble opinion, it's simply a matter of personal taste. (Though following the locals is always a good idea. The best *bacari* will always be bustling, with people spilling into the alleys and hanging around the adjacent canals.)

To facilitate navigation, we have divided our recommendations of Venice's best *bacari* according to their geographic location – popular and historic *bacari* near the Rialto Bridge (featured in this tip), the best *bacari* with a view of the Grand Canal (see tip 71), the best *bacari* near the Accademia (see tip 13), the best *bacari* near the Scuola Grande di San Rocco (tip 46), and the best *bacari* near Ca d'Oro (see tip 10).

To make the most of these recommendations, we suggest going on what is fondly known as an "*ombre* crawl"—a tour of two to four *bacari*, trying just a few items in each. A long session of meandering through Venice's alleys, sampling different wines and *cicheti*, can serve as a fun and unique dining experience.

The Rialto Bridge area is teeming with people and *bacari* of different styles, from the simplest and least expensive to the most costly and pretentious, so it's quite easy to walk around, survey the possibilities, and choose the one that attracts you most. If you are anything like us, you will be immediately drawn to the more "local" spots, which are packed with authentic charm.

Al Merca is a tiny, hole-in-the-wall *bacaro* and is quite popular with the locals, who come here for a quick Spritz and one of Al Merca's mini-sandwiches. Some grab a drink and go, while others linger around the town square and chat. A reasonable selection of local wines is also available.

Then, don't miss the famous local favorite, **All'arco**, just 50 meters away. Tourists, dock workers, office clerks, and people from all walks of life mingle here enjoying the traditional *cicheti* of a true Venetian institution. All'Arco has been in operation for over 50 years and has remained as popular as it was in the 1960s. Don't count on finding a seat, but rather do as the locals do—stand, chat, eat, and enjoy. Try typical *cicheti* such as *baccala mantecato* (creamed cod), *sardine in saor* (sardines in a sweet and sour sauce), fried squid, and *crostini* with asparagus and boiled eggs. *Buonissimo!*

Next, visit the historic **Cantina Do Mori,** where brass and copper pots hang from the ceiling, reminding guests that this *bacaro* has been serving patrons since 1462. Cantina Do Mori is a treasure trove of wines and local liquors, packed together in small wooden barrels ready to serve thirsty patrons. In fact, every self-respecting Venetian stops here once in a while. Their selection of *cicheti* is slightly limited but very tasty, especially the roasted *polpo* (squid) in olive oil and the tiny sandwiches, and the wine they generously pour will put you in a good mood right away. Next door, make a quick stop at **Osteria alla Ciurma**, locally known for their excellent deep-fried delicacies – *baccala* croquettes, batter-covered anchovies, and tiny *arancini* (Sicilian-style rice balls with scrumptious filling); they are all delicious, and help balance out the alcohol.

End your *bacaro* crawl in style, with a stop at either **Vinaria** or **Ostaria dai Zimei.** Located right off the Rialto Bridge, along Riva del Vin, **Vinaria** is a modern wine bar and restaurant that offers a more stylish experience. Vinaria's selection of dishes includes stewed octopus on a bed of polenta, beef fillet with a coffee-based sauce and, for those who are in desperate need of some fresh vegetables to counterbalance all the wine and deep fried mozzarellas, various salads. There is seating inside, overlooking the Rialto Bridge, and even a tiny garden from which you can do some people watching while you enjoy your leisurely drink.

Ostaria dai Zimei, on the other hand, is more of a locals' spot, but unlike the previously listed *bacari*, it also offers outside seating, which is a major draw. The bar displays that day's *cicheti*, and the selection is excellent—come early, before they run out of the good stuff! The crostini with various toppings come particularly recommended.

Al Merca,
Fondamenta Riva Olio. Open Monday-Saturday, 10:00 a.m.-2:30 p.m. & 6:30 p.m.-9:00 p.m. ★★★

All'arco,
Sestiere San Polo 436 (Calle Arco), Tel: 041.520.5666. Opening hours tend to vary. The *bacaro* is usually open Monday-Tuesday, 8:30 a.m.-2:30 p.m.; Wednesday-Friday, 8:30 a.m.-7:30 p.m. Closed weekends. ★★★★

Cantina do Mori,
Sestiere San Polo 429.
Tel: 041.522.5401. Opening hours vary. In high season, the *bacaro* is usually open Thursday-Tuesday, 8:00 a.m.-2:00 p.m. & 4:30 p.m.-7:30 p.m.; Wednesday, 8:00 a.m.-2:00 p.m. ★★★★

Osteria alla Ciurma,
Sestiere San Polo 427. Open Monday-Saturday, 9:00 a.m.-3:00 p.m. & 5:30 p.m.-8:30 p.m. Closed Sunday. ★★★

Vinaria,
Riva del Vin 1097. Tel: 041.241.0665, www.vinariaristorante.it.
The bar is open daily, 11:00 a.m.-11:00 p.m.; the restaurant is open Monday-Friday, 12:00 p.m.-2:30 p.m. & 6:30 p.m.-10.30 p.m.; Saturday-Sunday, 12:00 p.m.-10.30 p.m. ★★★

Ostaria dai Zemei,
San Polo 1045/B. Tel: 041.520.8596. Open daily, 8:30 a.m.-8:30 p.m. ★★★★

Note that in all *bacari* the *cicheti* are served from 11:00/11.30 a.m.

04 Revel in an Aperitivo with a Breathtaking Panoramic View of Venice

There are literally dozens of bars, *enoteche* and *bacari* in Venice where you can enjoy a traditional Venetian aperitivo. And if you want to immerse yourself in the local culture and traditions, visiting one of those *bacari* is a great way to do so. But if you're after a memorable, breathtaking experience, one with fine cocktails and a view to remember, then a simple little neighborhood *bacaro* just won't do. When we are looking for that special something in Venice, here is where we go:

The best option, one that in our opinion simply shouldn't be missed, is the **Skyline Rooftop Bar** at the Hilton. Sitting on this uniquely positioned terrace as the day fades away, watching the entire city as the Venetian sky collapses into swirls of pinks and reds, is an enthrallingly surreal experience. Cocktail aficionados won't be disappointed by the Hilton's pricey but delicious drinks. This chic spot attracts quite a crowd, even more so during one of their events—jazz sessions, pool parties, and minglers. Be sure to consult their website to find out if any special events are planned during the time of your visit, and book a table in advance. When making a reservation, note that the bar is divided into three spaces: a swanky and modern closed hall and two terraces, one on either side. Naturally, we recommend booking a table on the terrace overlooking the city, and sitting as close as possible to the waterline.

If it's a smart, sophisticated experience you are after, preferably right on the Grand Canal, then look no further than the Gritti Palace's very own **Bar Longhi.** The Gritti is one of Venice's most exclusive

hotels, but even if you don't plan on staying in one of their exquisite suites, you can still enjoy the stylish ambiance and the fantastic views from its smart bar (or from the hotel's formal restaurant). And if you are willing to splurge and want a bit of exclusivity, this is one of the best choices in town. **Bar Longhi** has recently been renovated and today displays priceless 18th century paintings alongside artworks by local artisans, giving this space a sophisticated feel. Book a table on the terrace at sunset to enjoy a magical cocktail with a view of the Grand Canal and Basilica della Salute, Bladassare Longhena's Baroque masterpiece. Add some oysters and champagne to the mix, and you have irresistible romance.

Another fine option is the **Antinoo Lounge Bar and Restaurant** at the Centurion Palace Hotel. The Antinoo is divided into two sections: An interior dining space, which is pleasant but isn't the main draw, and a tiny exterior seating area right on the Grand Canal that is absolutely delightful—the water and the many gondolas passing by serve as a perfect accompaniment to a fun snack or meal. Order their Bellini cocktail, relax in front of the view, and be prepared to be envied by the many tourists who pass by aboard the *vaporetti*! Naturally, the Antinoo offers full meals, too, and those who appreciate a modern kitchen will be very pleased with the dishes on offer.

Alternatively, if you are looking for a more reasonably priced or more casual experience, we highly recommend **La Palanca**. This easy-going *osteria* and bar, which serves mostly locals, is quite different from the previous three recommendations in this tip. La

Palanca is modest and unassuming, and located far away from the bustle on Giudecca Island (across the lagoon from Dorsoduro). We especially enjoy coming here when mainland Venice is too crowded to be reasoned with. The menu is simple but tasty, and the lovely view, together with their well-prepared Spritz and tasty pasta dishes, make up for any possible disadvantages of this family-run eatery. If La Palanca is closed, **Trattoria Ai Cacciatori,** just a minute or two away, offers excellent pasta dishes and an equally beautiful view in a tranquil setting.

We cannot finish the list of recommendations for the best bars with a panoramic view without speaking of the Danieli Hotel. The Danieli, one of the most distinguished and historic hotels in Venice, offers both guests and non-guests a number of options for enjoying the city. For those who want a cocktail with a view, there is **La Terrazza Bar,** located right next to the famous La Terrazza restaurant (see tip 21) on the hotel's top floor. It is open from May to September, and guests can enjoy one of the best views of the Grand Canal in the city, second only to the view from the Hilton, in our opinion. Alternatively, if La Terrazza Bar is closed (off-season, or due to bad weather), you can find refuge at the Danieli's stunning Dandolo Bar. Though it can't rival La Terrazza's views, the décor and history of Dandolo make it a worthwhile choice in its own right, with its high ceilings, gold ornaments, and opulent marble columns. The fact that patrons such as Richard Wagner, Charles Dickens, Peggy Guggenheim and Steven Spielberg, just to name a few, have stopped here for drinks over the years only goes to show the uniqueness of this bar. In both Danieli bars, as you might imagine, the service is snooty and the prices are high (expect to pay north of €15 per cocktail). In their defense, the prices at similar historic cafes and bars in the city, such as Caffè Florian (see tip 29) and Harry's Bar, aren't any lower.

Skyline Rooftop Bar,
on the top floor of the Hilton Mulino Stucky Hotel. Giudecca 810. The nearest vaporetto stop is Pallanca, and you can also use the Hilton's shuttle boat, leaving from Zattere and Piazza San Marco. Consult the Hilton's website for the complete departure schedule. Tel: 041.2723.311, www.skylinebarvenice.com, info@hilton.com. Open daily, 5:00 p.m.-1:00 a.m. ★★★★★

Bar Longhi
(in The Gritti Palace hotel), Campo Santa Maria del Giglio. Tel: 041.794.611, www.thegrittipalace.com. Open daily, 11:00 a.m.-1:00 a.m. (the terrace overlooking the Grand Canal is open May-October only). Please note that the Gritti has a dress code (smart casual). ★★★★★

Antinoo's Lounge Bar and Restaurant,
Centurion Palace Hotel, Dorsoduro 173 (just a few meters from the Salute vaporetto stop). Tel: 041.241.3119, www.sinahotels.com. Open daily, 12:30 p.m.-2:30 p.m. & 7:30 p.m.-10:30 p.m. ★★★★

La Palanca,
448 Giudecca. Tel: 041.528.7719. The bar is open Monday-Saturday, 7:00 a.m.-9:00 p.m. (may close earlier off-season). The restaurant is open for lunch only, Monday-Saturday, 12:30 p.m.-2:30 p.m. Closed Sunday. ★★★★

Trattoria Ai Cacciatori,
Giudecca 320. Tel: 0415.285.849, www.aicacciatori.it. Open Tuesday-Sunday, 11:00 a.m.-11:00 p.m. Closed Monday. ★★★

Bar La Terrazza
(in the Danieli Hotel), Riva degli Schiavoni, Castello 4196 (next to the San Marco Zaccaria *vaporetto* stop). Tel: 041.522.6480. www.danielihotelvenice.com/en/bar-terrazza-danieli-terrace. Open May-September (weather permitting), 3:30 p.m.-6:30 p.m. ★★★★★

Bar Dandolo
(in the Danieli hotel), same hours of operation. ★★★

05 Stay in One of Venice's Most Romantic Hotels with a Garden

Venice is sensory intoxication. Beauty and charm tend to frame every moment of a stay here, and we must admit that at times it can be overwhelming, which is why choosing the right accommodations can be very important. Picking a small, romantic boutique hotel rather than one of the large, famous ones has many advantages. First and foremost, your stay will be far more intimate and unique. Second, prices at such hotels tend to be much more reasonable.

Our favorite venue in this category has to be **Pensione Accademia.** We still remember our first stay here, on a freezing weekend in January many years ago. We were nursing a nasty cold that was slowly developing into full-blown bronchitis, but despite our miserable health, the beauty of this 17th century villa-turned-hotel immediately enchanted us. If you are looking for an elegant lobby featuring comfy chairs surrounding an open fireplace, classically Venetian rooms, a charming garden, and a rich and tasty breakfast buffet, then Pensione Accademia is a fine option to consider. Booking a room here in advance is essential. There's no elevator, but the friendly staff will help you with the luggage. The location is perfect, too, right next to the Accademia, surrounded by quirky shops and neighborhood restaurants. The city center is about 15 minutes away (by *vaporetto*), which is just far enough from the hustle and bustle of the Rialto Bridge or the San Marco area to enjoy a calm experience.

Another favorite choice is **Oltre il Giardino**. This boutique hotel is a romantic oasis and the perfect spot for an inspiring stay. What makes Oltre il Giardino so special is its size and location. There are just six bedrooms, all of which are tastefully decorated and overhang the beautiful garden. The hotel is situated far enough from the crowds to guarantee a peaceful sojourn. Waking up to the fragrance of the magnolia trees, hydrangeas and aromatic herbs wafting in from the garden below is the best possible way to start your morning. The tasty buffet breakfast adds to the delight. The hotel has an interesting history, too. It was once the residence of Alma Mahler, wife of famous composer Gustav Mahler. She moved to Vienna in 1934, and some 50 years later the building was purchased and converted into a hotel.

Hotel Sant'Antonin is another excellent option to consider. Housed in a 16th century merchant's home in the Castello district, this elegant, refined hotel is surrounded by its very own garden—one of the largest and most beautiful privately owned gardens in Venice. Purchased by the current owners in the 19th century, the palazzo was remodeled, renovated and later turned into a hotel. The comfortable rooms are simply and elegantly furnished, and the common spaces are especially delightful. The garden is an oasis of peace and quiet.

Lastly, the enchanting **Hotel Palazzo Abadessa** is surely worth considering. Located between Ca' d'oro and Santa Sophia Church, it is a splendid 16th century mansion that has been transformed into a charming 4-star hotel. If you're after a quaint historical residence, this hotel, which has also been reviewed and admired by many magazines around the world, might just be what you are looking for. Stepping into the Abadessa feels like stepping back in time. The name of the hotel is a nod to its history; this period residence was once a convent, and Abadessa Ieromina Calba was the nun who oversaw its construction in 1540. Today the historic ambiance remains, thanks to the priceless art (including paintings attributed to artists of the Tintoretto school) and the original 18th century furniture. The rooms themselves are cozy and comfortable, and the junior suites, which are located on the top floor, are especially appealing and a good value. The Abadessa's private garden is one of the hotel's strongest selling points. Breakfast here, in a secluded corner of the garden surrounded by fragrant flowers and blooming trees, is a refreshing way to start your day.

Pensione Accademia - Villa Maravege,
Fondamente Bollani, Dorsoduro 1058.
Tel: 041.521.0188,
www.pensioneaccademia.it ★★★★★

Oltre Il Giardino,
Fondamenta Contarini, San Polo 2542.
Tel: 041.275.0015,
www.oltreilgiardino-venezia.com.
★★★★★

Hotel Sant'Antonin,
Fondamenta Furlani, Castello 3299.
Tel: 041.523.1621,
www.hotelsantantonin.com. ★★★★

Hotel Palazzo Abadessa,
Calle Priuli 4011. Tel: 041.241.3784,
www.abadessa.com. ★★★★

06 Lunch at a Homey and Authentic *Trattoria* near the Rialto Bridge

Like the challenge of finding a decent, affordable restaurant in the vicinity of Piazza San Marco, finding a reasonably priced, homey restaurant near the Rialto Bridge is a bit of a mission. But it can be done.

The first and most famous choice would probably be **Trattoria alla Madonna.** It's a Venetian classic, conveniently located right off the bridge, and tucked away in a small, crumbling alley. This no-frills eatery has been dishing out simple and authentic Venetian fare since 1954. For years, Trattoria alla Madonna was a meeting place for famous artists like Giorgio de Chirico and Emilio Vedova. Even though the crowd has changed, this trattoria stays true to its heritage, decorating the walls with paintings of local artists and preserving the simple but warm atmosphere that made it famous. At first glance the menu may seem limited, but there's a reason this trattoria is still buzzing with diners after 50 years—the food is good and reasonably priced, and the recipes haven't changed for decades. The owners rightfully claim that more than half a century of expertise is crafted into each offering, so don't be put off. You can enjoy staples of the local kitchen such as *granseola* (crabs served in their shells) and seafood risotto, as well as *spaghetti alle vongole* (spaghetti with clams), mixed seafood platters, *sardine in saor* (sweet and sour sardines), and *fegato alla Veneziana* (Venetian-style liver), but there are also many meat dishes, such as spaghetti with *ragu* (often mistakenly referred to by tourists as "Bolognese sauce") and ravioli.

Alternatively, move five minutes away from the Rialto, towards

Campo SS Apostoli (which is halfway between the Rialto and Ca d'Oro) to find **Osteria La Bottega Ai Promessi Sposi** (also mentioned in tip 10). The location is somewhat hidden—if you don't know what you are looking for, you'll never find the alley that houses this neighborhood restaurant. But once you are here, you won't be disappointed. Osteria La Bottega ai Promessi Sposi is a personal favorite, and with good reason. It is one of the very few authentic restaurants in a town of faux-neighborhood eateries that cater mostly to tourists. And what this place lacks in visual creativeness (which is our polite way of saying the interior design is very basic), it more than makes up for in culinary inspiration. In fact, the chefs here pride themselves on classic Venetian dishes with a southern Italian twist, which certainly explains why this place is packed solid every night of the week. Try their *saltata di cozze e vongole* (sautéed clams and mussels), *gamberetti fritti* (fried shrimp), or *tartara di manzo piemontese* (tartar of Piedmontese beef) for your *antipasti*, and continue with *spaghetti alle vonghole* (spaghetti with clams), *spaghetti al nero di seppia* (spaghetti with cuttlefish sauce), *orecchiette con tonno* (orecchiette pasta with fresh tuna, tomatoes and capers), or *tagliatelle* with duck ragout. For the *secondo*, try dishes like *seppie in umido con polenta* (cuttlefish cooked in tomato sauce, served with polenta), or *fegato alla Veneziana* (Venetian-style liver, served with polenta), or the excellent *orata* (sea bream) with potatoes. If you can't find a table here, or if you simply prefer a different restaurant, it is worth noting that just a few minutes away hides yet another highly recommended restaurant—Vini da Gigio, which is reviewed in tip 32.

Trattoria Alla Madonna,
Calle della Madonna, San Polo 594. Tel: 041.522.3824, www.ristoranteallamadonna.com. Open Thursday-Tuesday, 12:00 p.m.-2:30 p.m. & 7:00 p.m-9:30 p.m. Closed Wednesday. Reservations are only available for groups of four or more. ★★★

Osteria La Bottega Ai Promessi Sposi,
Sestriere Cannaregio 4367 (Calle dell'Oca, in front of Hotel Bernardi). Tel: 041.241.2747. Open Tuesday and Thursday-Sunday, 11:30 a.m.-2:15 p.m. & 6:30 p.m.-10:15 p.m.; Monday and Wednesday, open for dinner only, 6:30 p.m.-10:15 p.m. Advance reservations are recommended. ★★★★

07 Buy a real Venetian Mask

Characterized by their spectrum of bright, wild colors and their ornate design, Venetian masks have become an essential component of the famous Venice Carnival. Mask wearing is a custom unique to Venice, and started more than 700 years ago (with a brief intermission while Venice was under Austrian occupation). With time, the masks have come to symbolize the freedom and creativity of the city. In the past, masks allowed people to hide their identity. In a city as intimate and enclosed as Venice, covering one's face was often a necessity for royals and other nobles. Originally masks were made of leather, porcelain or glass, but today they are mostly made of *carta pesta* (paper-mache) or gesso, a white substance similar to that used for making casts. An obvious source of inspiration for mask designs was the Commedia dell'Arte, and even today many of the masks are of Commedia dell'Arte characters such as Arlecchino, Pulcinella and Brighella.

Today Venice is filled to the brim with tourist shops selling masks of every kind. However, they are obviously not all the same. Almost all the cheap masks are fakes made of plastic, mass-produced in China, and have nothing to do with Venice. If you are content with a simple mask that will serve as a basic souvenir, and aren't very particular about where it was made, then almost any shop will suffice. If, on the other hand, you insist on "the real thing" and prefer a mask with a pedigree, then check out one of our recommended shops.

Marega is an excellent choice, offering a wide selection of stunning handmade masks at a

variety of prices. They started 30 years ago in a tiny studio behind Basilica dei Frari and grew to become one of the leading shops in town, branching out and opening three different ateliers. They are also a favorite one-stop shop for those who attend the grand balls during the carnival (Marega also sells and rents beautiful period costumes, see tip 31).

Next on our list of favorites is **Cartapesta**, one of Venice's best traditional mask shops. The owners are friendly but seem to have lost patience with the endless stream of tourists coming in to ask questions. They came up with a unique solution—they moved their worktables to the front windows of the shop so passersby can watch and understand the intricate work involved in mask making. Those who enter the shop enter exclusively to buy. And what you can buy are some of the most original masks in town, all hand-decorated and prepared according to rigorous traditional techniques. The smallest masks are reasonably priced at €25 to €55.

Ca' del Sol offers masks that are authentic, handsome and reasonably priced (for the most part), and when you visit here you will enjoy the feeling of stepping back in time and exploring a crazy atelier full of surprises. They also offer theater costumes, perfect if you are planning to attend the carnival. The convenient location (near Piazza San Marco and just two doors down from the Marega atelier) makes this a very popular stop.

Sogno Veneziano is the atelier to go to if you are willing to do some serious spending (€150 and more) on a dramatic, one-of-a-kind mask. People come here for period clothes, too, before they attend the carnival ball. The masks are spectacularly grand and very classy, complete with eccentric feathers, pearls and many fine colors.

La Bauta, in Calle Maria Formosa (they have a second shop in Campo Tomà) is another very good option. The choice is ample and original, and includes some amusing animal masks children will love. The service is friendly and the prices remain absolutely reasonable.

Lastly, on Giudecca Island, **Bluemoon** (right off the *vaporetto* dock) is a serious atelier that still adheres to traditional production techniques, and produces some delicate and lovely handmade masks.

Marega,
Campo San Rocco 3046. Tel: 041.5221634, www.marega.it. The atelier is open daily, 10:00 a.m.-7:30 p.m. There are two more Marega shops, one in Fondamenta de l'Osmarin, and another at Calle de Mezzo (San Marco 4976). ★★★★★

Cartapesta,
Castello 5174/B (Calle Lunga S.Maria Formosa). Tel: 041.522.9995, www.papiermache.it. Open Monday-Saturday, 10:00 a.m.-7:00 p.m. (opening hours may vary). Closed Sunday. ★★★★

Ca' del Sol,
Castello 4964 (Fondamenta Osmarin). Tel: 041.528.5549, www.cadelsolmascherevenezia.com. Open daily, 10:00 a.m.-8:00 p.m. ★★★★

Sogno Veneziano,
San Marco 5009 (Calle delle Acque). Tel: 041.241.3252, www.sognoveneziano atelier.com. Open daily, 9:30 a.m.-7:30 p.m. ★★★★

La Bauta,
Campo San Tomà 2867 & Campo Santa Maria Formosa 5851. Tel: 041 740095. Open Monday-Saturday, 10:30 a.m.-7:30 p.m. Closed Sunday. ★★★★

Bluemoon
has two shops–the main shop and studio in Giudecca 607 (right off the Palanca vaporetto stop) is open Monday-Saturday, 10:00 a.m.-3:00 p.m. (the shop is usually open in the afternoon, too, but opening hours tend to change). Tel: 041.715.175. The second shop is near the Rialto Bridge, in Calle del Capeller. Tel: 041.5242567, www.bluemoonvenice.com. Open Monday-Saturday, 10:00 a.m.-7:00 p.m. Closed Sunday. ★★★

08 **Indulge in a Delicious Meal** in One of the Best Seafood Restaurants in Venice

In Venice tourists outnumber locals at a ratio of about 1:300, so your chances of discovering a tiny, locals-only *osteria* that serves heaping plates of pasta for less than €10 are, sadly, slim to none. However, that does not mean that you can't still find some classic, sophisticated Venetian eateries, the kind that savvy locals and well-informed visitors return to again and again. The restaurants in this tip aren't cheap, but they aren't unreasonably expensive, either. In our opinion, they are some of the best that Venice has to offer.

Far enough from the main tourist trail to be hidden from the crowd, but close enough to the center and to the Santa Lucia train station to be easily reached, are **Osteria Rioba** and **Anice Stellato,** two of the best seafood restaurants in Venice. Interestingly, they are within a 2-minute walk of each other, which means that if you haven't booked in advance and can't find a free table in one, you might find an opening in the other.

Anice Stellato is, simply put, a delight. It's the sort of place that hides a strong culinary statement behind a deceptively simple menu, and it has managed to gain the respect of both locals and tourists. Their menu is typically Venetian, but with obvious southern Italian influences. For your *antipasti,* try the *scampi in saor, pepe rosa e zenzero* (sweet and sour langoustines, prepared with ginger and pink pepper), or the *gazpacho e burrata* (a fresh gazpacho soup served with *burrata,* a cream-filled mozzarella), or perhaps the *piovra grigliata con ceci* (grilled octopus, served with chickpeas and drizzled with mint oil). For your *primo,* don't miss one of our favorites, the *tuffoli all'amatriciana di tonno e pesce spada* (hand-rolled Sicilian pasta with smoked tuna and swordfish sauce), or the *spaghetti con scampi alla busara* (spaghetti with langoustines in tomato sauce). The *secondi* are even more exciting: *seppie brune con polenta* (grilled cuttlefish in brown sauce with polenta), *guazetto con pesce del giorno* (a mixed platter featuring the day's catch), and *rombo chiodato con patate al forno* (oven-baked turbot with potatoes).

Ostaria da Rioba is a personal favorite and our go-to restaurant in town. It isn't quite as famous as its neighbor, Anice Stellato, but it is every bit as good. Rioba offers a strictly seasonal menu, which reinterprets the Venetian classics in a modern and sophisticated manner, setting it well apart from the competition. Add to that the charming location, right on a romantic little canal surrounded by colorful *palazzi*, with locals driving by in their boats saluting each other, and it quickly becomes clear why Rioba is always full, and why booking a table at least a day in advance (for dinner) is mandatory. The *antipasti* selection is tempting, but we would suggest skipping them in favor of the much more interesting *primi* and *secondi*. Specifically, the *spaghetti con vongole ed emulsion di corriandolo e bottarga* (spaghetti with clams and a rich bottarga and coriander emulsion) and the *cappellacci* pasta filled with goat cheese, served on a creamy base of mint-infused *straciatella* fondue, are both delicious. For the *secondi*, don't miss the *filetti di ombrina su mousse di melanzane* (Atlantic croaker fish fillet, served on a delicate aubergine mousse), a fantastic dish that is perfectly prepared and incredibly delicate. The *coda di rospo con spinaci e pomodori* (monkfish with a pistachio crust, served atop a spinach, ham, cherry tomato and spicy horseradish flake salad) is also very good. The extensive wine list and homemade desserts are also, naturally, recommended.

Lastly, **Trattoria Antiche Carampane** is a very good choice for those who prefer a more traditional venue. Very hard to find but worth your time, this restaurant serves some of the most authentic seafood delicacies we've tasted in Venice. While not cheap, prices are reasonable, considering the quality of the food. The menu here is varied and well thought out; as a matter of principle, the owner refuses to serve any "standard Italian dishes" (mainly pizza and lasagna), and sticks instead to local recipes. The *antipasto misto* is a great introduction to their cuisine, and while there is a very small selection of *primi* (we like the *spaghetti alla doge* and the *spaghetti cassopipa*), many head straight for the main dishes, such as the *fritto misto* (mixed fried seafood dish), which is delicious, or the fried soft-shell crab.

Anice Stellato,
Fondamenta della Sensa, Cannaregio 3272. Tel: 041.720.744, www.osterianicestellato.com. Open Wednesday-Sunday, 12:15 p.m.-2:00 p.m. & 7:15 p.m.-10:00 p.m. Tuesday, open for dinner only. Closed Monday. Advance reservations highly recommended. ★★★★★

Ostaria da Rioba
Fondamenta della Misericordia. Cannaregio 2553. Tel: 041.524.4379, www.darioba.com. Open Tuesday-Sunday, 12:30 p.m.-2:30 p.m. & 7:30 p.m.-10:00 p.m. Closed Monday. ★★★★★

Trattoria Antiche Carampane,
San Polo 1911. Tel: 041.524.0165, www.antichecarampane.com. Open Tuesday-Saturday, 12:30 p.m.-2:30 p.m. & 7:30 p.m.-11:00 p.m. Closed Sunday & Monday. ★★★★

09 Take a Romantic Gondola Ride

As the Eiffel Tower is to Paris, the gondola is to Venice. This traditional flat-bottomed Venetian boat was for centuries the primary means of transport on Venice's canals and the lagoon. Today it is primarily for tourists, and despite all the clichés, it remains an undeniably romantic experience. But, as you would expect, romance doesn't come cheap. A 30-minute ride for up to 6 people costs €80. For each additional 20 minutes after that, add €40. Between 7:00 p.m. and 8:00 a.m., a 30-minute ride is €100. And if you've always dreamt of having the gondolier serenade you as you float down the Grand Canal, you will be asked to pay an additional fee (also, note that not every gondolier can sing—serenading tours have to be booked in advance, see the information below).

Finding a gondola in Venice is easy; it's almost like raising your hand to stop a taxi in New York. There are several gondola docks, and the choice is up to you. The trick, in our opinion, is choosing the right location to depart from. Gondolas leave from several stops along the Grand Canal, such as: S. Sofia, San Marcuola, Roalto, S. Tomà, San Samuele, Santa Maria del Giglio, and Dogana. Of course, there are also gondola docks near Piazza San Marco and San Zaccaria, as well as a number of other little stops. We recommend skipping the area near the train station, as it isn't as scenic as the others, and departing from any point between the San Stae and San Marco stops. The area near Basilica della Salute, in our opinion, is particularly lovely, but there is something to be said for a tour of the small, peaceful canals, such as those that stretch between the Grand Canal and Querini Stampalia or the area around Santa Maria dei Miracoli.

If you'd like to book a gondola ride in advance, complete with a serenade (serenata, in Italian), consult websites such as www.venetoinside.com/it/tour-in-veneto/tour/gondola-serenade or www.gondolieritravel.com, or call the VeneziaSi information line (Tel: 041. 522.2264) to make your reservation. Note that serenading tours are only available in the spring and summer months, and usually leave in the evening (6:30 p.m. or 7:30 p.m.).
★★★★★

10 Go on a Particularly Delicious *Bacaro* Crawl near Ca' d'Oro

The **Ca' d'Oro alla Vedova** is probably the best known *bacaro* in this area. They've been reviewed in just about every guidebook and praised for their *polpette* (meatballs), and as a result this venue is usually absolutely packed. They open their doors at 6:30 p.m. and by 6:35 it's already swarming with people who are pushing their way to the bar to get their hands on some *cicheti*. And if we want to be honest, we should point out that there are actually better and far less crowded options in the vicinity.

Osteria ai Promessi Sposi is known mostly as a restaurant (see tip 6), but for locals, this is first and foremost a place to gobble up some delicious *cicheti*. The *osteria* is located in a tiny, narrow alley parallel to Strada Nuova, possibly as a way to keep the masses away—if you don't know it's there, you'll never find it. The young team that runs the place offers an interesting selection of local wines and some absolutely delicious *cicheti* to choose from. Their *polpette* (meatballs) and *baccala mantecato* (creamed cod, served on little slices of white bread) are some of the best we've tried in town. Other specialties are *sardine in saor* (fried and marinated sardines), *insalta di polpo* (squid salad), *sarde al beccafico* (a Sicilian dish of sardines filled with bread crumbs, spices, raisins, and nuts), *polpette al umido* (meatballs in tomato sauce), and other surprises. You can of course also sit down for a meal. (Booking a table in advance is essential.)

Once you are done, exit the tiny alley onto Piazza Santissimi Apostoli and turn left. Just a few meters ahead awaits **El Sbarlefo.** This modern spot, right in front of the popular Hotel Giorgione and Hotel Mignon (see tip 34), draws a local crowd and offers an ample selection of excellent *cicheti* and very well-prepared Spritz cocktails. Try their *baccala mantecato* served on tiny slices of roasted polenta, smoked salmon and cheese on mini-toasts drizzled with olive oil, plump *polpette,* or roasted artichokes, Veneto style. An expansive list of local and national wines (not just by the most well-known names, but from quality local producers, too) gives patrons the chance to sample some of the region's best blends.

Ca d'Oro alla Vedova,
Cannaregio 3912 (off Stradanuova, behind the McDonalds).
Tel: 041.528.5324. Open Monday-Wednesday and Friday-Saturday, 11:30 a.m.-2:30 p.m. & 6:30 p.m.-10:30 p.m.; Sunday, 6:30 p.m.-10:30 p.m.
Closed Thursday. ★★★

Osteria ai Promessi Sposi,
Sestriere Cannaregio 4367 (Calle dell'Oca, in front of Hotel Bernardi).
Tel: 041.241.2747. Open Monday and Wednesday, 6:30 p.m.-10:15 p.m.; Tuesday, 11:30 a.m.-2:15 p.m. & 6:30 p.m.-10:15 p.m.; Thursday-Sunday, 11:30 a.m.-2:15 p.m. & 6:30 p.m.-10:15 p.m.
★★★★★

El Sbarlefo,
Sestiere Cannaregio 4556/c (right off Campo SS Apostoi). Tel: 0415.246.650. Open daily, 10:00 a.m.-midnight. The *cicheti aperitivo* only starts around 11:30 a.m. ★★★★

11 **Stay at a Beautiful Mid-Range Hotel** in the Heart of Venice

It's no great revelation that Venice is an expensive city. And many tourists, knowing they will spend a limited amount of time in their rooms, rightfully decide not to blow most of their budget on lodging. That said, booking your stay in an underwhelming pension that is slowly falling apart around you is guaranteed to ruin your vacation.

If you are on the lookout for a sensible compromise between price and comfort, the hotels listed in this tip (and tip 14) will point you in the right direction.

Locanda Orseolo offers a fantastic solution for those searching for a good 3-star hotel. This elegant and welcoming hotel offers guests simple yet comfortable and well-designed rooms. Breakfast is good and the location—just a couple of minutes from Piazza San Marco—is enviable. Book well in advance, as rooms here fill up very quickly.

Hotel Casa Verardo Residenza D'Epoca is the kind of intimate hotel one might easily fall in love with. Guests enjoy a comfortable stay in this beautiful 16th century *palazzo* that has been converted into a 3-star hotel, just minutes from Piazza San Marco and Fondazione Querini Stampalia. There's a small courtyard where guests can relax, the rooms are air-conditioned, and the *vaporetto* stop is nearby, which makes the hotel a convenient base for exploration. In the summer months prices are higher, but off-season Casa Verardo offers very reasonable rates.

Lastly, **Hotel Becher** is a fantastic 3-star hotel with good value for money. It is located within walking distance of Piazza San Marco and just 50 meters from La Fenice (Venice's historic theater, see tip 45), and offers traditional (though somewhat small) Venetian rooms and comfortable amenities, making it one of the better choices in the area. If you are willing to splurge just a little bit, choose their junior suites, which are larger, more comfortable, and still very reasonably priced. The interior design is impressive, too; Murano glass lamps and baroque chandeliers are in most rooms, as well as many antiques from the owner's collection. In fact, one could easily be tricked into thinking they were in a higher-star hotel.

Locanda Orseolo,
Corte Zorzi, San Marco 1083.
Tel: 041.520.4827,
www.locandaorseolo.com. ★★★★

Hotel Casa Verardo - Residenza D'Epoca,
Castello 4765 (near Calle del Magazen. GPS coordinates: 45.435914, 12.341907). Tel: 041.528.6127,
www.casaverardo.it. ★★★

Hotel Becher,
San Marco 1857, Calle del Frutarol (across the bridge from Frezzaria).
Tel: 041.522.125,
www.hotelbecher.com. ★★★★

12 Hit the Hottest Shopping Streets in Venice

It is no wonder that Shakespeare set *The Merchant of Venice* in Venice; the city is today, as it always has been, a city of traders and retailers. It is almost strange talking about just one shopping area in Venice, as every part of the city is positively packed with stores. Everywhere you go, wherever you look, someone is selling something, be it souvenirs, glass, clothes, fabric or jewelry. Nevertheless, if you come to Venice in search of top Italian designers, or are keen on getting some serious shopping done, then knowing where exactly to go is essential. Because, contrary to popular belief, just roaming the streets around Piazza San Marco simply won't suffice.

For high-end clothing, from Fendi and Chanel to Bottega Veneta and Hermès, go to **Calle Vallaresso**, a street that starts from the San Marco Vallaresso *vaporetto* stop, leads to Piazza San Marco, and is packed with elite boutiques.

For excellent mid-range fashion, don't miss the area stretching from **Campo Bartolomeo** to **Campo San Luca** as well as the surrounding alleys, specifically **Campo San Salvador** and **Marzaria San Salvador** (just 2 minutes from the Rialto Bridge). Here you will find some of the best Italian brands, from Furla, Max Mara and Tosca Blu to Coccinelle, Bally, Massimo Dutti, Baldini, Twin-Set, Falconieri and Geox.

The prime location for menswear is **Campo San Luca.** Be sure to check Henry's Cottons for prêt-a-porter items, and the Black Watch boutique, which stocks some of the finest suits in town (during sales you can find beautifully tailored wool suits at half price). Just around the corner from Black Watch hides Boutique Elysee, in **Calle Goldoni,** with a good selection of jeans, jackets, bags and shoes for men and women. Down the road from Campo Luca, by the main entrance to the Hotel Bonvecchiati, sit Emporio Armani and the Boggi shop, both of which offer beautiful medium- to high-end Italian suits and shirts for men.

Calle Barcaroli and **Calle Frezzeria,** located just off San Marco, are two more streets to explore, and are full of interesting boutiques. Especially worth visiting here are the Frette shop (one of the best brands in Italy for linen), and Araba Fenice, a beautiful atelier priding itself on original, handmade clothes designed in-house.

Then, five minutes away from Campo San Luca hides Nina Boutique, an interesting find in an otherwise uninteresting town square (Campo Manin). Run by Daniela Soreca, a stylist with an eagle eye, the boutique is filled with beautiful clothes and classic collections by many of the best brands in Italy. The same owner operates another (much smaller) boutique, more avant-garde in style, in Campo San Rocco (just behind the Frari basilica). Lastly, if you are passionate about shopping, don't miss our recommendation about beautiful hand-made clothing from the Venice women's prison (see tip 49) and the best outlet shopping villages in the region (see tip 87).

Most shops in the area are open Monday-Saturday, 10:00 a.m.-1:00 p.m. & 3:30 p.m.-7:00 p.m. Larger stores remain open all day long, and don't close down at lunch.

Nina Boutique,
Campo Manin, Tel: 041.822.1085. Open daily, 10:00 a.m.-2:00 p.m. & 3:30 p.m.-7:30 p.m. The smaller shop in Campo Rocco is open Monday-Saturday, 10:00 a.m.-1:00 p.m. & 4:00 p.m.-7:30 p.m.
★★★★

13 | **Savor a Delicious *Aperitivo*** of *Cicheti* near the Accademia Museum

Cantinone Gia' Schiavi is possibly the best known *bacaro* in Venice. Continuing a three-generation tradition, Signora Alessandra and her sons run this ramshackle place, famous for the endless stream of people hanging in and around it. The interior, where the daily *cicheti* are on display, is charming, decorated with hundreds of bottles of wine that show the history of this *bacaro* better than any interior designer could. The staff is friendly and will happily fill your glass with a Spritz or one of their local wines. There's a very good offering of tasty *cicheti*, and the selection of toppings is almost dazzling: *bruschette* with ricotta and pumpkin; shrimp, artichoke and truffle; brie and nettle sauce; walnut cream and currants; or cheese and pesto are just a few of the options on display.

While Cantinone gia' Schiavi is the most famous, it certainly isn't the only option. Many tourists backtrack toward the Accademia once they have eaten, but that is a mistake. Instead, continue walking along that same calle, because just a few doors down you will come across another recommended spot, **Osteria Al Squero.** This *osteria* is tiny but accommodating, and enjoys an incredibly quaint position overlooking a colorful gondola boatyard, where experienced men are at work repairing boats. Al Squero is run by a charming couple who left their careers a few years ago to open this *bacaro*. The Spritz here is very good, as are the wines on offer, which have all been meticulously selected by the knowledgeable owners. The small but tempting selection of *cicheti* is a sure crowd pleaser, with favorites such as *panini* with San Daniele prosciutto, *crostini* with cream cheese with a radicchio topping, slices of mortadella sausage with hot peppers, and the omnipresent *baccala mantecato*.

Lastly, if you walk back 50 yards towards the Accademia, cross the bridge on your left and turn onto Calle Toletta, you will find the colorful **Bar alla Toletta**, which offers a fine selection of *tramezzini* (small sandwiches) with various fillings that cost €1.50 to €1.70 apiece (if you eat by the counter, as most Italians do). Try any number of combinations, from egg and crab meat to shrimp and mayonnaise to tuna and tomato, and you will complete what is surely a delicious tour, and a fine way to explore the area!

Cantinone Gia' Schiavi,
Dorsoduro 992 (Fondamenta Priuli). Tel: 041.523.0034. Open Monday-Saturday, 8:30 a.m.-8:30 p.m. Closed Sunday. ★★★★★

Osteria Al Squero,
Dorsoduro 943 (Fondamenta Nani, right after Cantinone Gia' Schiavi). Open Tuesday-Sunday, 9:30 a.m.-9:30 p.m. Monday, open in the afternoon only. ★★★★

Bar alla Toletta,
Dorsoduro 1191 (Calle Toletta). Tel: 041.520.0196. Open Monday-Saturday, 8:00 a.m.-8:00 p.m. Closed Sunday. ★★★

Note that all three *bacari* open early, but the *cicheti aperitivo* only starts around 11:30 a.m.

14 Stay at a Fantastic yet Reasonably Priced B&B or Hotel in the Heart of Venice

Ca' Bonvicini is a beautiful, reasonably priced and very welcoming B&B. The décor is typically Venetian and the obligatory red and gold appliqués can be found in most rooms, but the owners have shown impeccable attention to detail and take great pride in their little residence. Ca' Boncinci is located in a hidden, romantic corner of the city just a short walk from the bustling center and the Rialto Bridge. The rooms are spacious, comfortable and air-conditioned. As you might expect, rooms here fill up very quickly, so book well in advance.

Next on our list of favorites is **CimaRosa,** a wonderful boutique B&B in an enviable location. With its courtyard, modern amenities and beautiful rooms, this bed and breakfast is both inviting and a great find. You won't see the typical dramatic décor here. Instead, expect a clean and contemporary design, exposed wooden beams and a feeling of light and calm. The most expensive room is just under €400 and offers a view of the Grand Canal. Regular rooms cost between €140 and €200, and the San Stae *vaporetto* stop is nearby.

Lastly, **Ca' Gottardi** is a sophisticated and popular choice. The traditional 18th century ornamentation complements the intimate, romantic feel of the communal areas, and the rooms themselves are cozy, clean, and equipped with all the necessary amenities. The suite, the most sumptuously decorated room in the hotel, can double as a family room. The location of Ca' Gottardi is very convenient—just a minute from the Ca d'Oro *vaporetto* stop, and 10 minutes from Piazza San Marco.

Ca' Bonvicini,
Santa Croce 2160 (near Calle Agnello).
Tel: 0412.750.106,
www.cabonvicini.com. ★★★

CimaRosa,
Santa Croce 1958 (Just off the San Stae vaporetto stop). Cell: 333.354.8525,
www.cimarosavenezia.com. ★★★★★

Ca' Gottardi,
Cannaregio 2283 (right off the main street of Strada Nuova).
Tel: 041.275.9333,
www.cagottardi.com. ★★★★★

15 **Discover Cutting-Edge** Contemporary Art

Venice is a playground for art, history and culture enthusiasts. It's no secret that the city holds many treasures, from dazzling art work in grand baroque churches to world-renowned museums. Art lovers come to see timeless classics and masterpieces by painters such as Titian, Veronese, and Bellini, just to name a few. Architecture lovers and historians wander along the Grand Canal and find themselves face-to-face with renowned *palazzi* and churches by giants such as Andrea Palladio and Baldassare Longhena. Additionally, world-class 20th century art is on display in the Guggenheim Museum and the Ca' Pesaro Gallery.

But Venice is not a city to rest on its laurels. Intent on staying contemporary, Venice is home to one of the most exciting and famous art events in the world (the Biennale – find out more in tip 25). And if you want to further your journey and explore some cutting-edge contemporary work, there are three stops in town that you really shouldn't miss: Palazzo Grassi, Punto della Dogana and Prada Foundation. All three have opened in Venice in recent years, and have all but confirmed the city's continued commitment to inspiring art.

Punta della Dogana and Palazzo Grassi are the epicenter of contemporary art in Venice. Both belong to François Pinault, the French billionaire and collector and one of the most powerful people in the art world. The **Punta della Dogana** was once the customs house for the city of Venice, and today it is a fascinating 5,000-square-meter triangular building, restored and renovated by architect Tadao Ando, to house part of Pinault's vast collection. **Palazzo Grassi** is a favorite for many, and hosts several interesting exhibitions. Tadao Ando worked on this building, too, and his renovation masterfully highlights the museum's contemporary collection while giving credit to the baroque ceiling frescos and exterior of this 1749 neoclassic *palazzo*—the last to be built before the fall of the Venice Republic. A visit to the bookshop here is a must for art lovers. It is also worth noting that behind Palazzo Grassi hides a small gallery known as the **Teatrino**, which often hosts various cultural events, from screenings to concerts to theater shows (entry to many of these events is free of charge). Should you be interested in attending any of these events, check the Palazzo Grassi website in advance to find out more.

Lastly, the **Prada Foundation** is hosted in Ca' Corner della Regina, an 18th century former monastery and state archive. Beautiful and grandiose, the façade is covered in Istria stone, which adds to its captivating demeanor. The gallery is owned by the Prada Foundation and is the fruit of the long-held love of contemporary art by fashion designer Miuccia Prada and her husband Patrizio Bertelli. The couple have commissioned many works from various artists and launched a Milan exhibition space, and this is their Venetian "home base." Exhibitions don't open year-round, so it is worth checking in advance and stopping by if anything interesting is planned during the time of your visit.

Palazzo Grassi,
Campo San Samuele (right off the S. Samuele vaporetto stop). www.palazzograssi.it. Open Wednesday-Monday, 10:00 a.m-7:00 p.m. (the ticket office closes at 6 p.m.) Closed Tuesday. Combined tickets to Palazzo Grassi and Punto della Dogana are available. ★★★★

Punta della Dogana,
Dorsoduro 2 (near the Salute vaporetto stop). Punta della Dogana has the same hours of operation as Palazzo Grassi. Guided tours of the exhibitions can be booked in advance via email: visite@palazzograssi.it. ★★★★

Prada Foundation,
Santa Croce 2215 (Calle de Ca' Corner). Tel: 041.8109161, www.fondazioneprada.org. The foundation's hours of operation depend on the exhibitions it hosts. ★★★★

16 **Buy a One-of-a-Kind,** Uniquely Venetian Piece of Jewelry

Part of the thrill of visiting Venice is glimpsing the old-world glamour exuded by its *palazzi, campi* and bridges. And what better way to play the part of the elegant Venetian than by accessorizing with authentic jewelry? This tip guides the savvy buyer to two of our favorite jewelers in the city, one modern atelier and one classic antique shop.

Muranero was born out of the passion of two artists, Senegalese-born Niang Moulaye and Venetian native Emanuela Chimenton. Moulaye is a graduate of the Abato Zanetti Murano School of Glass, and can be seen working in the shop, creating stunning beads that are crafted into one-of-a-kind pieces by Emanuela. The designs here are smart and often amusing, reflecting the artists' free spirits and keen eye for structure and texture. And while

both artists do adhere to traditional manufacturing processes, they also incorporate their surroundings and different backgrounds into their style and design philosophy. One of the best features of this small atelier is that personalized items are not only available but actively encouraged, and since Moulaye prepares many of the glass beads on the spot, he can easily create a necklace or bracelet using the colors of your choice. Those who wish to complete the look with some swanky eyewear will be happy to know that Mantovani frames are on sale here, too (to read more about the famous Mantovani eyewear, see tip 33).

At the other end of the scale, **Le Zoie** specializes in intricately crafted antique jewelry, such as 18th century diamond pendants and brooches decorated with precious stones. The store has a number of collections on display, but our absolute favorite has to be the Theriaca Collection. Theriaca was a potent potion first used by the Greeks to cure various illnesses, and it continued to be a famous medicine throughout the Middle Ages. Venetian apothecaries were considered the most skilled in preparing this ancient potion, and each pharmacy had its own identifying seal on their individual bottles. The designers of the Theriaca collection have looped gold around these ancient seals, which come in a variety of colors, including beautiful deep reds and purples, vibrant blues and mustard yellows, and meticulously crafted them into necklaces, earrings and brooches. These are really one-of-a-kind pieces, imbued with a little piece of the city's history. Aside from jewelry, Le Zoie stocks other antiques, everything from period 18th century desks to 17th century glassware, and even an antique gonodola! They also have a selection of 20th century Murano glass items by some of the most famous names, such as Venini and Barovier. In short, Le Zoie is a treasure trove for design lovers.

Muranero,
Salizada del Pignater, Castello 3545 (about 10 minutes from Piazza San Marco). www.muranero.venezia.it. Open daily, 12:00 p.m.-8:00 p.m. ★★★★

Le Zoie,
Calle dei Boteri 1566 (near the Rialto Bridge). Tel: 041.275.8694, www.lezoie.com. The shop's opening hours tend to vary; stop by, or call in advance to book an appointment. ★★★★

17 **Celebrate the Most Beloved Local Festival in Venice** and Enjoy the Spectacular Fireworks

Carnival is undoubtedly Venice's most famous festival. Full of color and spectacle, it draws tourists from around the world, who flock to see the colorful masks and exuberant costumes. However, as famous as Carnival is, it is not necessarily the festival that truly captures the hearts of the locals. That honor is reserved for **Il Redentore,** a festival in July, when the city comes alive with fireworks and people decorate their boats, terraces and rooftops in celebration. Il Redentore is commonly regarded in Venice as the most authentic local event, so to speak, and participating in it gives visitors a chance to understand Venetian culture and enjoy an intimate glimpse into the beating heart of the city.

The **Redentore Festival** has been celebrated since 1577 and marks the end of a particularly violent episode of the plague in Venice, which killed thousands of Venetians, including the beloved painter Titian. To mark the city's emancipation from the grip of death, the wealthy merchants of Venice sponsored the construction of a new church. It is from that church, located on Giudecca Island, that the festival takes its name. Il Redentore takes place on the third weekend of July each year, and the festivities kick off on Saturday at sunset, when dozens of small boats packed with locals sail from every corner of Venice and park at St. Mark's Basin (the large section at the end of the Grand Canal, which opens onto the lagoon). As to be expected with any Italian festivity, the evening starts with a meal. Venetian classics like *pasta e fagioli* and *sarde in saor* are shared among family and friends, and Spritz cocktails and wine flow like water. Around 11:30 p.m. the impressive fireworks start, and dazzling colors illuminate the sky and reflect off the surface of the water, lighting up the lagoon like a mystical fairyland.

If you plan on dining out on this day, make sure you reserve well in advance, as everything is full. If you want to find a good place to see the fireworks, know that the streets, alleys, and waterways will be absolutely packed. You'd be surprised at the stamina of local elderly ladies who show up in the late afternoon with folding chairs and a determined look on their faces, ready to catch the best viewing spots for their families. The best places are, obviously, those that afford a good view of the water: Piazza San Marco; Fondamenta San Giacomo (on Giudecca Island), Fondamente Zattere Ai Saloni, and the Punta della Dogana.

To make your night even more special, consider booking a private viewing from an apartment or boat, with a private tour guide. Jacopo della Torre offers visitors access to historical events from select, private locations, for an unparalleled experience. Find out more here: www.jacopodellatorre.com, or consult the boat tour operators listed in tip 26; they all offer special tours and activities for the Redentore.

18 **Buy a Book** at Libreria Acqua Alta

Stacks and stacks of novels towering over a boat full of hardbacks? Piles of novels and magazines sitting beside a gondola packed with poetry? It must be Libreria Acqua Alta, Venice's quirkiest bookshop. This one-of-a-kind book seller hides in one of the most tranquil corners of Venice, and stocks a cavernous collection of literature all of kinds. Coming here is always an amusing adventure, as you get to peruse the collection and often end up purchasing some book or other about the history of Venice. Be sure to get some recommendations from the wildly eccentric owner, Luigi Frizzo. And take our word for it: There is method to his madness!

Libreria Acqua Alta,
Sestiere Castello 5176/B.
Tel: 041.296.0841. Open Monday-Saturday, 9:00 a.m.-7:00 p.m. (might close later in the summer). Closed Sunday. ★★★

19 Take an Exciting Helicopter Ride over Venice and the Dolomites

Driving around the Veneto countryside can be a pleasant experience, but if you are searching for an unforgettable way to explore the territory, why not appreciate the scenery from the unique perspective of a helicopter? Such rides, though expensive, are awe-inspiring and magical, a perfect way to create a lasting memory.

Alessandro, the friendly and professional pilot, will take you on a once-in-a-lifetime ride over the region. Various itineraries can be organized and personalized, but the most popular, without a doubt, is the "winged lion tour": you will fly over the lagoon and Burano, and then along the Giudecca Canal, where you will enjoy a spectacular view of Piazza San Marco. The flights are conducted in either a helicopter or a two-engined monoplane, and leave from Padova Airport. Your itinerary can even be extended to include a flight over the Dolomites (especially incredible on clear winter days), Verona, Lake Garda or the region's vineyards. Booking in advance is recommended (though same-day openings are sometimes available). Try not to schedule your flight for the weekend or for Monday—days when it can be hard to find an open booking.

Alessandro,
www.vfly-aerotaxi.it. ★★★★★

20 Dig into a Reasonably Priced Meal near the Accademia

The Dorsoduro area, especially the alleys surrounding the Accademia museum, offer their fair share of un *bacari*. But if you aren't in the mood for a *cicheti* crawl to satiate your hunger (see tip 13) and prefer a real restaurant instead, then **Taverna San Trovaso** is just the spot. It has reasonable prices, tasty food, generous portions and tends to please all (even children), so it's no wonder the Taverna is almost always full. The style here is unassuming and homey, like a meal cooked by someone's grandma (albeit a talented one!). Choose between simple and popular crowd-pleasers, such as the meaty lasagna or the gnocchi *quattro formaggi* (gnocchi served with a creamy four-cheese sauce), or try more complicated dishes, such as gnocchi *newborg* (with tomatoes, shrimp and cream), or spaghetti with clams. Under *specialita' dello chef* (the chef's specialty) you will find dishes such as *ossobuco* with polenta, or one of our favorites – *bavette alla busera* – a flat type of pasta served with *scampi* (langoustines), hot chili flakes and fresh tomatoes. While this isn't gourmet cooking, it's absolutely satisfying. The fact that most *primi* cost under €10 and most *secondi* are less than €15 is in itself a reason to stop by. If you come at lunchtime, their €15 fixed menu is worth considering.

Alternatively, if you prefer something more sophisticated (and don't mind spending just a little bit more), walk five minutes toward Campo San Barnaba, where two absolutely delightful restaurants await – Oniga and La Bitta. **Oniga,** on the main *campo,* is a great choice, and offers a seasonal menu featuring all of the classic Venetian staples (their menu is heavily oriented towards seafood).

Alternatively, vegetarians and meat lovers will be happy to discover **La Bitta,** which is just half a block away. This no-frills neighborhood restaurant specializes in meat and vegetable-based dishes, with not a fish or shellfish in sight. Try dishes such as grilled radicchio salad with melted Taleggio cheese, potato gnocchi with artichokes and salty ricotta, any of their delicious homemade pasta dishes, braised pork, and traditional and hearty bean and spelt minestrone.

Taverna San Trovaso,
Sestiere Dorsoduro 1016 (across the bridge from Calle Toletta, and near Pensione Accademia).
Tel: 041.520.3703,
www.tavernasantrovaso.it.
Open daily, 12:00 p.m.-2:45 p.m. & 7:00 p.m.-9:45 p.m. ★★★

Oniga,
Dorsoduro 2852 (Campo San Barnaba, near the Ca' Rezzonico vaporetto stop).
Tel: 041.522.4410, www.oniga.it. Open daily, 12:00 p.m.-3:00 p.m. & 7:00 p.m.-11:00 p.m. ★★★★

La Bitta,
Calle Lunga de San Barnaba, Dorsoduro 2753. Tel: 041.523.0531. Open Monday-Saturday for dinner only, 6:30 p.m.-11:00 p.m. Closed Sunday. Note that this restaurant does not accept credit cards, only cash. ★★★★

21 **Revel in a Gourmet Meal** with a Spectacular View

Whether they are located in sun-filled courtyards or in tiny little hideaways by quiet backwater canals, Venice is teeming with excellent restaurants of various kinds. Visitors who want to experience the quintessential Venetian dining experience in a romantic little *trattoria* by a canal will be spoiled for choice. But if you are searching for something different, a restaurant that offers majestic views as well as divine flavors, then this is the tip for you (to read more about an *aperitivo* with a view, see tip 4). Listed below are four restaurants that we believe have the best combination of an exclusive location, dazzling views and, of course, quality food. Whichever you choose, you'll be sure to have an unforgettable evening. For all four of these restaurants, we highly recommend that you book a table in advance.

Note that in all four, the lunch menu is less costly (and less elaborate) than the evening menu.

On the top floor of the historic Hotel Danieli you will find the number one choice for lunch or dinner with a view in Venice. **La Terrazza's** outdoor terrace steals the show in this unimaginably romantic setting, with views overlooking the Grand Canal. At night, when the marble-covered *palazzi* glow in the soft moonlight and the island of San Giorgio can be seen from afar, the ambiance is bewitching. The setting outside is matched inside with a stylish interior décor, but, naturally, it's the terrace that draws the crowd, so don't settle for anything but an outside table with a view. If you book well in advance, you might be able to reserve the best table in the house – a table for two at the farthest angle of the terrace, with an uninterrupted panoramic view. La Terrazza specializes in an eclectic menu, featuring a locally sourced range of seafood dishes that, for the most part, lives up well to the quality of the surroundings. Some of the dishes you can expect to enjoy include seared *scampi* with zucchini and crispy seaweed wafers, risotto with a creamy broccoli sauce, or mussels served with goat's cheese and citron mignonettes. Meat and vegetarian options are available, too. Unsurprisingly, such a beautiful setting comes at a price. Expect to pay €140 to €170 per person if you opt for the à la carte menu (or about €120 for the tasting menu—wine excluded). Note that the terrace section of the restaurant is only open in high season, when the fine weather permits outdoor dining (usually May to September). If you are visiting off-season and can't sit outside and enjoy the view, you might want to consider other dining options instead.

Second on our list of favorites is **Cip's Club,** at the Belmond Cipriani Hotel. The Cipriani is one of the most famous and exclusive hotels in Venice. It has been home to the jet-set crowd for decades and is used to catering to stars, directors and globe-trotting celebrity designers when they come to town. The Belmond Cipriani is located on Giudecca Island, across the canal from Piazza San Marco, giving guests that quiet intimacy that's so hard to come by in tourist-heavy Venice, yet it is just five minutes (by water taxi) from the heart of the mainland. The hotel has a number of dining venues, including their flagship restaurant, **Ristorante Oro,** but in our opinion, the choice that tops the list every time is Cip's Club. While not quite as formal as the Oro, it remains suitably glamorous and sophisticated. Best of all, it is located on a beautiful terrace right on the water, giving you unparalleled views of Piazza San Marco and the lagoon. The food here is good, for the most part (but not exceptional); stick to one of their classic dishes, such as the thinly sliced beef tartar seasoned with the Cipriani's original secret sauce, or the sole fillet in sweet and sour sauce, served with white polenta and sautéed onions. The spaghetti with lobster and tomatoes is always a popular choice, too.

Last on our list of favorite spots with a view is **La Cusina,** located in the Westin Europa hotel on the Grand Canal. Sophisticated yet not overly so, La Cusina is simpler than our previous two recommendations, and offers visitors the chance to enjoy a pleasant lunch with a wonderful view without spending a fortune. (Though it certainly isn't cheap—expect to pay around 25€ per serving, and note that the dinner menu is much pricier than the lunch menu.) La Cusina is situated just across the Grand Canal from the Basilica della Salute, which means it affords particularly charming panoramic views to those who choose to dine on its terrace. Add to that its proximity to Piazza San Marco, and you will understand why we consider La Cusina a worthy option. Seating outside on the terrace is limited, so booking in advance is recommended. If you are enjoying a romantic city break, know that La Cusina also offers private seating arrangements (that must be booked in advance).

La Terrazza,
Hotel Danieli, Riva degli Schiavoni 4196. Tel: 041.522.6480, www.terrazzadanieli.com. Open daily, 12:00 p.m.-3:00 p.m. & 7:00 p.m.-10:30 p.m. Dining on the terrace is possible in fine weather only. ★★★★★

Cip's Club,
in the Belmond Hotel Cipriani, Giudecca 10. Tel: 041.240.801 (reservations: 0185.2678.451,) www.belmond.com. Open daily, 12:30 p.m.-2:30 p.m. & 7:30 p.m.-10:30 p.m. ★★★★

La Cusina,
San Marco 2159 (between the San Marco Vallaresso and the Santa Maria del Giglio *vaporetto* stops). Tel: 041.2400.794, www.lacusina.it. Open daily, 12:00 p.m-2:30 p.m. & 7:30 p.m.-10:00 p.m. ★★★★

22 **Buy Stunning Hand-Crafted** Paper Artifacts

Along with so many other fine inventions, the humble italic font (type) is an Italian innovation, and has its roots in the papermaking industry of 15th century Venice. This sloping, light-bodied and compact letterform was invented in 1501 by Francesco Griffo and popularized by Venetian printer Aldus Manutius. Manutius hoped that the new font would save space and make his books cheaper. His font became well-loved, and his competitors, unwilling to pay to use the innovation, created their own version of the font and named the style after Italy, thus the "italic" font was born. This small anecdote is just one example of many that demonstrate Venice's long history with paper and print. In fact, Venice has always had a reputation for making beautiful, quality paper, and the industry is as intrinsic to the city as mask making or glass manufacturing. Today, whether you are looking for traditional marbled paper or more modern designs, you will find it among Venice's artisans. And handmade and hand-printed notebooks, wrapping paper and frames make for delightful and authentic souvenirs.

There are a number of famous shops in town that have been hooted and tooted in guidebook after guidebook, but there are actually many other lesser-known yet equally excellent craftsmen worth discovering. **Il Fabricharte** is a case in point. Run by a passionate young artist named Andrea Andreatta, the shop hides in a slightly less touristy section of Venice (though very accessible), right next to the Hospital and the Scuola Grande San Marco (not to be confused with the Scuola di San Rocco). It's surrounded by other tiny and interesting shops, and this whole area is worth a quick tour, perhaps on your way to other, better-known attractions. Andreatta offers handmade papers in traditional prints, as well as custom designs made to your specific taste (when we came in, he was working on a traditional Venetian box for one client's son's Nintendo DS). Don't miss one of the best items on sale—the "Book of Venice," a gorgeous notebook in which every page is illustrated with 19th century images of Venice and the Grand Canal. We bought one and found it to be the perfect pad to jot down our impressions of the city. All items can be personalized with calligraphy, too. The prices are absolutely reasonable and the service is friendly and helpful, giving you an added reason to stop by.

Legatoria Polliero is another personal favorite. This is a delightful little shop right on Campo dei Frari, next to the famous Basilica dei Frari. The papermaking here adheres to traditional processes and the selection of products is beautiful. We love the reproductions of authentic 18th century designs and the classic leather-bound notebooks, but there are also some more modern items and fabulous stationery. Anselmo Polliero, the current owner, is the third-generation Polliero to run this family business.

Another fine choice is **Paolo Olbi,** which has been in operation since 1962 and is a true Venetian institution. Paolo, the owner who gives the shop its name, is a dedicated artist and has a genuine passion for what he does. The shop stocks a wonderful selection of products: pencil holders in vivid primary colors, photo albums with intricate designs, diaries in various sizes, and unique stationery. Everything, naturally, is handmade.

Finally, **Il Papiro** is a small chain of shops that offer clients in Tuscany and Veneto several beautiful handmade paper products, everything from elegant stationery to delightful albums, envelopes and even items of clothing. Their Venice shop is centrally located and irresistible for those who love handcrafted paper.

Il Fabricharte,
Castello 6477/A (Calle del Cafetier). Tel: 041.200.6743, www.fabricharte.org. Open Wednesday-Monday, 11:00 a.m.-7:00 p.m. Closed Tuesday. ★★★★

Legatoria Poliero,
Campo dei Frari (left of the Basilica), San Polo 2995. Tel: 041.528.5130. Open Monday-Saturday, 10:30 a.m.-12:30 p.m. & 4:00 p.m.-7:00 p.m. Closed Sunday. ★★★★

Legatoria Paolo Olbi,
Dorsoduro 3253 (by the Ca' Foscari bridge). Tel: 041.523.7655, www.olbi.atspace.com. Open Monday-Saturday, 10:00 a.m.-12:30 p.m. & 3:30 p.m.-6:30 p.m. Closed Sunday. ★★★★

Il Papiro,
Calle del Piovan, S.Marco 2764 (there's a second shop in Calle delle Bande - Castello 5275). Tel: 041.522.3055, www.ilpapirofirenze.it. Open daily, 9:30 a.m.-8:30 p.m. ★★★★

23 Relax with a Glass of Fine Wine at the Charming Bar Foscarini

Foscarini is, in our opinion, the prime stop for a glass of wine before or after a visit to the Gallerie dell'Accademia. It is perfectly located and manages to create a sense of intimacy even though it is constantly surrounded by tourists. The tiny gondola dock on the other side of the canal is perfect for people watching, and if your hand is wrapped around a glass of bubbling Prosecco, your break will be that much better. Most importantly, Bar Foscarini has a beautiful view – the Accademia Bridge on your left and the elegant Palazzo Loredan directly opposite. The palazzo, which features a striking 15th century Gothic facade, today houses the Veneto Institute of Science, Literature and Arts. Though it can't be visited regularly, the institute does open its doors when temporary exhibitions are held on the premises. If you have some extra time on your hands, it is worth checking in with the local tourist office to find out if any interesting events or shows are planned during the time of your visit.

Foscarini,
Dorsoduro 878/C (by the Accademia Bridge). Tel: 041.522.7281. Open daily, 9:00 a.m.-9:00 p.m. ★★★

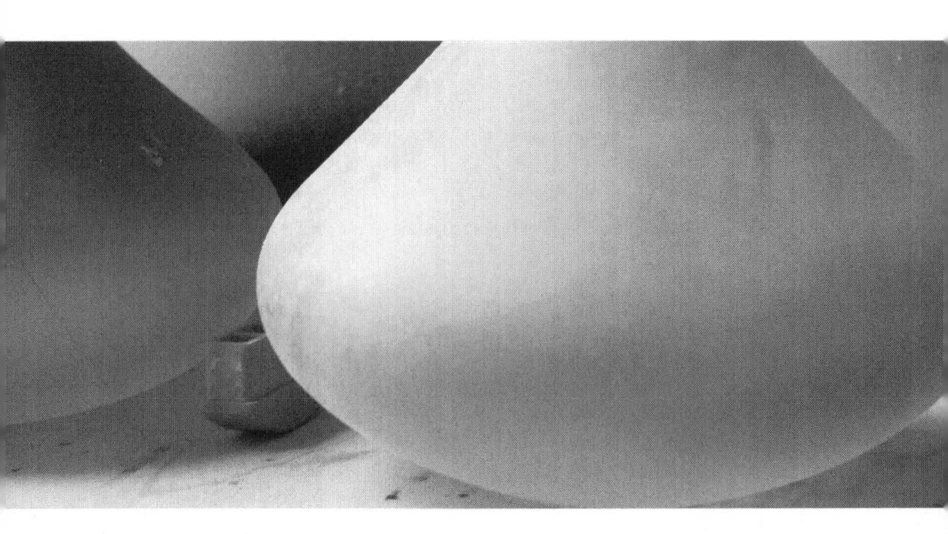

24 Stroll the Streets around the Guggenheim Museum for Swanky Souvenirs

The area that stretches from Gallerie dell'Accademia to the Guggenheim Museum is home to a wonderfully eclectic array of shops, many of which stock swanky items that you won't find in regular tourist haunts. If you are searching for a unique piece, here are some interesting stops in the area that shouldn't be missed:

The Guggenheim Museum gift shop is a must-visit, whether you plan on entering the museum or not. (Though we absolutely recommend you visit the museum, naturally. It's one of the most exceptional attractions in Venice.) There are actually two shops: one inside the museum that requires a ticket for access, and one outside on the street, for the general public. The shop in the museum has a better selection of art books, whereas the shop outside has a better selection of artifacts. You will find some delightful items here, everything from handmade Milanese pottery to stylish jewelry from local designers. The typical fare of museum shops, such as postcards, posters, and magnets, is also on sale.

A block away from the Guggenheim you will find **Schiavon Art Team,** with their selection of vibrant and contemporary Murano glass sculptures. This well-known boutique is considered by many to be a must-stop for designers. You will find everything from jewelry to artistic vases, all produced by this family of famous glass blowers, which has been in the business for six generations and today exhibit their work in galleries across the globe. Prices aren't cheap, but if you choose smaller items, like a beautiful set of handmade Murano glasses, they can be affordable.

Mariana and Susanna Sent is another obvious stop. Their

sophisticated handmade glass jewelry and vases are sold at many galleries and museums, not just in Venice itself but abroad, too (including the MOMA shop in New York). The Sent sisters' style is modern and light. Today they operate three shops in Venice: the first, located on Calle Larga Marzo, is absolutely tiny (and can probably be skipped); the second is near the Guggenheim Museum; and the third is on the island of Murano, where most glass blowers keep an active studio and boutique.

Also in the area are the intriguing **Pop Art Gallery** and the **Antiquus Gallery,** offering jewelry by the Carla C. studio. The former has some quirky Murano glass items and wildly colorful glasses, while the latter has a captivating selection of dramatic pieces, as well as vintage silver and antique paintings and artifacts that will grab your attention.

The selection of shops and galleries continues after you pass the Guggenheim Museum, too. **Genninger Studio,** in Campiello Barbaro right next to the exit from the museum, will tempt you with some classic Murano jewelry, as well as beautiful lamps and tableware, designed by American-born Leslie Ann Genninger. Next door, antique collector **Claudia Canestrelli** sells some surprising, quaint antiques and collectibles that will entice you to hang around just a little bit longer and rummage a little harder to discover hidden treasures.

Finally, don't miss Calle del Bastion, a street that runs parallel to the canal and connects the Guggenheim Museum exit to the Salute *vaporetto* stop. This narrow alley is filled with stylish and interesting shops, and our absolute favorite is **Nason Ermanno,** a boutique that overflows with colorful and whimsical Murano glass items (most are reasonably priced). Don't be put off by the touristy exterior—this shop actually sells many quality items, including the work of famous Murano artist Ermanno Nason (or rather, his studio. Nason passed away four years ago).

Guggenheim Museum gift shop, Dorsoduro 710 (about 50 meters before the museum's entrance). Tel: 041.2405.422, www.guggenheim-venice.it. Open Wednesday-Monday, 10:00 a.m.-6:00 p.m. Closed Tuesday. ★★★★

Pop Art Gallery, Dorsoduro 880/B. Tel: 041.522.8585. Open Monday-Saturday, 10:00 a.m.-6:00 p.m. ★★★

Antiquus Gallery, Dorsoduro 873 (Calle Nuova S.Agnese). Tel: 041.241.3725, www.carla-c-venice.com. Open Monday-Saturday, 10:00 a.m.-1:00 p.m., & 3:30 p.m.-6:00 p.m. Closed Sunday. ★★★★

Genninger Studio, Campiello Barbaro 364 (20 meters from the Guggenheim Museum exit). Tel: 041.522.5565, www.genningerstudio.com. Open Monday-Saturday, 9:30 a.m.-1:00 p.m. & 3:00 p.m.-6:30 p.m.; Sunday, 11:00 a.m.-6:00 p.m. ★★★★

Claudia Canestrelli, Campiello Barbaro 364, Tel: 041.522.7072. Hours of operation tend to vary, but the shop is usually open Monday-Saturday, 10:00 a.m.-12:00 p.m. & 3:30 p.m.-6:00 p.m. ★★★

Nason Ermanno, Calle del Bastion, Dorsoduro 192. nasonermannove@gmail.com. Open Monday-Saturday, 10:30 a.m.-6:00 p.m. ★★★★

25 **Discover Cutting-Edge Art** at the Venice Biennale

The Venice Biennale is one of the most famous art exhibitions in the world. It takes place every two years (hence the name) in the late spring, and consists of a number of separate but interconnected events, which include biennales for art, music, theater, and architecture, the International Festival of Contemporary Dance, the International Kids' Carnival, and the Venice Film Festival (see tip 72). The biennale was established in 1893 to celebrate the silver anniversary of King Umberto I and Queen Margherita of Savoy. In 1895 foreign artists were invited to participate, and after a few technical delays (this is Italy, after all...) the first official international biennale was inaugurated, attracting a huge crowd of more than 220,000 visitors.

While the architecture biennale and the dance festival are quite famous, when people speak of the Venice Biennale, they are usually referring to the prestigious art exhibition, which has over the years drawn some of the best-known artists in the world, from Pablo Picasso and Gustav Klimt to Anish Kapoor and Jeff Koons. Undoubtedly, the glamorous and exclusive parties, closed auctions and high-brow seminars that accompany the exhibition today have all added to the allure of this event. Visiting the biennale is a special experience for seasoned art lovers, but it can also be intriguing for curious passers-by. With such a wide array of events and exhibitions, it is more than likely that you will find something that will pique your interest.

The main venue for the biennale is the **Biennale Gardens,** where the pavilions for each country participating in the event are located, but several additional exhibitions are scattered around Venice in various private *palazzi*. Touring these annexed exhibitions is a unique opportunity not only to see innovative contemporary art from around the globe, but also to get a peek inside some of Venice's most beautiful mansions, which are normally closed to the public.

Lastly, since many of the exhibitions remain open long after the biennale has officially ended (most exhibitions are open until November), it's always a good idea to check and see which events are still available during the time of your visit. Find out more here: www.labiennale.org.

26 **Tour the Lagoon** in a Historic Boat

Venice draws its life from the water, so what better way to get intimately acquainted with the city than to do as the locals do and sail the lagoon? Touring the water and the little islands at a leisurely pace is a wonderful way to connect with the ancient pace of Venice. If you are visiting off-season, in the autumn, for example, when the entire lagoon is covered in mist, the experience can be mysterious and bewitching.

Il Bragozzo is a friendly tour operator, offering a wide variety of customized tours of the lagoon. Take a romantic ride at sunset or spend the day exploring the hidden corners, monasteries, and natural beauty spots. Tours include trips to San Giorgio Island, any of the lagoon's smaller islands and even down the Brenta River, along the historic route that connects Venice to Padova. Special activities are on offer, too, everything from gondola rowing classes to sailing classes to fishing expeditions. During the Festa del Redentore (see tip 17), Il Bragozzo offer seats on their boats headed to St. Mark's Basin, where you will be able to participate like the local Venetian families and enjoy a meal and the fireworks show from the water.

Alternatively, try a tour with **Sior Cioci.** Captain Vito will take you across the lagoon aboard his 1955 *bragozzo* boat, a beautifully restored craft—the perfect authentic vehicle for sailing to whichever hidden spot in the lagoon you desire to discover.

Cavana Tintoretto offers interesting tours, too. They focus on a variety of subjects, from the lagoon's flora and fauna to the famous (and controversial) MOSE project. These professional tours can easily be adapted and personalized to visitors' interests.

Alternatively, those who wish to experience the lagoon in a more adventurous and alternative way will greatly enjoy the kayak tours offered by **Venice Kayak.**

Il Bragozzo,
Dorsoduro 2408. Cell: 388.182.6009, www.ilbragozzo.it. ★★★★

Sior Cioci,
Cell: 327.924.9084, www.siorcioci.com. ★★★★

Cavana Tintoretto Boat Tours,
Cannaregio 3333. Tel: 041.722.818, www.cavanatintoretto.com. ★★★★

Venice Kayak,
Via Servi di Maria 41 (activities leave from the Certosa island). Cell: 346.477.1327, www.venicekayak.com. ★★★★

27 **Book a Delectable Meal** at Alle Testiere, one of Venice's Top Restaurants

In recent years alle Testiere has become one of the most discussed restaurants in town. With every foodie and guide singing its praises, it seems almost redundant to mention it. However, this restaurant really is quite good and shouldn't be ignored, as it is, together with Da Rioba, Venissa and Anice Stellato (see tips 8 and 57), one of the best seafood restaurants in town.

Serious but far from austere, respectable but never stuffy, alle Testiere was born of the owner's frustration with the abundance of Venetian restaurants that served mediocre food for ridiculous prices, destroying Venice's culinary reputation. The result was this tiny family-run osteria, where the chef cooks exclusively what he knows and loves best—fine seafood dishes made with the freshest possible ingredients. Alle Testiere's menu changes regularly, depending on what's available at the Rialto fish market. When we were here, we found dishes such as gazpacho with fried octopus, scallops with a delicate orange sauce and thinly sliced and sautéed organic leeks, *grancevola alla veneziana* (a typical local dish of whole crabs), creamed *baccala* with polenta, ravioli filled with swordfish, potato ravioli served with fresh shrimp, and more. The commitment to quality can be witnessed in the smallest details, such as the choice of *polenta* flour (alle Testiere uses a coarse white flour, which gives their polenta a surprising consistency) or the way they prepare their cuttlefish. The fine wine list, focusing on local offerings, is fantastic—allow the knowledgeable staff to recommend the right pairing for your dish. Lastly, don't miss the homemade desserts. We promise the sweet ending will make your meal even more delectable. There are only 22 seats in the house, which means that finding an empty table without a reservation is impossible. Additionally, note that there are two dinner turns, one at 7:30 p.m. and one at 9:00 p.m., which, honestly, creates a bit of a stressful dining experience for those who book an earlier meal. For that reason we prefer coming for lunch or for the later evening round.

Alle Testiere,
Calle del Mondo Novo 5801 (in the narrow alley between Campo Santa Maria Formosa and Salizada San Lio). Tel: 041.522.7220, www.osterialletestiere.it. Open daily, 12:30 p.m.-3:00 p.m. & 7:00 p.m.-10:30 p.m. Advance reservations are recommended. ★★★★★

28 Relax at Some of the Most Fashionable Beaches on the Lido

The Lido is often overlooked by tourists in favor of the more picturesque Burano Island, or the famous glass industry island of Murano. But the island of Lido does throw in a few surprises and perks that are worth checking out. The days here are filled with relaxing beach activities, renting bikes and setting off along the beautiful shoreline, stopping here and there to top up your tan. Golf enthusiasts will even find a golf course in which to practice their swing. In late August, the Lido is buzzing with people and events. At night you can experience the fashionable beach parties and during the day you can buy tickets for public screenings of one of the movies featured in the Venice Film Festival (see tip 72) and ogle the parade of VIPs making their way on the red carpet near the Palazzo del Cinema.

Regardless of the glamorous allure of the Venice Film Festival, the first and foremost reason to come to Lido is for that all-important, precious beach time. The choice for beachgoers is vast—there are free beaches, standard beaches and luxury beaches. The free beaches are located right at the end of Viale Santa Elisabetta, the avenue that leaves from the *vaporetto* docking station and connects it to the waterline. As soon as the street ends, at the roundabout, you'll see a sign in front of you directing you to the free beaches. If you turn left at the roundabout, you will find a series of family friendly standard beaches (such as Blue Moon, Paradiso and San Nicolo' beaches). These require a fee to enter and to rent a chair. Alternatively, if you turn right at the roundabout and walk along Viale Marconi, you will see a series of exclusive beaches that belong to the most famous hotels in the Lido, starting with the **Des Bains Beach,** which is even mentioned in Thomas Mann's *Death in Venice,* and continuing all the way to the **Excelsior Beach** by Hotel Excelsior (a favorite shooting location for directors, including Martin Scorsese). Entry to these beaches starts at €25 per person per day, and can go up to €180 if you want the most coveted spots and a private couch. If you have your heart set on spending the day on one of the exclusive beaches, it's worth calling the beach association's info line (Tel. 041.2716808) in advance, as they sometimes offer last-minute reductions for spaces that haven't been booked or have been cancelled. Many of the exclusive beaches offer a 50% discount for those who come during the afternoon (though you should know that most beaches close down at 7:30 p.m., so you will only have a few hours to enjoy the waves).

All that swimming and tanning makes a person hungry, and the eateries on the Lido have the typical beach town ambiance. There are a number of friendly restaurants along Viale Santa Elisabetta, and a few unjustifiably pricey restaurants attached to the exclusive hotels. Ideally, limit your culinary sampling of the Lido to a chic *aperitivo* with a view and enjoy dinner on mainland Venice (which is just 20 minutes away by *vaporetto*). There are several beach bars to choose from, naturally, but if you are looking for a calmer and more upscale option, then try the bar and restaurant at **Hotel Villa Laguna.** The hotel is located next to the Lido *vaporetto* docking station (stand with your back to the docking station, turn right and walk about 100 meters) and the restaurant is open to non-guests, too. If you book a table close to the water, you will enjoy a lovely view of San Giorgio Island and the lagoon. Far in the distance you will spot Piazza San Marco's bell tower. In the evening, the sunset turns everything into magic. Whichever place you choose, dressing the part can go a long way toward ensuring friendly service.

The Beach Association's Info Line,
Tel. 041.271.6808

Venezia Beaches,
www.veneziaspiagge.it

Hotel Villa Laguna,
Via Sandro Gallo 6, Lido di Venezia.
Tel: 041.526.1316, www.villalaguna.hotelinvenice.com. ★★★

29 Drink an Espresso at Casanova's Favorite Spot: the Historic Caffé Florian

Venice is awash with popular cafés, where locals and tourists flood in to savor a finely roasted and smooth espresso before heading out to see the city. And while some may make a very fine cup indeed, none can compete with the Florian's rich history.

Coffee may seem a more recent Italian obsession, but Italians have actually been enamored with the fragrant black liquid for centuries. The Florian, Europe's oldest coffee house, was founded in 1720, when Venice was still a powerful and vibrant maritime republic. Venetian merchants trotted the globe and brought back with them scents, tastes and secrets from east and west. One of these treasures was coffee, a mysterious drink first reported by the Venetian ambassador to Turkey in 1581, and described as a potent potion that helped one stay awake. Initially coffee was reserved for noble families and kings, but the drink quickly gained fame and popularity among the general public, too; eventually, the Florian and other public coffee houses were established. Word of the Florian spread quickly and, according to local legend, it was Giacomo Casanova's favorite hangout. In fact, the famous lover even risked imprisonment for a final cup of their flavorsome brew; right after he escaped his prison cell he called in one last time before embarking on a boat that took him away from Venice forever.

Today the Florian cashes in on its fame, and prices here are ridiculously high. That said, it is still one of those places that history buffs and those romantic at heart will probably want to visit at least once when in Venice. And on hot summer nights, when the cafe's orchestra is playing, you can dance under the moonlight, or simply sip your cappuccino or a pricey but expertly mixed Tintoretto (the Florian's signature cocktail) and get some people watching done. Alternatively, you can sit inside and take a step back in time. The interior of the Florian is lavishly decorated with opulent, dramatic frescoes. It is hard not to be dazzled by the resplendent riches on offer as you walk past gold mirrors, fancy chandeliers and classic antique Italian furniture, and it takes only a tiny bit of whimsical fantasy to imagine that the year is 1715, and you are taking your coffee with the exclusive affluent of 1700s Venice.

Caffè Florian,
Piazza San Marco 56-59,
Tel: 041.520.5641,
www.caffeflorian.com.
Open daily, 9:00 a.m.-midnight. ★★★

30 **Book a Cooking Class** and Learn How to Make Authentic Italian Delicacies

Italy is all about food. Crisp pizza, satisfying pasta dishes, creamy risottos, tender and flavor-packed meat, fresh seafood, long lunches and even longer dinners—Italians adore and celebrate their mouth-watering cuisine. Italian food and culture go hand-in-hand, so what better way to understand the rich local culinary heritage than by taking a fun yet professional cooking class? While cooking classes are never cheap, they are not ridiculously expensive either. For aspiring chefs or hungry foodies, they become a gift that keeps on giving, as you transfer what you have learned during your vacation to your kitchen at home and straight to the plates of hungry friends and family. This tip includes two of the best cooking schools the city has to offer, in our opinion, so don't forget to pack your apron!

Enrica Rocca has, in recent years, become somewhat of a celebrity on the local cooking scene. Her courses are a little pricey but professional and great fun, not least because instead of cramming into a restaurant kitchen-turned-school, you are invited into her beautiful Venetian mansion, inside an 18th century *palazzo*, where you will cook and then eat, accompanying your meal with fine wines. The full-day cooking class includes a guided tour (led by Enrica or her assistant) to the famous Rialto Market, where you will learn about selecting seafood. Then, after a glass of Prosecco in a nearby *bacaro*, you will return to Enrica's home to cook. The half-day cooking class is similar, but doesn't include the Rialto Market tour.

Alternatively, **Acquolina Cooking School** offers fun and professional cooking classes run by a well-established chef, Marika Seguso, who has worked in top restaurants in New York and Milan. Upon her return to Italy she decided to start offering lessons, too. Classes are held on Lido Island, away from the hustle and bustle of mainland Venice, and are meant to let visitors get up close and personal with authentic, homey, everyday Italian cooking. Chef Marika is passionate about sharing the beauty of Italian cuisine with her students, exploring everything from pasta to Venetian fish dishes to appetizers and desserts. Half-day classes, priced at €160 per person (including lunch), are the most popular choice, but full-day adventures can be booked, too, which feature a visit to the Rialto fish market, a tour of two *bacari*, a cooking class and then a fine dinner, naturally, to enjoy the fruit of your labor.

Enrica Rocca Cooking School,
Calle San Domenico, Dorsoduro 568/A.
Cell: 338.634.3839,
www.enricarocca.com. ★★★★

Acquolina Cooking School,
Via Lazzaro Mocenigo 10, Lido (Venice).
Tel: 041.526.7226, www.acquolina.com/cooking-school. ★★★★

31 Celebrate the Venice Carnival in style
with Exclusive Tickets to the Masquerade Ball

No other event captures the magic of Venice like its famous carnival. It is no surprise, then, that people from all over the world flock to the city to feast on this centuries-old spectacle of color, glamour and magic. The Venice Carnival has been running since 1162, inspired, it is said, by a victory of the Serenissima Republic against the Patriarch of Aquileia, Ulrico di Treven. From the Renaissance and into the 17th century, the carnival's fame grew, along with that of its native city. In 1797, under the rigid rule of the King of Austria, the festival was banned; however, the spirit of the carnival continued and certain traditions were privately kept alive. In 1979 the government of Venice officially reinstated the spectacular event, and each year since then it has grown in size and impact. There is an impressive selection of events that take place every year, many of which are open to the general public (pick up a leaflet detailing all the events and festivities on offer at the local tourist office, or consult this website: www.carnevale.venezia.it/programma-eventi), but if you want more than the "regular" celebrations in Piazza San Marco and the standard parades, then this particularly hedonistic tip is for you.

During the carnival a number of private parties, dinners, and, most importantly, masked balls are organized by various associations. Entry to one of these glamorous events requires both advance booking and preparation (first and foremost, renting period costumes and wigs). Prepare yourself to spend a hefty sum wherever you go; this is one experience that does not come cheap. And while some of the balls do offer less expensive tickets, experience has taught us that in this case, the difference in the service you get can be substantial. So if you "only" buy one of the cheaper tickets that allow entry to the party after dinner, or one of the tickets that offer a table in one of the side halls instead of the main hall, bear in mind that you might be forfeiting part of the real experience.

The **Casanova Grand Ball** is one of the most impressive events of the carnival. At €690 for a ticket (that includes a full dinner), it doesn't come cheap. If that price tag is outside your budget, it is possible to get your hands on an after-dinner ticket that is a more affordable at around €200.

The **Mascheranda Grand Ball** takes place in a beautiful *palazzo* right on the Grand Canal—Palazzo Pisani Moretta—a magical venue for a fairytale night. This opulent mansion is decorated with sumptuous 18th century frescoes, and dinner is accompanied by live performances by dancers and musicians. This party will enable you to enjoy the incredible experience of a Venetian ball without spending an exorbitant sum (unlike the Ballo del Doge, see below). Prices start at €250 and go up to €650 for the best seats in the main hall.

The **Ballo del Doge** has a reputation for being one of the most lavish celebrations in Venice. Though the theme of the ball changes yearly, you can be certain it will be a colorful and dramatic night that will dazzle your senses. The ball takes place in the Palazzo Pisani Moretta, a magnificent historic *palazzo* that is usually closed to the public. This mansion is simply remarkable—the detailed frescos in the grand halls and the bejeweled chandeliers will transport you into the world of the 18th century nobility, a beauty that you will be reluctant to leave behind even long after the party is over. As can be expected, the prices match the feelings of grandeur. The most basic ticket costs €800, and will give you entry to the party at 11:30 p.m. A €2,000 ticket (yes, you read that correctly...) will grant you entry at 8:40 p.m. and a dinner along with the late night festivities. Getting the all-star treatment will cost about €3,000; this super-VIP ticket will secure you the best table, dinner and access to the ball, and includes a fantastic costume and wig to rent.

If these prices strike you as complete madness, then know that more reasonably priced options do exist, such as the party at the **Luna Baglioni Hotel.** The event here is quite lively and costs around €320 per person, though this excludes the cost of renting a costume. A welcoming cocktail by the fireside will give you plenty of time to take in the handsomely decorated hall before enjoying Commedia dell'arte performances in Italian. Then take part in the traditional dance in the Marco Polo Ballroom and enjoy a hearty dinner.

All of the events listed here are 18th century-themed masked balls, and require all attendees to dress like nobles from the period. It is these fabulously decadent costumes and amusing wigs, along with the glamour of the beautifully decorated mansions where the balls take place, that guarantees the charm of these events. Renting the mandatory ensemble is actually simpler than it sounds. Most grand-balls will refer you the atelier they usually work with, and you can of course also search for a favorite shop on your own. Many head directly to **Atelier Marega,** one of the most famous shops for masks in Venice (see tip 7), where lavish costumes are available to rent. Another worthy option is the **Tragicomica Workshop,** which should be able to fit you with the very finest 18th century-style clothes.

Please note that booking should be done exclusively through official and authorized representatives, to avoid fraud.

For the **Doge Ball (Ballo del Doge),** contact Maison Antonia Sautter Creations & Events, San Marco 1652 (Frezzeria). Tel: 041.241.3802, www.ilballodeldogegallery.com, booking@ballodeldoge.com. Costumes can be rented through their offices, or independently. ★★★★★

For the **Luna Baglioni Hotel Ball,** contact the hotel directly, www.baglionihotels.com. ★★★

For the **Mascheranda Ball** contact Tragicomica (www.tragicomica.it), who also provide the official costume design and rental service for the event. ★★★★★

For the **Casanova Grand Ball,** contact one of the official ticket agencies in Venice, such as www.veneziaopera-tickets.eu; or www.ticketsvenice.com. ★★★★

Alternatively, consult with a serious travel agency that will be able to take care of everything, including booking your tickets and renting your costumes. Try **Venice Events,** a British-Italian agency specializing in such activities, www.venice-carnival-italy.com. This website can also provide more information about all the events and balls organized during the carnival (including a few parties that aren't listed in this tip). Whichever ball you choose, make sure to book well in advance!

32 Enjoy an Intimate and Delicious Meal at Ristorante Vini da Gigio

There's a very good reason why Vini da Gigio is so popular and often fully booked year-round. With a simple and romantic ambiance and a classic but understatedly suave interior design, this restaurant will put you right at ease. The service can be a bit neurotic, but that takes nothing from the restaurant's charm. Add to that the excellent food and a very convenient location (just minutes from Ca' d'Oro), and it becomes quite clear why this restaurant should be high on your "restaurants to consider" list for Venice.

When coming here, we usually order their mixed Venetian platter for our *antipasto*, as it is a good way to enjoy some of the most typical Venetian delicacies, expertly prepared—polenta with tiny shrimp, a delicious seared ball of creamed *baccala*, scallops in a tangy sauce, and *sarde in saor* served with a small slice of roasted polenta. The pasta is good by any standard, particularly the *tagliolini con pesto e coda di rospo* (tagliolini with pesto and monkfish) and the spaghetti with *caparossoli* (clams). Ask for the day's specials; on our last visit we enjoyed a particularly good dish of homemade ravioli with a creamy fish filling topped with a delicate tomato and langoustine sauce. Those who prefer meat will be happy to find that unlike so many other restaurants in town, Gigio's offers an ample choice of seafood-free *antipasti, primi* and *secondi,* everything from classic Venetian liver with polenta and beef tartar to tagliatelle with duck ragout, lamb shank with roasted vegetables, and even a rich *ossobuco*. Vegetarians will also be happy to see that they haven't been left out of the feast; the spaghetti with cheese and pepper sauce, deep fried Taleggio, and potato gnocchi with truffles are all scrumptious. For dessert, try their tiramisu or the semifreddo. Alternatively, hop to **Gellateria Grom** just down the street for one of their excellent ice creams.

Vini da Gigio,
Cannaregio 3628 (near the church of San Felice). Tel: 041.528.5140, www.vinidagigio.com. Open Wednesday-Sunday, 12:00 p.m.-2:00 p.m. & 7:00 p.m.-10:00 p.m. Closed Monday & Tuesday. ★★★★

33 Buy Original and Cool Eyewear in Venice!

Ottica Mantovani is a bubbly little shop that specializes in statement eyewear that is unique in shape, color and design. The friendly owners quite rightfully pride themselves on their collection of wild, light-hearted and imaginative glasses. A stop here is a must for those looking for something "different." The location is perfect for seasoned shoppers, too. Pick up a pair of glasses and then continue, with enhanced vision, into the shopping district that surrounds the shop!

Another recommended stop for lovers of fashion and originality is **Ottica Urbani.** This hip and smart boutique is a personal favorite, and stocks some of the most original and beautiful frames we've seen. It's also a historic shop, and since 1952 they've had their fair share of famous clients, including Hemingway, Elton John, and various Italian designers. Whether you are in the market for a classic model or something fun, a sophisticated metal frame or a surprising creation from their limited collection, we recommend stopping here and seeing what they are up to.

Ottica Mantovani,
San Marco 4860 (Mercerie del Capitello). Tel: 041.522.3427. Open daily, 10:00 a.m.-7:30 p.m. On Sunday the shop usually closes earlier, at 7:00 p.m. ★★★★★

Ottica Urbani,
S. Marco 1280 (Frezzeria). Tel: 041.522.4140, www.otticaurbani.com. Open Monday-Saturday, 9:30 a.m.-12:30 p.m. & 3:30 p.m.-7:00 p.m. Closed Sunday. ★★★★★

34 **Sleep at a Centrally Located** and Very Reasonably Priced Hotel

Finding a good, reasonably priced hotel just off the Rialto Bridge, in the heart of Venice, sounds like an impossible dream. But the recommendations in this tip—Hotel Serenissima and Hotel Mignon—are proof that you can have your cake and eat it too.

Hotel Serenissima is located on Calle Goldoni, just two minutes from the Rialto and in the heart of the shopping district (so whatever you save on lodging may end up being spent on beautiful Italian fashion...). This private mansion was converted into a hotel and has been managed by the Dal Borgo family since 1960s. The ambiance here is intimate and welcoming; the rooms are simply decorated but comfortable, light, airy and well-proportioned (even the bathrooms are good-sized). Some noise penetrates from the street, but generally speaking, this hotel provides excellent value for the money, and the breakfast buffet is one of the most bountiful we've seen in Venice (quite a surprise considering this is just a two-star hotel).

The second option to consider is the delightful **Hotel Mignon**. The Mignon isn't as well-known as it should be. That's a little strange, because it has everything you could want from a city hotel: reasonable prices, friendly staff, comfortable rooms and a central location. Then again, maybe it's a good thing the word hasn't gotten out just yet. It's one of our most frequent ports of call when visiting the city! Hotel Mignon lives up to its name; it is small and quaint, and located just two minutes from Ca' d'Oro and five minutes from the Rialto Bridge. There are several restaurants in the area (such as Beppi 54, a classy and traditional fish restaurant, and Ai Promessi Sposi—see tip 6), as well as several shops. The rooms are very Venetian in style but not overbearingly so, and the great deals one can often find here, especially off-season, make up for anything the rooms may lack in size or amenities. In short, both Hotel Mignon and Hotel Serenissima offer the budget-conscious traveler a cozy and affordable stay in the heart of Venice.

Hotel Serenissima,
Calle Goldoni 4486 (right off campo S.Luca). Tel: 041.520.0011,
www.hotelserenissima.it. ★★★

Hotel Mignon,
Cannaregio 4535, Calle dei Preti (right off Campo Santi Apostoli),
Tel: 041.523.7388,
www.mignonvenice.com. ★★★

35 Buy Beautiful Antique Venetian Fabric

By the 13th century, Venice had begun to establish itself as a hub for the fabric trade. Silk and cotton were imported from the East, worked with, and exported as luxurious finished products, including clothes, tapestries, drapes, religious vestments and wall coverings, to northern and western Europe. Today, much of the old fabric industry has been consolidated, but some of the tradition remains. Those who want to use fabric from Venice to add accents to select pieces at home can easily find some beautiful, authentic items. Naturally, you don't have to go fully baroque and cover your walls with golden Damask fabric, but a throw or pillow will lighten up a room and provide a unique memory of your time in the city.

When one thinks of luxurious Venetian fabric, the first name that comes to mind is **Rubelli.** This exclusive and much sought-after atelier is loved by fashion and interior designers. It offers both classic Venetian designs and high-end, very modern fabrics and items that will add a sense of sophistication to any home. Prices, as you might expect, are far from cheap, but the quality is impeccable. Clients may visit the historic Rubelli shop on the banks of the Grand Canal, or set up an appointment if any special assistance or advice is required.

Another must-stop is **Bevilacqua.** Bevilacqua have been manufacturing the city's most exclusive fabric and upholstery for years, and specialize in the exuberant, opulent, dramatic, and luxurious—just like Venice itself. If minimalism is your stylistic preference, then Bevilacqua isn't the shop for you; but if you are looking for traditional fabric or items to add color to interior furnishings or upholstery, then this is your material mecca. In other parts of Italy, Bevilacqua sells directly to retailers. However, Venice is their home town, and they have opened up two locations for the general public. The first is run by Mario Bevilacqua and is located at Piazza del Giglio. Here you will find some stunning examples of their work, all of the highest quality: rolls of plush Damask fabric and colorful velvet, cushions, drapes, and table runners of all kinds. A second shop, smaller but equally charming, is run by another family member, Paola Bevilacqua, and can be found right behind Piazza San Marco. (Exit the piazza and walk toward the Diocesan museum. The shop will be on your right, before the bridge and the museum.)

Rubelli,
Palazzo Corner Spinelli, San Marco 3877. Tel: 041.523.6110, www.rubelli.com. Visit by appointment. ★★★★

Bevilacqua,
Campo Santa Maria del Giglio, San Marco 2520. Tel: 041.241.0662; San Marco 337 (Fondamenta della Canonica), Tel: 041.5287581). www.bevilacquatessuti.com. Both shops are open Monday-Saturday, 10:00 a.m.-7:30 p.m. Closed Sunday. ★★★★

36 Gamble in Style at Venice's Historic Casino

You don't have to be an avid gambler to enjoy a visit to Venice's historic casino. The real draw is the building in which the casino is housed—the glorious 18th century Ca' Vendramin Calergi—and the chance to play at tables that once hosted the most famous nobles of Europe. Upon arrival you will already be impressed with the Renaissance-style façade and the opulent interior—beautiful paintings, traditional marble flooring, sculptures and baroque ceiling murals come together to complete the experience. There are a number of entertainment and dining venues within the casino, and various cultural events are organized throughout the year. First and foremost are the gambling tables and machines, which are, naturally, the main attraction. Additionally, the casino's restaurant, **Ristorante Wagner,** named after the famous yet controversial composer who once lived in this palazzo, is a tasteful and refined space, divided into three halls, all of which are elegantly decorated with original artwork. The lounge bar **La Capsula** is a far livelier place. Unlike the restaurant, which is formal and traditional, La Capsula attracts a younger crowd who flock here for the cool music and modern atmosphere. The bar is an extension of the original *palazzo* and is housed in a glass structure decked out with luxurious leather sofas and dramatic chandeliers—the perfect setting for a night of hedonism by the water. The casino is easily accessible by the free water taxi which departs from Piazzale Roma. Don't forget to ask your hotel concierge for free-admission coupons, otherwise entry is €10. If you feel like trying your luck, you can get your entrance fee returned to you in chips, which you can then use at the various game tables.

Casino di Venezia,
Ca' Vendramin Calergi, Sestiere Cannaregio 2040 (right by the San Marcuola *vaporetto* stop).
Tel: 041.529.7111, www.casinovenezia.it. A free shuttle is available for guests of the casino; it leaves from Piazzale Roma every 20 minutes (Sunday-Thursday) or every 10 minutes (Friday and Saturday). The casino has a **dress code**–casual elegant for the slot machines and obligatory jackets for the gambling tables. The slot machines are open daily, 11:00 a.m.-2:45 a.m. The gambling tables are open daily, 3:30 p.m.-2:45 a.m. (Mid-June to August 31, the tables are open 4:00 p.m.-2:45 a.m.).
★★★★

37 Savor a Delicious Lunch on Burano, Venice's Most Colorful Island

When people talk about Venice, they mean the mainland—Venice itself, where Piazza San Marco, the Rialto Bridge, and the Accademia Museum can be found. But there are several small islands scattered in the lagoon that are popular destinations in their own right. The island of Murano (see tip 67) is known for its glass production, the island of Lido (see tip 28) is home to a world-famous film festival every August, and the island of Torcello (see tip 70) is a relaxed and half-abandoned oasis. But the most captivating island of them all has to be Burano, famous for its incredibly colorful houses. Touring Burano is an easy and delightful experience, and it is hard to resist the urge to take an unreasonable number of photos of the scenic canals and homes. Many legends circulate about why the houses are colored. Some say it is to keep away ghosts, but most believe it was designed to aid fishermen in seeing their homes from afar. Nowadays the color code is strictly controlled by the local government, helping to preserve the childlike fun of the island.

When the time comes to sit down for lunch, head to **Gatto Nero.** This family-run establishment is hugely popular, so try to book a table in advance. The food here is fresh, simple, and delicious, especially the *tris alla griglia* (grilled clams, razor clams and comb shells), the *spaghetti alla scogliera* (mixed seafood spaghetti), the Burano-style risotto, and the *tagliatelle* with *scampi* (langoustines). Unlike many other restaurants on the island, there is a good selection of non-fish dishes too, perfect for those who are fed up with any sort of dish involving the sea and just want some pasta with ragout. Whatever you pick, don't forget to order a glass of wine, preferably a crisp white, to wash everything down and complete your experience.

Those who prefer a more upscale dining experience will enjoy **Riva,** a fabulously located venue offering a good selection, for the most part, of local specialties. Try the *antipasti* platter, which changes daily depending on what the local fishermen pull in from their morning catch, and the *Risotto di Go,* the typical Burano risotto made with fish exclusively from the lagoon. For the best dining experience book the restaurant's "romantic table", located on the roof. This is the perfect spot for an intimate evening, where you can enjoy the fine food and wine and watch Burano life unfold in all its color.

To end the list we must share a different sort of favorite. **Al Fureghin** is a simple but delightful Burano eatery. Michele, the owner, runs this completely unpretentious neighborhood tavern with the charm of an experienced host. Come here only if you love seafood, are not intimidated by the occasional bizarre dish, and are happy to eat with your hands. The fish, scallops, and langoustines are all fresh and delicious—even more so if accompanied by some good wine! Prices aren't cheap (nothing in Burano ever is), but the quality is very good.

Gatto Nero,
Fondamenta della Giudecca 88, Burano. Tel: 041.730.120, www.gattonero.com. Open Tuesday-Saturday, 12:00 p.m.-3:00 p.m. & 6:30 p.m.-8:30 p.m.; Sunday, open for lunch only. Closed Monday. May close down off-season. ★★★★

Riva Rosa,
Via San Mauro 296, Burano. Tel: 041.730.850, www.rivarosa.it. Open Thursday-Tuesday, 12:00 p.m.-4:00 p.m. Closed Wednesday. ★★★★

Osteria Al Fureghin,
Sestiere S. Martino Sinistra 888, Burano. Tel: 041.527.2250, www.osteriafureghin.it. Open for lunch only, Tuesday-Sunday, 12:00 p.m.-3:30 p.m. Closed Monday. ★★★

38 Buy Fine Handmade Lace on Burano

Burano is famous not just for its colorful houses but also for its centuries-old lace industry. For over 500 years the women here have developed this meticulous labor into an art form, creating lace so beautiful it was worthy of royalty and could be found in the homes of most noble families in Europe.

Like so many traditions, Burano's fascination with lace is attributed to a miraculous story. Legend has it that a local sailor set out to sea, leaving his young fiancée behind. During his travels a siren tried to seduce him, but despite her beauty, he remained loyal to his love. As a reward, the siren struck the waves with her tail, foam flew up, and a delicate and intricate piece of lace landed in the hands of the faithful sailor. This piece of lace was used to prepare the young bride's veil, and inspired the art of lace on Burano. Many of the finer examples of lace made by the women of Burano can still be seen in Burano's lace museum, but today much of the handwork has been replaced by machines, and some of the production doesn't come from Burano at all, but is made in China. And yet, here and there you can still find islands of quality among the rubbish and buy an authentic souvenir to take home.

Martina Vidal is a historic and very famous atelier that has catered to the most exclusive clientele for many years. It is also one of the few shops where you can still get the "real stuff"—everything from womenswear to accessories to linen to tapestries, baby clothes and even a cashmere collection. (Though that has very little to do with Burano.) Prices are, as you might expect, quite high, but you don't have to buy the most expensive items – a lovely handkerchief could make a great souvenir at a reasonable price. Martina Vidal also has a little museum, featuring some stunning pieces made by the atelier (book a guided tour in advance), and if you've always dreamed of learning the fine art of needlepoint lace making, there are even courses available.

Another luxury atelier worth visiting is **Emilia.** They work on a large scale and specialize in stunning and classic linen, which they have been manufacturing for four generations. They also collaborate with other famous brands, including Aston Martin, to create signature linen collections. Don't miss their flagship store, at Piazza Galuppi 205.

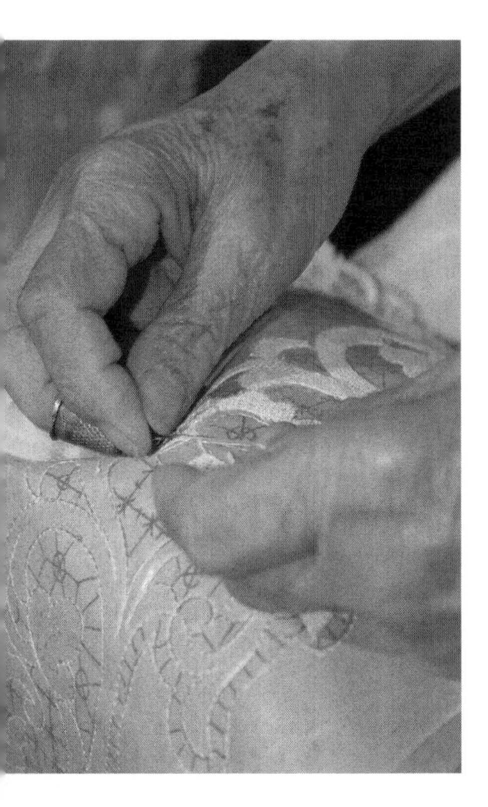

Lastly, in **Dalla Lidia's Lace Shop** you will find some cute handmade items at various prices, a little museum of the atelier's creations, and friendly service. The shop is located right on Burano's main canal.

Martina Vidal,
Via San Mauro 309, Burano.
Tel: 041.735.523, www.martinavidal.com. Open daily, 9:30 a.m.-6:15 p.m.
★★★★

Emilia,
Piazza Galuppi 205, Burano.
Tel: 041.735.299, www.emiliaburano.it.
Open daily, 9:30 a.m.-6:00 p.m. ★★★★

Dalla Lidia's Lace Shop,
Via Galuppi 215, Burano.
Tel: 041.730.052, www.dallalidia.com.
Open daily, 9:30 a.m.-6:30 p.m. ★★★

39 Catch a Concert in Style

Venice is a hub of art and music, the city that gave birth to some of the greatest Italian musicians, including Antonio Vivaldi, Italy's finest baroque composer and violinist (and responsible for the world's most popular on-hold music). It is only natural that in his home town, where he and others taught music and created some of their most recognizable works, there are many concerts for tourists to enjoy. The selection is wide, and you will find pamphlets in just about every hotel in town, advertising the various shows. However, not all concerts are of the same level and value.

Opera buffs and curious viewers will enjoy the dramatic shows organized by **I Musici Veneziani.** This group performs at the Scuola Grande di San Teodoro, which provides wonderful acoustics and an elegant setting. More importantly, the shows are performed in full 18th century period costumes. The repertoire focuses on famous arias by the likes of Donizetti, Mozart, Puccini, and Vivaldi, and occasionally includes an entire opera, such as *La Traviata.* Tickets cost around €35 and booking in advance is advised.

Other shows to dazzle are those held at the **Scuola Grande di San Giovanni.** The concerts here are sporadic, so you'll have to consult their website to see if anything is planned (sadly, in Italian only: www.scuolasangiovanni.it). But if you are lucky enough to visit Venice when a good concert is planned, do book a ticket. The setting is nothing short of magnificent, and the majestic marbled *Sala delle Colonne* (Hall of Columns) where the shows usually take place is the perfect backdrop for any cultural event. Naturally, you can also just visit the Scuola Grande di San Giovanni as a tourist attraction, regardless of the concert schedule.

Another good choice is **Interpreti Veneziani.** This ensemble of talented musicians regularly tours the world, and when in Venice, usually performs in Chiesa San Vidal (San Vidal Church), across the bridge from the Accademia Museum. For serious music lovers, this is one of the best options to consider.

Lastly, if you are a hard-core Vivaldi fan, know that the ensemble **I Virtuosi di Venezia** stages chamber orchestra concerts at the Ateneo di San Basso, right off Piazza San Marco. The setting, though slightly more modest than the others, was chosen for historical reasons—this is where Vivaldi himself worked when he lived in Venice. The ensemble performs various pieces by Vivaldi, mainly *The Four Seasons,* naturally. Tickets cost between €20 and €26.

Scuola Grande di San Teodoro
Campo San Salvadore (near the Rialto). Tel: 041.521.0294, www.imusicivenezianі.it. ★★★★

Scuola San Giovanni,
www.scuolasangiovanni.it. (Near the Venezia Santa Lucia train station). ★★★

Interpreti Veneziani,
Chiesa San Vidal (across the bridge from the Accademia). Tel: 041.277.0561, www.interpretiveneziani.com. ★★★★

I Virtuosi di Venezia,
Ateneo di San Basso (near Basilica San Marco). Tel: 041.528.2825. www.virtuosidivenezia.com. ★★★

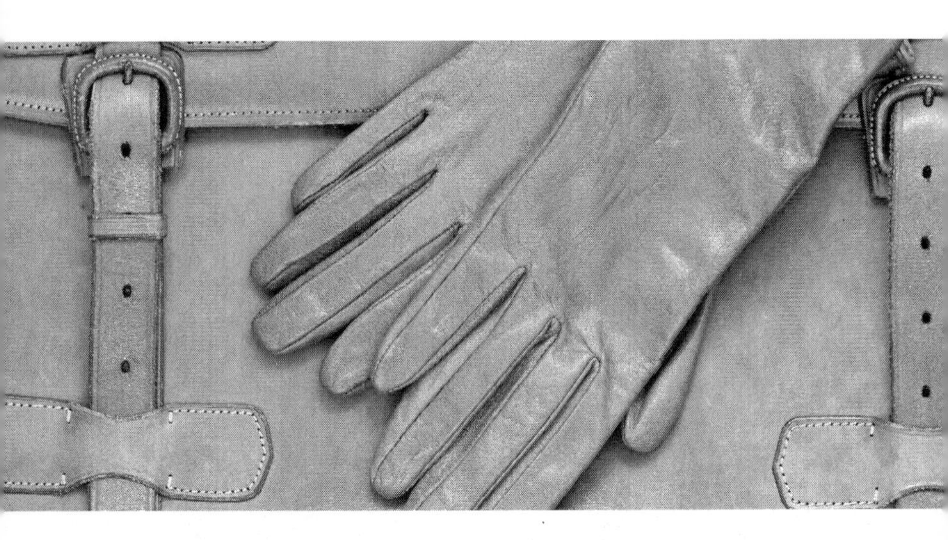

40 Buy Elegant Handmade Handbags and Gloves

Venice isn't as famous as Tuscany for its leather industry, but if you know where to look, there are interesting discoveries to be made—boutique shops where you can pick up some stylish and hand-crafted pieces. Fanny Gloves and Raggio Veneziano are two such shops.

Fanny Gloves is one of Venice's most-loved glove shops. The owners, Claudia and Giorgio, hail from the Santia neighborhood of Napoli, which is famous for its many artisan shops. When Claudia's family moved to Venice, they brought with them an intimate understanding of leatherworking that is reflected in the stock the shop carries. Here you will find everything from the classic and elegant to the quirky and eccentric, all made of quality leather and hand sewn. Try a pair of funky leather gloves with a polka dot design or a graceful, soft leather set with cashmere lining (silk and rabbit's fur linings are also available).

Raggio Veneziano specializes in artisanal leather bags and accessories. Their style is modern and playful, slightly rustic, yet clearly anchored in a classic base. Color infuses most of the designs and everything is handmade, often using centuries-old techniques and tools; the process of coloring, for example, is achieved through vegetable and plant extracts. The best thing about shopping at Raggio Veneziano is that each bag is one-of-a-kind. There is no production line, and even blemishes in the leather or color become part of the authenticity of the design. In both cases, we recommend consulting the shop website before visiting, to make sure their style matches your taste.

Fanny Gloves
operates two locations in Venice - the larger shop is located in Campo San Polo 2723 (Calle dei Saoneri), Tel: 041.522.8266, and is open daily, 9:30 a.m.-1:30 p.m. & 2:30 p.m.-7:00 p.m. It may close an hour earlier on Sunday. The second shop is located in Cannaregio 1647 (a few meters from the shop-packed Lista di Spagna street), and has similar hours.
Tel. 041.244.0338,
www.fannygloves.it. ★★★★

Raggio Veneziano,
Campo Santo Stefano (San Marco 2953).
Tel: 041.241.2712,
www.raggioveneziano.com. Open Monday-Saturday, 10:30 a.m.-7:30 p.m. Closed Sunday. ★★★

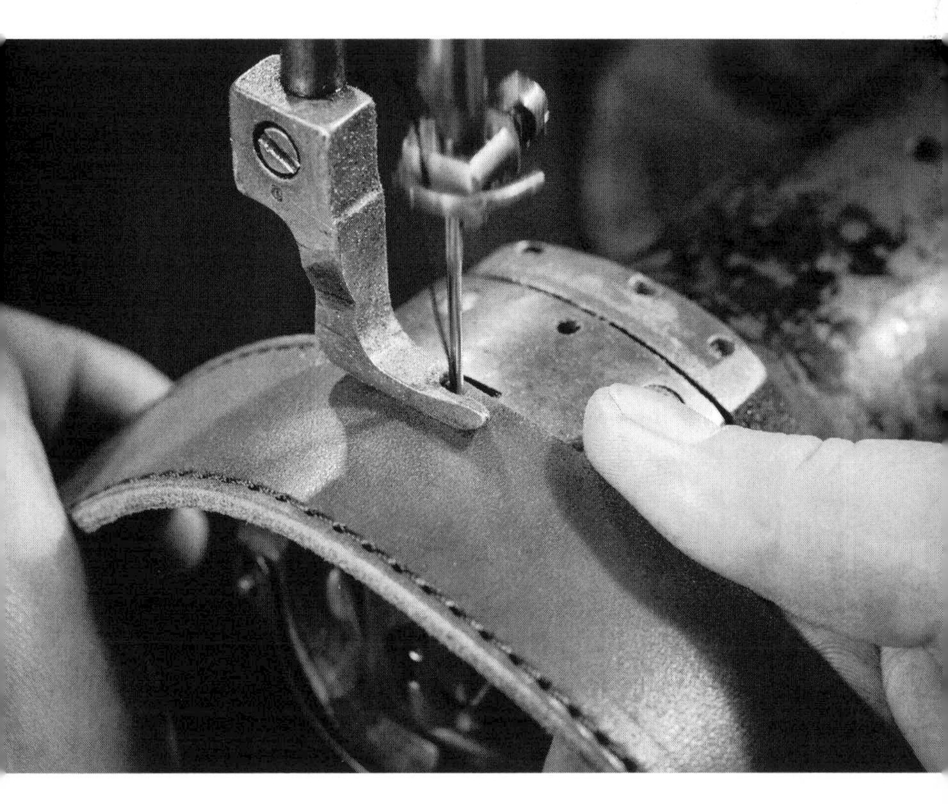

41 **Stay in One of Venice's** Finest Boutique Hotels

Ca' Maria Adele is Venice's self-proclaimed sexiest hotel. We will leave you to decide whether it lives up to this high title, but what we can say is that this hotel works hard to create an experience for all the senses, from sight to smell to touch, and the staff pay great attention to the smallest details. The hotel has 12 rooms divided into three categories: deluxe, concept and suites. We adore the uniqueness of the concept rooms, and you can choose which style suits you the best. Draped in deep red brocade and heavy damask fabric, the *Sala Del Doge* is sumptuously sensual. The *Sala Noir,* with its black Murano glass chandelier and white tapered ceiling, is deliciously decadent. And the *Sala Orientale,* with its gold wallpaper and Asian antiques, is sensual. The owners perfectly understand the attraction of their decadent rooms and organize breakfast in bed at no extra charge. If you can tear yourself away from your room, there is a beautiful little terrace that is perfect for relaxing after a long day of sightseeing. The Salute *vaporetto* stop is just a few meters away. Ca' Maria Adele has, somehow, remained a bit of a secret, perhaps because this boutique hotel hides away in the artistic and romantic neighborhood of Dorsoduto, a stone's throw away from attractions such as Gallerie dell'Accademia, the Guggenheim Museum and Francois Pinault's Punta della Dogana. Prices are far from cheap, but if you are planning a romantic getaway, this exclusive little hotel is certainly worth considering.

Ca' Maria Adele Boutique Hotel,
Dorsoduro 111 (50 meters from the Salute vaporetto stop).
Tel: 041.520.3078,
www.camariaadele.it. ★★★★

42 Shop at Venice's Top Luxury Boutiques

Venice may not be a fashionista's city like Milan, but it certainly does offer shoppers several interesting options to explore, from the high-end and luxurious to the hip and modern. Additionally, rows of shops punctuate the streets in the city center, making Venice seem at times like one huge outdoor shopping mall (see tip 12 for the best shopping streets in Venice).

For luxury brands, hit **Calle Larga XXII Marzo** and **Calle dei Fuseri,** where it is easier than ever to fulfill fantasies and empty pockets. If Louis Vuitton, Salvatore Ferragamo and Burberry aren't enough, head to two of Venice's most famous one-stop luxury boutiques—La Coupule and Pot-Pourrì.

La Coupole is a bit of an institution. It is one of the largest and best-known boutiques in town, offering brands such as Zagliani, Kenzo, Iceberg, Red Valentino, Gianfranco Ferrè, and Brunello Cucinelli, all under one roof (well, actually under three roofs—the women's, men's and baby collections can be found in three different shops, all in the same area).

Similar in style is **Pot-Pourrì,** an exclusive boutique that boasts a classic, elegant look. It may not cater to your day-to-day shopping taste, but you may very well find certain exclusive pieces for special events, so make your way among the coiffed Venetian women with their strings of pearls and closely examine the newest arrivals.

If La Coupole and Pot-Pourrì are more elegant, classy choices, then **Al Duca d'Aosta** is their wilder alternative sister. Here you will find exclusive clothing and accessories from the best Italian and foreign designers, including Marni, Valentino, Gucci, Isabel Marant, Dries Van Noten, Fendi, and Alexander McQueen. It's located quite close to the Rialto Bridge and during the *saldi* (sales season) there are some surprisingly great finds.

La Coupole,
Sestiere San Marco 2366 & 2414 (Calle Larga XXII Marzo). Tel: 0415.224.243 / 041.296.0555. Open daily, 10:00 a.m.-7:00 p.m. ★★★★

Pot-Pourrì,
Ramo dei Fuseri 1810,
Tel: 041.241.0990, www.potpourri.it.
Open Tuesday-Saturday, 10:00 a.m.-1:00 p.m. & 3:30 p.m.-7:30 p.m.; Monday, 3:30 p.m.-7:30 p.m.; Sunday, 11:00 a.m.-6:00 p.m. ★★★★

Al Duca d'Aosta,
San Marco 284 (Calle Larga Mazzini).
Tel: 041.520.4079,
www.alducadaosta.com. Open Monday-Saturday, 10:00 a.m.-7:30 p.m.; Sunday, 11:00 a.m.-7:00 p.m. ★★★★

43 Stop for Afternoon Drinks at Ristorante San Giorgio to Enjoy a Beautiful View of San Giorgio Island and the Lagoon

Riva degli Schiavoni, which runs west from Piazza San Marco to the Arsenale, is one Venice's most famous quais and home to some of the most coveted real estate in the city. Many famous hotels are situated here, including the Danieli (see tip 4). Walking down this grand road while gazing across the glistening water is blissful, especially at sunset. It will also provide you with some particularly beautiful photo ops. There are several restaurants along the route that compete for the visitor's attention, but many of them are incredibly touristy and aren't worth your time. Instead, we prefer a small venue slightly farther along from which the view is better.

Ristorante San Giorgio is located right across from San Giorgio Island (hence the name) and is ideal for people watching. It is small but elegant; the white chairs and simple but stylish setting wonderfully juxtapose against the turquoise of the lagoon. We usually come for the drinks, not for the food (we prefer the ambiance to their cooking), but the food actually isn't bad at all. And unlike so many other restaurants in Venice, the kitchen is open all afternoon, which means you can eat a late lunch if you want—a rare treat in Italy! Since San Giorgio is just far enough away from Piazza San Marco to enjoy some relative peace and quiet, you will be able to recharge before heading back to the center, or before visiting the Arsenale, which is just 50 meters away.

Ristorante San Giorgio,
Riva di Cà di Dio 2185 (right off the Arsenale *vaporetto* stop).
Tel: 041.523.1993,
www.ristorantesangiorgio.it.
Open daily, 12:00 p.m.-10:45 p.m. ★★★

44 **Visit the Secluded and Peaceful San Lazzaro degli Armeni Convent** and Follow in the Footsteps of Lord Byron

Over the centuries Venice has inspired some of the world's most renowned thinkers and writers. Though more often associated with Italian artists, who found patronage among the city's elite, Venice has also played the muse for many international authors, actors, and poets. It is no surprise, then, that the English poet Lord Byron, with his turbulent and romantic soul, found stimulation and refuge in this endlessly charming city. Lord Byron was undoubtedly inspired by Venice, but he returned the favor. He resided for a while on the Grand Canal, and spent many days on Lido Island, where he strolled for hours in the ancient Jewish cemetery or swam. But Byron's most important relationship was with the monastery on the tiny island of San Lazzaro degli Armeni, where a small community of Armenian monks had been living since early 18th century. Through an interesting turn of events, Lord Byron became enamored of the monks inhabiting the island. He lived in their small community and created surprisingly strong and meaningful ties. Byron took part in their activities, learned Armenian, and even helped author an English-Armenian dictionary. Today he is honored with a small museum on the premises. Following the footsteps of Lord Byron into this tranquil and small hideaway on the lagoon can be an interesting and inspiring tour for those who have already seen Venice's most famous sites. This is by no means a "must-see," but if you want to explore lesser-known ground, this monastery is certainly a valid option. The monastery, library and museum can be toured with a guide (tours leave just once a day), a mission that one of the monks who still live here will be happy to undertake.

San Lazzaro degli Armeni Convent.
Visits take place at 3:20 p.m. daily (Sundays may be a bit more complicated–call in advance). You can reach the island using public transportation on *vaporetto* line 20, or book a private ride (try www.vni.it/eng/tour-and-itineraries/san-lazzaro-san-giorgio-salute or www.cristianobrussa.it). If you use the public vaporetto, make sure to check its precise departure and return times in advance, as it runs only a few times a day, and you wouldn't want to be stranded on the island. ★★★★

45 **Catch a Show** at the Historic La Fenice Theater

There are a number of music performances in Venice with repertoires based on the works of well-known composers who were based in town, such as Vivaldi (see tip 39). But none of these shows, as enjoyable as they may be, can compete with "the real thing"—watching a concert or opera at the grand La Fenice Theater, one of the most famous theaters in the world. The construction of La Fenice came toward the end of Venice's dominance of the high seas. The city's new interests lay in culture and cultivation, and the theater became the epicenter of the flourishing arts scene, as elaborate, extravagant productions of operas by the likes of Rossini were staged here. Construction of La Fenice began after the city's previous leading theater burned down, and when it finally opened in 1792, it instantly became the most celebrated theater of its time—until it burned down in 1836. But Venice without opera was unthinkable, and a year later a new La Fenice, whose name means "phoenix," rose from the ashes in triumph and once again became a cultural hub. Unfortunately, La Fenice's history is bathed in flames; in 1996 the theatre was reduced to ashes once again, and two electricians were found guilty of arson.

Despite the initial shock, the theatre was restored once more, and no expense was spared in returning this iconic opera house to its former glory. And it truly is glorious. The neoclassical exterior of the theater dominates its Campo San Fantin location, while the interior, replete with gold gilt detailing, elaborate stucco and a stately ceiling mural, is majestic. In a nod to the authenticity with which the restoration was undertaken, the fabric came from the same Venetian company, Rubelli (see tip 35), that upholstered the theatre close to a hundred years earlier. Even the original fabric patterns were used. You can visit the theater on an expensive but interesting guided tour that includes walks through the most important sections of the building and a complimentary *aperitivo*, or simply catch a show—there is a fine selection to choose from, thanks to a rich yearly program that attracts both locals and tourists. Lastly, music lovers won't want to miss La Fenice's book shop, which sells, among other things, a large selection of CDs and DVDs of their best shows and operas.

La Fenice,
San Marco 4387. Tel: 041.786.672, www.teatrolafenice.it. Open daily, 9:30 a.m.-6:00 p.m. (opening hours and tour availability depend on planned shows and events in the theater). ★★★★

46 **Enjoy a Delicious *Cicheti* Meal** near the Frari Basilica and Scuola San Rocco

The Basilica di Santa Maria Gloriosa dei Frari, commonly referred to simply as the Basilica dei Frari, is one of the best-known churches in Venice. And since it is located right next to the grandiose Scuola Grande di San Rocco (a stunning artistic treasure which no tourist should skip), it is likely you will be spending at least a couple of hours in the area. If you are feeling peckish after your visit, but the cafés and uninspiring restaurants around the Basilica don't seem that tempting, don't despair. Exit the Basilica, cross the bridge in front of you, turn left, cross another bridge, and you will immediately find yourself in Campo San Satin, where a little surprise awaits. **Il Vizzietto** sits unimposingly in the right-hand corner of the *campo*, and is one of the area's best-kept secrets. Dario, the owner of this tiny *bacaro*, is meticulous about his ingredients and puts careful thought into the gourmet *cicheti* he prepares daily. For that reason, the selection is small but impeccably made, and includes such delicacies as *bruschette* with aged *lardo* and truffle cream, artisanal cold cuts, and cheeses from the finest producers in northern Italy. Vegetarian options are available, too, such as delicious sandwiches with roasted vegetables and *robiola* cheese. Order a few of these *cicheti* and a glass of wine or a Spritz, and you will enjoy a perfect light lunch. End with a fine cup of espresso.

Alternatively (or in addition), make a stop at one of the most famous *cicheti* bars in the area – **Mondo di Vino.** A butcher shop turned *bacaro*, the bar is immediately recognizable, thanks to the signs outside and the illustrations of cows inside, attesting to the owner's former occupation. Mondo di Vino is friendly and inviting and the selection of *ombre* (wine) and *cicheti* is extensive. The décor adds to the atmosphere: a long dark wood bar, clay vases hanging from the ceiling, and locals everywhere. What's not to like?

Il Vizietto,
Campo S. Stin, San Polo 2532.
Tel: 041.244.0259, www.facebook.com/ilvizietto. Open Sunday and Tuesday-Friday, 6:00 p.m.-midnight; Saturday, 10:00 a.m.-midnight. Closed Monday. ★★★

Mondo DiVino,
Sestiere Cannaregio, 5984/A.
Tel: 041.521.1093. Opening hours tend to change. Usually open Monday-Saturday, 10:00 a.m.-3:00 p.m. & 5:30 p.m.-10:00 p.m. In July and August, often closed on Thursday. ★★★

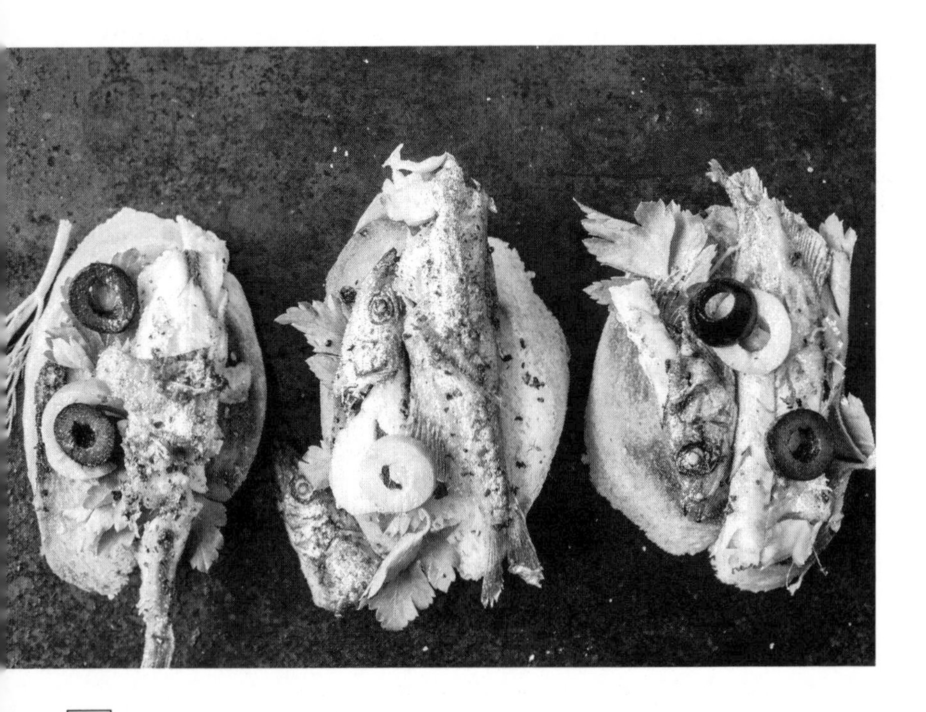

47 **Learn How to Row** like a True *Gondoliere*!

Watching the gondoliers masterfully navigate Venice's canals, one can't help but wonder what it's like to work in one of the city's oldest professions. Luckily, the team at **Row Venice** can help you discover exactly what being a *gondoliere* means. The company will take you out on a *batelina*, a historic boat that was once the most popular vessel in Venice and is considered safer and more suitable for lessons than the iconic traditional gondola. During the lesson you will learn all of the tricks of the trade, like how to row without moving, how to properly use the oar, and how to steer a gondola. Naturally, this activity is especially suitable for families with kids, but really anyone who is young at heart can enjoy this adventure. If you'd like to add a decadent streak to your day, opt for the *bacari* boat tour; your rowing lesson will be followed by a much-deserved *aperitivo*, during which you will visit two *bacari* and sample their *cicheti* and wine. A 90-minute basic lesson costs around €80 for one or two people (€140 for a group of four). Booking in advance through their website is recommended, and lessons are available in English. If you prefer a different means of transportation, such as kayak, check **Kayak Venice's** tours in tip 26. Whichever tour you choose, this is a wonderful and fun adventure to incorporate into your Venice experience.

Row Venice,
Cell: 347.725.0637 / 340.341.3448,
www.rowvenice.org, ★★★★

48 Buy an Authentic Gondolier's Uniform

The shop front of **Emilio Ceccato** feels like a film set for a production about historic Venice. The window sports a colorful display of quaint traditional gondolier's garb, and the best thing about this shop is its authenticity—real gondoliers come here to buy the clothes they wear as they row along the canals. Of course, the owners of Emilio Ceccato have realized that those iconic stripes also serve as delightful souvenirs, and over the years the shop has become popular with tourists. For that reason, prices aren't cheap, but the selection of shirts, scarves and sweaters is unbeatable. The kid's collection is especially cute. The location is very accessible – the shop is at the foot of the Rialto Bridge (on Ruga dei Oresi), so even if you don't think you will buy, pop in to have a look around. It's quite a sight!

Emilio Ceccato,
San Polo 16 (right off the Rialto Bridge). Tel: 041.522.2700 / 041.531.5301. Open Monday-Saturday, 10:00 a.m.-1:00 p.m. & 3:30 p.m.-7:00 p.m. ★★★

49 Buy Gorgeous Handcrafted Items from the Venice Women's Prison

It may come as a surprise, but Venice is home to a small prison—the correctional center for women, located on the island of Giudecca. The women in the facility regularly interact with the public through a number of rehabilitation programs, the most famous of which is the weekly vegetable market, held every Thursday morning by the prison gate—a representative comes out and sells fresh fruit and vegetables from the prison's *orto* (vegetable garden). The produce is organic, reasonably priced and quite good, which explains the number of determined Venetian grandmas who show up 15 minutes before the market opens to make sure the zucchinis don't sell out.

Lesser-known, but just as intriguing, is the fashion atelier **Banco Lotto n. 10,** where some beautiful items made by the inmates are sold. The draw here isn't just the unique origin of the clothes, but the fact that they are simply stunning. The dresses and blouses are very feminine, handcrafted down to the last stitches, and often made using better materials than many "regular" shops in town. If you are in the Castello neighborhood, making a stop here is highly recommended.

Banco Lotto n. 10,
Salizada Antonin 3478, Castello.
Tel: 041.5221439,
www.ilcerchiovenezia.it. The shop is open Monday-Saturday, 10:00 a.m.-1:00 p.m. & 2:00 p.m.-7:00 p.m. ★★★★★

50 Book a Memorable and Opulent Stay at the Most Luxurious Villa in Venice

Imagine the scene. You board a private shuttle boat at Piazza San Marco, cruise across the lagoon to Giudecca Island, and dock at a palatial 16th century villa. Your bags are taken from the boat as you are guided past three acres of private gardens and through grand glass doors into an oak-paneled reading room. You are then shown upstairs to your 3,229 sq. ft. apartment. Through the floor-to-ceiling windows, you look out across the glittering lagoon to busy Piazza San Marco in the distance. This is your home for your stay in Venice. Well, it's home if you can afford it; the price tag here might cause your heart to skip a beat or two. But if money is no object and you are set on booking the most luxurious accommodations in Venice, then look no further than Villa F.

Villa F was once home to a series of noble Venetian families, and over the years it has hosted a wide range of intellectuals and artists, including Gabriele d'Annunzio and Eleonora Duse. Today it has been lovingly restored and divided into 11 serviced accommodations, the largest of which is Residenza F (described above). The smallest is suitable for two people. Each has a view of the lagoon or the private garden, and some have a view of both. You can also rent the whole property, which can accommodate a party of 38. Each room displays the owner's keen eye for design and detail. All the interiors feature an eclectic mix of the modern and the antique, as well as innovative flourishes crafted with fine materials. Little touches create charm, from the original frescoes and antiques to the silk and linen sheets and dramatic baths. Guest have access to the adjoining Palladio Hotel & Spa (which belong to the same owners, see tip 61), where they can go for additional rest and relaxation. The private garden of the villa is the largest in Venice and has a beautiful meditation pool. Common areas in the house include a reading room and a wine bar with working fireplaces and a winter garden lobby, all turning this villa into the definitive Venetian luxury, and a fantastic spot for a romantic getaway.

Villa F,
Giudecca 50. Tel: 041.520.7022,
www.villfvenezia.com. ★★★★★

51 Visit Two Unique Murano Glass Artisans in Venice

There are many, many glass shops in Venice, some of which are internationally famous, such as Barovier, L'Isola and Venini, to name just a few. But to us, **Massimo Micheluzzi's** studio stands apart from the rest, and we are confident in saying that despite its tiny size, it is one of the most interesting shops we've come across. Micheluzzi's studio isn't your typical showroom, and you certainly won't be buying any colorful reproduction cups here. Rather, this is the very personal atelier of an artist who crafts just one of everything, and turns glass into palpable art. Micheluzzi is a Venetian native, born and raised in the city, in a family of art lovers who ran their own antique gallery. He studied at Ca' Foscari University and began his career as a photographer, but when he was commissioned by the world-famous Venini Atelier to shoot their catalogue, his artistic life took a turn. He fell in love with glass, and eventually decided to start sculpting in glass himself. He quickly gained fame, and today his work is shown in museums around the world, including the Metropolitan Museum of Art and the Museum of Arts and Design in New York. As you might expect, the prices are high, but his work is unique and intelligent. His monochromatic vases are particularly beautiful, more reminiscent of sculpture than tableware. If you are passionate about glass and art, this is a stop you will want to make.

Another singularly interesting artist (though very different in style) is **Luigi Camozzo.** His work is vibrant, colorful and distinctive, and his delicate and intricate glass carvings, as well as the more classic Murano sculptures, are all marked by quality and exquisite craftsmanship. Camozzo uses an etching technique that creates shaded and textured pictures with a three dimensional appearance. He draws inspiration from nature, and the designs often feature wildlife and natural scenes. His Murano sculptures come in unusual shapes and feature almost-tribal designs with great explosions of color.

Both studios can be visited by appointment.

Massimo Micheluzzi,
Dorsoduro 1071 (off Calle Toletta). Tel: 041.528.2190. ★★★★★

Luigi Camozzo,
Fondamenta Venier Sebastiano 3, Murano. Cell: 349.092.1087, www.luigicamozzo.com. ★★★★

52 **Combine History and Shopping** when Hunting for Antiques in Venice

There is real excitement about hunting for antiques. There's not only the feeling of pleasure associated with seeking out bargains or unique pieces, but also the wonderful sense of delving into history. Venice's history is as long as it is dramatic and entangled, so you can expect to make some particularly interesting discoveries in the city. There are a number of options for antique aficionados visiting Venice, the first and most obvious being the antique market. Up until a few years ago, the *mercato* was located near the Rialto Bridge, but due to a number of bureaucratic constraints, it was moved to Campo San Maurizio, a peaceful town square near Campo Santo Stefano. This market has limited opening dates, and may be closed in January, February, and June-September, so be sure to check their website before setting off.

Alternatively, there are several antique shops scattered around the city, and many of them offer tempting and interesting finds. **Antichità Marciana** and **Antichita' Zanutto** are two of our favorites. Both are just a couple of minutes from La Fenice Theater and both have fascinating collections, everything from 19th century paintings to 17th century tableware, precious objects, statues, and other surprises.

The antique shops in Calle De le Botteghe (the boutique-strewn alley behind Palazzo Grassi), such as **Antichita' San Samuele** and others, hold museum-worthy tableware, and are absolutely worth exploring, too. For the pricey items, **Antichita' Pietro** near Gallerie dell'Accademia is the place to go. Despite the occasional rude and unpleasant service, they do have a fine and unique collection. **Antichi Splendori** is another excellent choice, and fashion lovers will be glad to find that they also have a spectacular collection of fine vintage jewelry. Finally, for an interesting selection of antique lamps, including some gorgeous 19th century hanging Murano lamps, go to **Luca Sumiti-Cose Antiche.**

All of the shops listed below tend to have variable opening hours. Generally speaking, they are open Monday-Saturday, 10:00 a.m.-12:30 p.m. & 3:30 p.m.-6:30 p.m., but more often than not these hours change. If there's a specific shop you are interested in, we recommend calling in advance to make sure someone is manning the shop.

San Maurizio Antiques market,
www.mercatinocamposanmaurizio.it. ★★★

Antichita' Zanutto,
Fondamenta Corner Zaguri, S.Marco 2013. Tel: 041.523.5359, www.antichitazanutto.com. ★★★

Antichita' San Samuele,
S. Marco 3130 (Calle Madona). Tel: 041.520.4900. ★★★★

Antichita' Pietro Scarpa,
1023 Dorsoduro (just left of the Accademia). Tel: 041.522.2697 / 041.523.9700. ★★★★

Antichita' Marciana,
S. Marco 1864 (half a block from La Fenice theater). Tel: 041.523.5666, www.antichitamarciana.it. ★★★★

Antichi Splendori,
Castello 5545 (on Salizzada San Lio, near Alle Tetstiere restaurant). Tel: 041.523.9265, www.antichisplendori.com. ★★★★

Cose antiche-Luca Sumiti,
Castello 5274 (Calle delle bande). Tel: 041.520.5621, www.coseantiche.eu. ★★★

53 **Book ARRRRomantic Dinner** on a Lively Pirate Boat

We pride ourselves on digging out tips that are off the typical tourist trails, but every once in a while one of those oh-so-touristy attractions grabs us and presents itself as an amusing alternative to the usual list of Venetian activities. The Jolly Roger is a large pirate-style wooden ship that traverses the lagoon from Punta Sabioni to Murano to Piazza San Marco carrying merry guests. The vessel is actually a replica of an ancient galleon which was used by the Serenissima Republic of Venice over 300 years ago for battle and transporting goods and precious commodities. When you step on deck you will be immediately welcomed by a Prosecco *aperitivo*. Once settled on board you will be served a four-course meal while enjoying the view, passing by sights such as Sant'Erasmo (Venice's tiny vegetable-growing island), San Francesco del Deserto, where a small community of monks live, and, of course Venice itself, including Piazza San Marco.
The meal changes by season and includes dishes such as sea bass carpaccio, langoustine *antipasto* with a lemony vinaigrette, creamy seafood risotto, and salt-baked sea bream served with ratatouille and rosemary potatoes. The whole experience lasts three hours, and we recommend that before booking, you check both the proposed menu (since it's fixed) and the weather forecast (since their cancellation policy is very strict, even in case of bad weather). Aside from normal dinners, special festival parties are organized during the year, which are great fun. Dinners typically take place three to five times a month, and advance booking is required (at least 48 hours prior to the dinner date). At €110 per person, the whole experience isn't cheap, but it

certainly is unique. Cheaper seats are available for €10 less, but these aren't recommended as the price difference is so trivial, and you will be seated in a spot with a less panoramic view.

Jolly Roger,
Tel: 0421.380.006, www.jollyroger.it.
★★★

54 **Relax with a Glass of Wine** at a Good Local *Enoteca*

The word "*enoteca*" originally derives from Greek and means wine repository. But today in modern Italian vernacular an *enoteca* (plural - *enoteche*) is a wine shop that stocks local wines that are available for tasting and purchase. Though the concept has spread to other countries, the *enoteche* are a very Italian custom, and they are often run in collaboration with local grower's organizations. And if you have no intention of leaving Venice and following one of our recommended wine routes (see tips 88, 93, 94 and 96), then a good *enoteca* is the perfect place to enjoy the wonderful wines of Veneto – one of the top three wine-producing regions in Italy – without stepping out of the city.

Centrally located and very welcoming, it's quite clear why **all'Amarone** is so popular. This is a lively *enoteca* not far from Piazza San Marco, and, as you might have guessed from the name, a locale that has a good selection of Amarone and Valpolicella wines, as well as many other national favorites. The owners are creative and enjoy using technology to enliven the experience, and you can consult their website to find an updated wine list and the day's dishes. The combination of fine wines and simple and tasty food makes this a fun option for a pleasant lunch or a pre-dinner *aperitivo*.

If you are trying to escape the crowds, then head to **Al Prosecco,** a small but well-stocked *enoteca* in a slightly calmer area of town—Campo San Giacomo da l'Orio (10 minutes from the Jewish Ghetto). Make the trip out here if you have had it with the masses, or if you feel like unwinding and sharing a drink with the locals. Trust the *enoteca*'s staff—their recommendations are usually spot-on. You can accompany your drink with one of their little dishes or snacks to complete the experience.

all'Amarone,
San Polo 1131 (Calle degli Sbianchesini, between Campo San Silvestro and Campo San Aponal). Tel: 041.523.1184; www.allamarone.com. Open Thursday-Tuesday, 10:00 a.m.-11:00 p.m. Closed Wednesday. ★★★★

Al Prosecco,
Campo San Giacomo da l'Orio, Santa Croce 1503. Tel: 041.524.0222, www.alprosecco.com. Open Monday-Friday, 10:00 a.m.-8:00 p.m.; Saturday, 10:00 a.m.-5:00 p.m. Closed Sunday. ★★★

55 **Experience a Sophisticated Meal** at one of Venice's Top Modern Restaurants

Il Ridotto is one of Venice's best-known restaurants – a Michelin-starred venue where savvy locals come seeking a fusion of novelty and quality. Located just off of Piazza San Marco, this is the place to go if you are in a daring mood and want to delve into something slightly more creative than the traditional Venetian fare. Opt for their €80 five-course tasting menu, a good way of getting to try many of the delights on offer. You will be able to sample dishes such as San Pietro fish in black rice crust, baked scallops, pasta in an aromatic fish broth, red wine risotto (made with one of Veneto's most celebrated wines, the famous Amarone), and cuttlefish with a creamy green bean sauce. If you choose to order à la carte, you will probably end up paying more. Their fixed lunch menu is much cheaper (€28 for three *cicheti* and one dish of the day, excluding water, desserts, and wine), but it isn't as interesting or impressive.

Alternatively, try **Osteria di Santa Marina.** Intimate, high-class and tempting, it's no coincidence that so many Venetian chefs and journalists recommend it as one of the top restaurants in town. Upon arrival, you will be seated in one of two elegant dining rooms. Alternatively, book in advance a table outside in the *campiello* (little *campo*) for a candle-lit dinner al fresco. The menu here is seasonal, and tends to break from tradition and venture into more innovative territory. It should also be noted that the selection of dishes is highly oriented toward seafood, and meat lovers or vegetarians will find it lacking. Try their tasting menu (€70), which is both a good deal and delicious, and features dishes such as raw scallops with smoked foie gras, king prawns wrapped in bacon served on a Jerusalem artichoke cream, eggplant mille-feuille, baked turbot fillet with tomatoes and capers, mixed fried fish and shellfish, calamari stuffed with snowpeas and vegetables, and more. You can of course also order à la carte. It goes without saying that in a place like this the pasta is handmade, and almost all the ingredients used in the kitchen are locally sourced. The desserts are quite delicious, too.

Il Ridotto Restaurant,
Castello 4509 (Campo SS. Filippo e Giacomo, behind Basilica di San Marco).
Tel: 041.520.8280, www.ilridotto.com.
Open Friday-Tuesday, 12:00 p.m.-1:45 p.m. & 6:45 p.m.-9:45 p.m.; Thursday, open for dinner only.
Closed Wednesday. ★★★★

Osteria di Santa Marina,
Campo Santa Marina 5911.
Tel: 041.528.5239,
www.osteriadisantamarina.com.
Open Tuesday-Saturday, 12:30 p.m.-2:30 p.m. & 7:30 p.m.-10:00 p.m.; Monday, open for dinner only.
Closed Sunday. ★★★★

56 **Shop at Il Prato,** a one-stop shop for all that is Venetian

Normally we love to recommend small, old-world ateliers where one can find the fruits of original and loving labor. But once in a while we come across a larger shop that offers customers a quality selection of original souvenirs, and then we can't resist the urge to pop in. **Il Prato** is a case in point. The shop is centrally located, right on Campo Santa Maria del Giglio, and inside awaits an ample selection of everything that is Venetian, from beautiful handmade paper to lively and colorful Murano glass items to figurines, leather-bound diaries and much more. Everything is gracefully displayed on large wooden shelves, challenging customers to limit their selection and choose just one (or two...) souvenirs to take home with them.

Il Prato,
Calle delle Ostreghe 2456 (just off Campo Santa Maria del Giglio).
Tel: 041.523.1148,
www.ilpratovenezia.com.
Open Monday-Saturday, 10:00 a.m.-7:30 p.m.; Sunday, 11:00 a.m.-7:00 p.m. ★★★

57 **Savor a Magical Dinner** in a Secluded Corner of Venice

Venissa is one of the most unusual restaurants in Venice. Located on the tiny island of Mazzorbo (connected by a simple wooden bridge to Burano), this Michelin-starred venue is surrounded by vineyards and apple orchards, allowing guests to enjoy the light breeze from the lagoon and the tangy smells of fresh fruit and herbs when they sit down for their meal. Stepping into this colorful and peaceful oasis, you will feel as if you have been transported to a different world, quite apart from the maddening crowds on the mainland. The seasonal menu is original and bold, proudly setting Venissa apart as one of the few nouvelle cuisine restaurants in town. The dishes are created using local produce, including fruit and vegetables from nearby Sant' Erasmo Island, and wine from Mazzorbo itself. The tasting menus, such as the €105 ten-course menu (€150 with wine pairings for each course), are usually your best bet and will enable you to try some of the kitchen's finest creations. If you decide to go à la carte, there are a number of excellent options, including beef carpaccio with blackberry vinegar, oysters served with a creamy potato cheese fondue and noisette butter, and roasted barley and herbs with local fish roe and sea urchin. Other options are the langoustine bisque infused with licorice and rosemary, spaghetti with red turnips and roasted squid, smoked risotto flavored with cumin and tomatoes, and candied lagoon shrimp with fennel blossoms.

The restaurant closes off-season (October/November to April), but even when it shuts its doors, **Via della Vigna,** the owners' smaller (and simpler) *enoteca*, is usually open (though January and February might be tricky; call before making your way here). Reservations are required, and it is important to remember that the island of Burano (hence the restaurant, too) is about one hour away from the mainland (by *vaporetto*). The staff can help you with transportation to the restaurant with a water taxi from a fixed location—call the restaurant a few days in advance to find out more and book a ride.

Venissa is also a boutique resort, and offers guests various exclusive activities to enjoy, everything from rowing lessons in the lagoon to fishing expeditions with the locals to cooking classes, wine tastings and even photography lessons, which will help you capture the beauty of this incredibly scenic little haven. Consult their website to find out more.

Venissa Ristorante,
Fondamenta Santa Caterina 3, Mazzorbo (Burano). Tel: 041.527.2281. www.venissa.it. Open Wednesday-Monday, 12:30 p.m.-2:00 p.m. & 7:00 p.m.-9:00 p.m. Closed Tuesday. ★★★★★

58 **Watch the Regata Storica,** the Best Rowing Competition in Town

Rowing has been practiced in the Venetian lagoon for more than 1,000 years. Venice's wealth came from its maritime location and the rich supplies that travelled down its canals and into the city from faraway lands. Strong oarsmen who could navigate Venice's waterways were the lifeblood of the city, and much emphasis was put on their training. Hundreds of races, designed to hone skill and encourage new talent, emerged. Today, the most famous regatta (of the 100-plus that still take place) is the Regata Storica. The first recorded occurrence of the Regata Storica (Historical Regata), which takes place on the first Sunday of September each year, dates back to the mid-13th century. In a dazzling nod to the past, the event begins with a parade of dozens of multicolored 16th century-style boats, powered by traditionally dressed oarsmen. At the head of the parade are the Doge and the Doge's wife, played enthusiastically by local actors, together with the rest of the high-ranking Venetian officials.

The Regata has always featured various races with different kinds of boats, which originally included galleys, bucentaurs, and barges. Nowadays the event is split into four races, divided by age group. The *Campionissimi su Gondoloni,* or the *gondolini* regata, is the most famous race and sees experienced gondoliers race small sport gondolas down the Grand Canal to reach the Ca' Foscari Palace. Here they meet the spectacular floating stage: the *machina*. St Mark's Bay and the Grand Canal are packed with boats and the quays are lined with excited spectators cheering for their favorite gondolier.

To find out more about the Regata and the yearly program, visit www.regatastoricavenezia.it. ★★★★★

59 Buy the Famous Fortuny Lamps

Fortuny lamps are immediately identified with Venice. Named after Spanish designer Mariano Fortuny, who found both fame and success here, these iconic cascading lamps ooze charm and style and add a touch of beauty and decadence to any home. Fortuny lamps are crafted from silk and other fine materials, and synthesize aspects of Oriental and Venetian designs. The details in these famous hanging lamps—from the hand-painted motifs to the multi-layered structure—are the legacy of Fortuny's personal obsession with every aspect of the production process.

Today you can buy the iconic lamps, together with accessories and bags made with the signature Fortuny fabrics, at the exclusive **Venetia Studium** shops in Venice. If you are passionate about design we highly recommend you make a stop here. And if you are a non-EU citizen, you can save quite a lot of money by filling out a tax-refund form when you pay for your purchases.

Additionally, we recommend that you check the designs at **Archeo Venice.** They offer a tasteful collection that draws inspiration from Venetian museum pieces and then integrates contemporary functional elements. By using the finest materials, including 20-karat gold plating, brass finishings and hand-blown Murano glass to recreate historic items, they manage to breathe new life into historical designs, including their own version of Fortuny lamps (which they make from glass instead of silk).

Venetia Studium
has two shops in Venice. The Flagship store can be found in Dorsoduro 180/A (Calle del Bastion, between the Guggenheim Museum and the Salute *vaporetto* stop). Tel: 041.521.0187. A second shop can be found in S. Marco 2428 (Calle delle Ostreghe, at the end of Calle Larga XXII Marzo). Tel: 041.520.0505, www.venetiastudium.com. Both shops are open Thursday-Tuesday, 11:00 a.m.-6:00 p.m. Closed Wednesday. ★★★★★

Archeo Design Venice,
Bressagio 30, Murano.
Tel: 041.583.9749,
www.archeovenicedesign.com.
Visit by appointment. ★★★★

60 Enjoy a Splendidly Romantic Dinner by the Water at Ristorante Riviera

Riviera has maintained its position as one of the best-loved restaurants in Venice for a number of years now, and that in itself is a testament to their culinary abilities. The location, right on the bank of Giudecca Canal, is intimate and romantic. There is an indefinable elegance to the contrast between the greenish-blue water and the crisp white linen tablecloths, especially when seated right on the water line. The service here is friendly and informative, and the owners take great pride in their kitchen and the dishes they create, many of which offer a bit of a modern twist to "old" favorites. Try specialties such as scallops with braised leeks, pepper pesto and a green salad, ricotta gnocchi with crunchy broccoli and sea bass cubes, or thick *chitarrucci* spaghetti with calamari sauce and red chicory. The *secondi,* such as the stewed veal cheek served on a bed of potatoes and sautéed carrots, are quite good, but even better is the house specialty—a selection of the day's fish, raw, marinated, grilled, or baked in salt. Unlike in many other Venetian restaurants, the desserts here are excellent, and make the perfect ending for such a splendid dinner. Our favorite is the milk parfait with grappa, coffee sauce and chestnut purée, but their tiramisu and cake have their fans, too. Since this is such a popular spot, be sure to book in advance. After your meal, you can end your evening with a long stroll by the water, enjoying the magic of Venice at night.

Ristorante Riviera,
Fondamenta Zattere al Ponte Longo 1473 (50 meters from the Zattere *vaporetto* stop). Tel: 041.522.7621, www.ristoranteriviera.it. Open Tuesday-Sunday, 12:30 p.m.-3:00 p.m. & 7:00 p.m.-10:30 p.m. Closed Monday.
★★★★★

61 **Indulge the Senses** at Venice's Best Spas

When exploring Venice's grand *campi* and hidden alleys, traversing bridges and navigating canals, tired feet are to be expected. By the end of the day you might even discover you are simply too exhausted to move. But help is at hand (or at foot!). A number of spas in town offer first-rate treatments to revive the weary senses. It should be noted, however, that most spas in Venice are located in top hotels, so while that does add to the feeling of pampering, it also adds to the final bill.

The best spa in town, in our opinion, is in the **Bauer Palladio Hotel**. Often referred to simply as "the Palladio," this refined and luxurious hotel is a haven of tranquility and good taste. It is located on Giudecca Island, away from the hustle and bustle of the center, right next to the Belmond Cipriani Hotel. The first-rate service and the opulent décor make it clear why many choose this hotel as their base for touring the city. And while a night here will cost north of $500, the spa treatments are far more accessible, and are available for non-guests, too. The Palladio offers wonderful couple's packages, such as the "Ritual of Dreams," a sumptuously pampering choice that includes a Turkish bath, a scalp massage, a Feng Shui facial massage and a foot massage, ending with a dip in their king-size Jacuzzi. Other options include detoxing Dr. Vitalis steam baths, purifying sea salt, algae and quartzite silver rituals, and a variety of excellent wellness, anti-stress, energetic and oriental massages and facials. Prices range from about €90 for a 50-minute reflexology session to €250 for a complete pampering package. For a particularly lovely experience, book the Magnolia Massage outside in the garden, surrounded by the fragrant blooming trees and accompanied by the relaxing sound of Tibetan bells.

Next, the **Reali Wellness Spa** at the Ai Reali Hotel is another good option to consider. The spa is located on the top floor of the hotel, and the owners have gone to great lengths to combine form and function with a touch of class. Neutral colors are used throughout, which contrast beautifully with some oriental influences. The aesthetic sets the perfect mood for relaxation. The facilities here include a Finnish sauna, a Turkish bath, aromatic showers and outside and inside relaxation areas. Naturally, you will also find a number of massages and facial treatments on offer, executed with the finest products. As there is a strong Eastern theme here, there is also a selection of Thai massages, including Thai foot massages. The signature Ai Reali Massage includes a combination of Thai, Hawaiian Lomi Lomi and classic Swedish techniques and is a particularly indulgent way to relax.

Next, **Lanna Gaia** is slightly simpler but still very professional, and it's a pleasant way to unwind. It is located in the famous Ausonia & Hungaria Hotel on Lido Island, a 20-minute *vaporetto* or a water taxi ride from the mainland. This traditional oriental spa is named after the ancient kingdom of Lanna, one of the earliest kingdoms of Thailand, and Gaia, the goddess of the earth. Their philosophy of balance and connecting with your core guides the array of detoxing and relaxing treatments on offer. Here you will find more traditional Thai massages which hail from Northern Thailand, reflexology, aromatic massages and the four-elements massage. Because Thai massage aims to penetrate deep into the muscles, talk to your masseuse before you start the treatment about the level of strength you'd prefer, especially if you are not used to strong massages. As an alternative, try the Lanna Signature Massage, which focuses on relaxing the body and releasing tension and pressure. Body treatments, including body scrubs and firming treatments, are also available. A favorite with many is the four-hour pampering package: 30-minute sauna and steam baths, followed by a body scrub, a body massage, and then facial hydration (€230 per person, €430 for a couple). The Lanna Gaia ritual, which includes a 30-minute sauna followed by relaxing aromatic massage, is a good deal at €105.

Bauer Palladio Hotel & Spa,
Giudecca 33. Tel: 041-2703867, www.spa.bauerhotels.com. The spa is open by appointment, 11:00 a.m.-8:00 p.m. ★★★★★

Ai Reali Hotel & Reali Wellness Spa,
Campo della Fava, Castello 5527. Tel: 041.241.0253, www.hotelaireali.com. The spa is open daily, 10:00 a.m.-9:00 p.m., and all beauty treatments and massages should be booked in advance. ★★★★

Lanna Gaia Spa
(in the Grande Albergo Ausonia & Hungaria), Via Doge Michiel 17, Lido. Tel: 041.526.9703, www.lannagaia.com. The spa is open daily, 3:00 p.m.-8:00 p.m. The rejuvenation center is open daily, 10:00 a.m.-10:00 p.m. All treatments must be booked in advance. ★★★★

62 Ride *Vaporetto* Line 1 along the Grand Canal Early in the Morning

Perhaps the only drawback of Venice's famous beauty is the inevitable crowds of tourists it attracts. During the high season, especially, it can be nearly impossible to find a quiet corner to enjoy the city in peace. Instead, you will often find yourself submerged by thousands of visitors snapping away furiously with their cameras and smartphones.

Considering how difficult it is to find an intimate spot from which to appreciate this magnificent city, we made it our mission to uncover places of (relative) tranquility. Rather unexpectedly, we found just what we were looking for one morning, while making our way home from a party that ended just as the sun was rising. We felt there was no point in heading to bed so late (or early), and instead decided to hop on the nearest *vaporetto* and ride Line 1 along the Grand Canal. What started as a makeshift solution turned into a lucky discovery because for the first time in a long time we enjoyed the uninterrupted beauty of Venice, blushing with the bright pink light of the early hours of the morning, and almost empty, as most tourists, and even most of the locals, were still tucked under the covers. Now, every time we return to town, we try to repeat the experience, and tour along the city's main *vaporetto* route in the early hours of the morning. And, as long as getting up early on your hard-earned vacation doesn't strike you as heresy, we recommend you give it a try.

There are two lines that make their way along the Grand Canal from start to finish – lines 1 and 2. Both ply the same route, but Line 1 moves more slowly, makes far more stops, and allows you more time to take in the sights. Once you board the *vaporetto* go straight for the best seats—don't waste your time on inside seating, where glass windows will ruin your view and your pictures. Instead, plant yourself outside right at the front, in the open air (sometimes there are outside seats at the very back of the *vaporetto*, too), where there is nothing in your way to distract from Venice's many wonders. Some *vaporetti* don't have seats in the front, but most do. Arm yourself in advance with one of the colorful local guide books that illustrate the many *palazzi* of the Grand Canal, to get a better understanding of what you are looking at. Many of these stunning *palazzi* were built by rich and powerful noble families and have an interesting history. The most impressive section of the canal starts around the San Stae stop, continues past the Accademia, then Santa Maria della Salute, and finishes up around the Piazza San Marco-Zaccaria. Along this segment you will enjoy architectural and artistic treasures such as Ca' Rezzonico, the church of Santa Maria della Salute, Ca d'Oro, Ca' Pesaro, Palazzetto Pisani, Punto della Dogana, and many other jewels that make the Grand Canal one of the most famous tourist destinations in the world.

Naturally, you can skip the *vaporetto* experience altogether and avoid the masses by organizing a private tour of the Grand Canal—simply rent a **water taxi** for half an hour and ask to be taken along the classic route (from Santa Lucia to San Marco). This option is worth considering if you have your heart set on a more intimate and exclusive experience and don't mind paying for the pleasure.

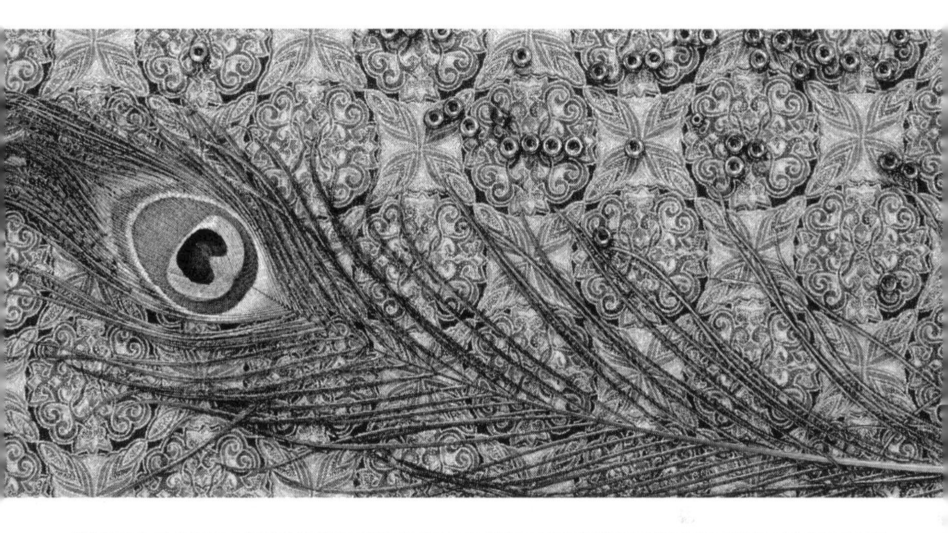

63 Buy Stylish Italian Fabric from the Best Designers

Aspiring designers and those in the market for something a little more affordable and modern than the classic, antique ateliers described in tip 35, will find many smaller boutiques that are worth exploring in Venice. These shops have a wider, more modern selection, and get their stock from some of the best designers in Italy.

Il Canape – tessuti per l'arredamento is a small but excellent boutique, selling items by Fornasetti, Edmond Petit, Le Crin, SAHCO, Manuel Canovas, and others. Gino and Anita Stefani run this beautiful shop, and will help you navigate your away across their large showroom, discovering not just fabric but also furniture and tableware, lamps, cushions and more.

Ca' Nova is another first-rate stop, and it's very close to the Rialto Bridge and Campo San Luca (in the heart of the shopping district, see tip 12). This small but high-end boutique has been supplying demanding clients for over 40 years, and will delight anyone who is interested in interior decorating or looking for a special gift to bring back home. The selection at Ca' Nova focuses on the leading modern Italian brands, everything from colorful and stylish Missoni towels to rows and rows of the finest fabric and soft, delicate cashmere throws. Hand-stitched blankets and items by Jab, Etro and Voghi are also on display, and there's a tempting selection of handmade linen by Dea House, an exclusive boutique in Florence, which could make for a lovely gift for newlyweds.

Il Canapè,
Dorsoduro 3736 (right off Campo San Pantalon). Tel: 041.714.264, www.ilcanape.it. Open Monday-Friday, 10:00 a.m.-12:30 p.m. & 3:00 p.m.-7:30 p.m. From June to September the shop closes down on Saturday afternoon. The shop is closed on Sunday year-round. ★★★

Ca' Nova,
San Marco 4264/A (right off Campo San Luca). Tel: 041.520.3834, www.canovatessutitendaggi.com. Open Monday-Friday, 9:00 a.m.-12:30 p.m. & 3:30 p.m.-7:30 p.m.; Saturday, 9:00 a.m.-12:30 p.m. Closed Sunday. ★★★

64 **Stay at the Magnificent** and Historic Metropole Hotel

Time can be said to be the greatest measure of quality. If a hotel can build and maintain a reputation over decades—it is doing well; over centuries—that is unique. The Metropole Hotel is just such a place. Located on Riva degli Schiavoni, a few minutes from Piazza San Marco and overlooking the lagoon, it is a refined, upscale and historic stay. Unlike some of the newer, glitzier hotels that have opened in recent years, the Metropole adheres to the principles of old-world hospitality and exudes the charm of a bygone era. The service feels ordered, elegant and grand, and perhaps this feeling and ambiance come from the hotel's illustrious history: When it was still a private residence, Vivaldi lived and taught here, and, since its conversion to a hotel, guests have included Marcel Proust, Sigmund Freud and Thomas Mann (who composed part of his celebrated novella *Death in Venice* within the walls of the Metropole). That old-world charm is reflected in the décor; the aesthetic is clearly Venetian, and luxurious period furniture and Damascus fabrics create a sense of grandeur. Eclectic artworks and antique furniture compete for the eye.

There are 67 rooms in total, each decorated in a different manner. The deluxe double rooms are especially beautiful and, if you are interested, book in advance to secure a room with a private terrace overlooking the lagoon. If money is no object (and be warned—this hotel is far from cheap!), then book one of the dramatic suites, such as the Damascus suite, which is the owner's favorite and offers spectacular waterfront views. Their large buffet breakfast is included in the price (for those who reserve their room directly through the hotel and not through various booking websites), and is served in the gazebo in the small but beautiful courtyard garden, fragrant with the smell of jasmine and citrus. The hotel also has a bar (open to non-guests, too); the Oriental Bar is the perfect place to stop for a drink after a long day of touring the city. For a fine dinner, consider the hotel's Michelin-starred restaurant, the Met, a worthy choice in its own right.

Hotel Metropole,
Riva degli Schiavoni (near the S. Zaccaria *vaporetto* stop).
Tel: 041.520.5044,
www.hotelmetropole.com. ★★★★★

65 **Rub Shoulders with the Locals** at Two Easy-Going Neighborhood Eateries

Fancy dinners aside, having a fun meal surrounded by locals (a rare sight in Venice) is a great experience. And despite the onslaught of tourists, there are still a few spots in town where such meals can be enjoyed.

Al Portego is, simply put, a zero-frills neighborhood *bacaro* par excellence. It isn't as cheap as a neighborhood eatery would be in any other city (this IS Venice, after all), but it is the kind of fun and noisy place where people get up from their tables to walk over and chat with friends seated across the room, and then forget to go back. And while it's famous for its tasty *cicheti*, Al Portego is actually also an *osteria*, where you can expect to find a simple but satisfying lunch or dinner. Our recommendation is to come here for a pre-dinner *aperitivo* and hang out by the bar, trying various delicious *cicheti* and chatting with a glass of white wine in hand. Wherever you go next, you will surely be in a good mood!

Alternatively, head to **Il Paradiso Perduto,** another locals' favorite. It's situated on Fondamenta della Misericordia, just past the Jewish Ghetto, and many tourists don't make it this far, leaving the scene to young Venetians who come here in droves and gobble up the *cicheti* and the Spritz. *Aperitivo* hour is especially merry—come armed with patience (the waiters often look like they are about to have a nervous breakdown) and in a good mood. This isn't the place for a serious dinner; there are far better restaurants just down the street (see tip 8). But it is certainly a fun stop to make before you sit down for your meal. If you prefer to order something more substantial, try the Paradiso Perduto *antipasti* platter (€29 for two people), which is tasty and a good deal.

Al Portego,
Castello 6014 (just off Calle Forneri). Tel: 041.522.9038. Open daily, 11:00 a.m.-3:00 p.m. & 5:30 p.m.-10:00 p.m. ★★★

Il Paradiso Perduto,
Fondamenta della Misericordia (Cannaregio 2540). Tel: 041.720.581, www.ilparadisoperduto.com. Open Thursday-Sunday, 11:00 a.m.-midnight. May close down in July for the summer break–call before making your way here. ★★★

66 **Book a Private After-Hours Tour** and Have the Treasures of Venice All to Yourself

Tired of fighting off crowds to get a glimpse of that Veronese? Sick of being bumped into while gazing up at Tintoretto's masterpieces? Navigating the daily crowds at Venice's magnificent museums can be tiring even for the most hardy traveler. But it doesn't necessarily have to be this way. If you are truly passionate about Venice's great artists, or simply want to add a memorable VIP experience to your travels, think about booking an exclusive after-hours tour to discover the magic of the museums by night. Currently, after-hours tours of 11 of Venice's museums are available, including Ca' Rezzonico, Palazzo Fortuny and even the Natural History Museum. Best of all, and we are sure you will agree, is the chance to see the beauty of Palazzo Ducale (the Doge's Palace) in the silence and intimacy that only a private night tour can afford.

Private after-hours tours can be booked (in advance) through the Venice Tourism Board: www.visitmuve.it/it/mostre-eventi/aperture-straordinarie, or email: eventi@civicimusei.com.
★★★★★

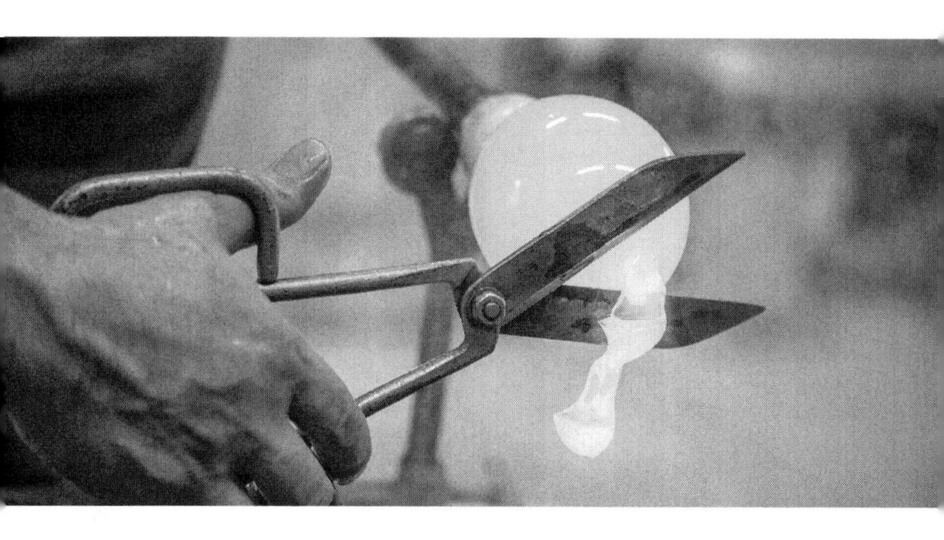

67 **Visit Murano and Buy** One-of-a-Kind Handmade Glass Souvenirs

Murano, a small island just 15 minutes off the mainland, is world-renowned for its glass production. It all started in 1291, after the reigning Council of Venice decreed that glass makers would have to move their studios to a different island, to limit the loss of life and property resulting from fires caused by the many glass furnaces (and to make sure the secrets of glass production remained in Venetian hands, protected from prying eyes...). So Murano became the "island of glass," and the industry quickly grew and flourished. Masters developed techniques to create some of the most intricate and beautiful glass artistry in the world. In fact, glass was such a prestigious and profitable occupation in medieval Venice that only the sons of *vetrai*, glass men, were allowed to marry into noble families.

While the heyday of artisanal glassblowers is long past, the tradition is still alive in pockets of Murano. Today you can buy classic items, such as handblown glass sets and jewelry, or invest in spectacular pieces of modern glass art. Many of the finer hotels in Venice have Murano chandeliers, and several of the upscale restaurants serve their drinks in Murano glasses. Buying real Murano glass can be tricky. First, be aware that the cheap stuff found in most souvenir shops is not real Murano glass, and probably comes from China. It is unlikely that artisans will sell their handmade work for €10. Second, try to avoid the annoying guides on the mainland who offer free rides to Murano. The rides are indeed free, but many of them will strongly insist that in return you visit a specific shop that they collaborate with (and from which they receive a commission for every sale). Murano is connected to the mainland by the regular *vaporetto* system (see technical info at the end of this tip) and can easily be reached from both the train station and Piazza San Marco. It is actually easier to make your own way to the island, get off at the first stop, and visit one of the many recommended artisan shops without being followed around by an overly-persistent guide.

Antica Murano is a tiny shop just meters from the Murano Colonna *vaporetto* stop, which seems to go to great lengths to hide its existence from potential clients. The shop is located on Fondamenta Manin 1, inside the building with the huge sign that says "Vetreria Gritti." Vetereria Gritti no longer exists, but if you walk inside, and pass through the maze of corridors, you will reach this tiny family-owned business run by Andrea and Diego. Antica Murana doesn't organize any proper glass demonstrations, but if you come early enough, you might catch them feeding the 1,000-degree furnace, preparing for the day's work. The selection here is limited but beautiful, and greatly depends on what is available on the day of your visit. We once came only to discover an almost-bare showroom,

but a week later we found a most beautiful set of colorful glasses, which made for a perfect wedding gift for some friends.

As you continue your stroll along Fondamenta dei Vetrai and Fondamenta Manin, it quickly becomes clear that the choice of glass shops is endless, and that the various boutiques cater to all tastes. Some of our favorites are **Fornace Mian** (for modern and reasonably priced items), **BF Signoretti** for modern artwork and vases, and **Lu Murano,** for extraordinary modern chandeliers. Then, of course, there is **Venini,** one of the most famous shops in Venice, offering incredible craftsmanship and stylish items at very hefty prices. Venini regularly collaborates with leading internationally famous artists, and in the past they have worked with Carlo Scarpa and Ettore Sottsass. Their designs can also be found in their flagship shop on Piazza San Marco. For sculptures, try **Zanetti Murano;** they have some fascinating and elegant artwork. If you want to see artists at work, we recommend **Vetreria Estavan**—the shop is very touristy, and somewhat overpriced, but it is one of the few places on the island that still organizes regular glass blowing demonstrations. Guided tours can also be booked by advance reservation. Lastly, to find out more about the best Murano glass in Venice itself, consult tips 24, 51, and 56.

Antica Murano,
Fondamenta Manin 1, Murano.
Tel: 041.739.556, www.anticamurano.it.
Open Monday-Friday, 8:30 a.m.-4:30 p.m.
Closed Saturday and Sunday. ★★★

Fornace Mian,
Fondamenta Vetrai 143, Murano.
Tel: 041.73.92.85, www.fornacemian.com. Open daily, 10:00 a.m.-5:00 p.m. (They offer no tours of the glassmaking facilities.) ★★★★

BF Signoretti,
Calle San Cipriano 48, Murano.
Tel: 041.527.4294, www.signoretti.it.
(Near the Murano Serenella *vaporetto* stop). ★★★★

Venini,
Fondamenta dei Vetrai 47 & 50, Murano.
An additional shop can be found in Piazza San Marco 314 (left of the Basilica).
Tel: 041.273.7211, www.venini.com.
★★★★★

Lu Murano,
Calle del Paradiso 14, Murano.
Tel: 041.736.176, www.lu-murano.it.
Visit by appointment only. ★★★★★

Zanetti Murano,
Fondamenta Serenella 3, Murano,
Venezia 30141, Tel: 041.739.163,
www.zanettimurano.com ★★★★

Vetreria Estevan,
Fondamenta Navagero 50, Murano
(near the Murano Navagero *vaporetto* stop). Tel: 041.739329,
www.rossettomuranoglass.com. ★★★

68 **Become an Artist for a Day** and Learn How to Make Traditional Glass Items in Murano

Murano glass is one of Venice's most cherished crafts, a tradition honed over hundreds of years by Italy's finest glassblowers. For lovers of this elegant workmanship, or those wanting an intimate insight into the industry, hands-on workshops led by some renowned craftsmen are available. The largest school in Murano is **Abate Zanetti**, which was founded in 1862 and is today considered a center of excellence. The Zanetti school offers a number of courses and workshops, usually lasting at least four days. The school focuses on the techniques and methods of traditional and contemporary artistic glassmaking. Creative glass jewelry design is the most popular course, but there is a rotating schedule that also includes fusing workshops, lamp work, and stained glass classes, among others. Consult their website to find out more and book a class.

Abate Zanetti Glass School,
Calle Briati 8, Murano. Tel: 041.273.7711,
www.abatezanettimurano.com.
★★★★★

69 | **Book a Guided Tour** to Discover the Mysteries of Venice

What we love about guided tours are the anecdotes—the fascinating and often surprising little stories about buildings, monuments or people that bring the city alive. But we have been on enough guided tours to know the opposite is also possible—lifeless, boring guides who reel off memorized scripts. Luckily, in a competitive city such as Venice, you can find some fantastic tours that are worth your time and money. Here are our favorites:

Discovering Venice offers well-executed, fun, and reasonably priced tours that you can enjoy privately or as part of a group (bringing the price down to about €50 per person). The three professional guides who operate Discovering Venice, Antonella, Eugenia, and Federica, are all very experienced and ready to show you the treasures of the town.

Photographers should check out **Venice Photo Walk,** led by photographer Marco Secchi. These expensive but serious tours are aimed at those who want to professionally capture the city with their cameras.

Walks of Italy provides well-researched and fascinating walking tours, with a focus on particular areas of Italian culture, art, history or food. Their list is pretty extensive, so there is something to suit everyone.

Finally, **Luisella Romeo,** an independent tour guide, is one of Venice's best. Her tours are booked solid, so make sure you contact her early. She is friendly and extremely knowledgeable about her town. Chat with her to plan your perfect day, as she offers customized tours.

Discovering Venice,
www.discoveringvenice.com. ★★★★

Venice Photo Walk,
Cell: 041 963 73 74 (Marco),
www.msecchi.it. ★★★★

Walks of Italy,
US number (toll-free): 888.683.8670.
Italian number: 069.480.4888.
www.walksofitaly.com. ★★★★★

Luisella Romeo,
Cell: 349.0848.303, www.seevenice.it.
★★★★★

70 Visit the Mysterious Island of Torcello

Torcello was first inhabited during the Roman Empire and was once the most prosperous island and a center of activity in the Venetian lagoon. However, its fortunes began to decline during the 15th century, parallel to the growth and success of Venice. There was no place in such a small lagoon for two main islands. Today the island of Torcello is almost completely abandoned. And yet something about its magic draws a surprising number of tourists every year to wander this piece of land that seems to have been frozen in time. Torcello is just a few minutes from Burano by *vaporetto*, and is considered somewhat of a refuge from the crowds. If you've already seen Venice's main sights and now have the time for something different, we highly recommend coming here to follow the trails Hemingway once walked on his hunting trips, and to discover hidden archeological treasures that tell of Torcello's impressive past.

Walk here to discover monuments such as the Santa Maria Assunta church, built 1,400 years ago, which is still decorated with Byzantine mosaics; the Ponte del Diavolo, one of Venice's most ancient bridges; and the 1,000-year old Church of Santa Fosca, a beautiful example of Venetian Byzantine architecture. You can even make a stop at the immediately enchanting Locanda Cipriani, Hemingway's preferred restaurant and pension.

Locanda Cipriani,
Piazza Santa Fosca 29, Torcello. Tel: 041.730.150,
www.locandacipriani.com. ★★★★

71 Mingle and Enjoy a Chic *Aperitivo* Right on the Grand Canal

Cicheti, as explained in tip 3, are the perfect way to sample some of Venice's most authentic treats. Small, light and reasonably priced, these tempting Italian-style tapas offer the perfect compromise for foodies with limited time. While there are several spots in town that offer a more "authentic" experience, few can compete with the ambiance of the *bacari* reviewed in this tip. All three are centrally placed, one next to the other, on the highly popular Campo Beccaria (just meters from the Rialto Mercato *vaporetto* stop). All three have ample outside seating right on the water, and the food served at each is similar—a classic Venetian *aperitivo* alongside full entrees and main dishes, prepared using fresh ingredients from the nearby market. Prices reflect the coveted location; a ten-piece *cicheti* plate at Al Pesador, for example, costs about €24.

Al Pesador offers modern, imaginative cuisine and sophisticated presentation: Meticulously cut meats and fish are colorfully decorated with herbs and spices and served on slabs of granite or glass plates. Dishes include larded scallops with chanterelle mushrooms, rabbit terrine with herbs and porcini mushrooms, and fresh pasta with fish sauce.

Next door, **Al Bancogiro** is located in a 17th century warehouse, and offers a selection of smart and elegant dishes of its own. If you choose to stand outside, nibble some *cicheti* and mingle with the crowd, the experience will be less costly than sitting down for a full meal. A glass of Spritz or Prosecco and three or four tasty *cicheti* cost around €15. If you decide to stop for a proper meal, perhaps at lunch time, when you can enjoy the constant flood of people going by, try dishes such as the San Daniele prosciutto platter, goose terrine, salads, gnocchi with boar ragout, tagliatelle with fish sauce, and green *bigoli* (a typical local pasta) with mushrooms. The wine selection, as you might expect, is ample, and includes local wines from Veneto, as well as a large selection of Prosecco and rosé wines, which have been making a comeback in recent years. Note that this *osteria* is open on both ends; one side overlooks the Grand Canal, and the other overlooks the bustling Campo San Giacomo di Rialto.

Naranzaria is right next door, and is slightly more modern than the previous two recommendations. Their menu features both traditional dishes as well as some Asian-influenced plates, such as tasty yakitori chicken, and their "Venetian sushi." On hot summer nights, the *campo* in front of this popular *bacaro* bubbles with life, and it becomes a top place in which to rub shoulders with the locals and make new acquaintances. Try their cocktails (the staff here knows its way around a shaker), munch on a plate of *cicheti,* and gaze at the gondolas slowly drifting under the Rialto Bridge.

Al Pesador,
San Polo 125 (Campo San Giacometto), Tel: 041.523.9492, www.alpesador.it. The bar is open daily, 11:00 a.m.-midnight. The restaurant is open daily, 12:00 p.m.-3:00 p.m. & 7:00.p.m.-10:00 p.m. ★★★

Al Bancogiro,
Campo San Giacometto 122. Tel: 041.523.2061, www.osteriabancogiro.it. Open Tuesday-Sunday, 9:00 a.m.-midnight. Closed Monday. ★★★

Naranzaria,
San Polo 130. Tel: 041.724.1035, www.naranzaria.it. Open daily, 12:30 p.m.-3:00 p.m. & 7:30 p.m.-10:30 p.m. In high season, hours of operation are often extended and the bar remains open all day long. ★★★★

72 **Visit the Star-Studded** Venice Film Festival

For about ten days in late August or early September, Venice becomes the center of the cinematic world. Movie stars, film critics, journalists, directors, and producers from all over the world descend on the city in droves to explore the latest trends and developments and enjoy hundreds of films. The Venice Film Festival is one of the world's most respected cinematic events, and while most screenings are for industry members only, there are also some screenings for the general public, enabling you to watch critically acclaimed films long before they are released in theaters and enjoy the glamorous ambiance, often in the presence of the stars themselves. The festival started back in 1932, making it one of the oldest film festivals in the world. The first edition attracted 25,000 visitors and officially became part of the biennale (even though the festival is held every year, not once every two years).

The festival takes place on the island of Lido, just 20 minutes from the mainland. The streets around the aptly named **Palazzo del Cinema**, where the iconic red carpet is spread, buzz with life. But the real business happens at the Hotel Excelsior, where stars, filmmakers, producers, and executives mingle behind closed doors before and after screenings. The big drama, of course, centers on the question of who will take home the most prestigious prizes—the Golden Lion and the Grand Jury Prizes (awarded to the best film), the Silver Lion (awarded to the best director) and the Volpi Cup (awarded to the best male and female actors). If you are in the mood for a cinematic evening, check the festival's website to find out what is planned this year. Booking in advance is essential if you want to get good seats (or any seats at all).

The Venice Film Festival
(in Italian: Mostra Internazionale d'Arte Cinematografica),
www.labiennale.org/cinema.

Verona

73 **Take in the view** from one of Verona's Top Panoramic Spots

It is only when you get to enjoy an unobstructed view of Verona that you can truly appreciate the all-consuming elegance of the city and understand just why William Shakespeare referred to it as "fair Verona."

Piazzale Castel San Pietro is, in our humble opinion, the Number 1 spot for a panoramic vista in town. The views from here are simply stunning. If you are fit enough, you can walk up the 250 steps that lead to the Piazzale from Teatro Romano. Alternatively, drive up or take the hop-on/ hop-off bus from Piazza Bra. Once you have taken about 100 photos, you might want to consider staying in the Piazzale for a meal or a good cup of coffee. If so, we recommend **TeodoricoRe**, a pleasant *aperitivo* bar and restaurant that overlooks the view.

Another great option, though not quite as incredible, is **Torre dei Lamberti.** This 84-meter high, 500-year-old tower is located at the heart of the historic center, right off Piazza delle Erbe, and affords some beautiful views.

Lastly, we've always enjoyed taking our coffee on the terrace of **Bar al Ponte.** It doesn't offer a panorama like the previous two suggestions, but it does overlook the Ponte Pietra, Verona's prettiest bridge, and it's a pleasure to sip a cappuccino here in the morning while gazing at the river and the colorful houses that surround the bridge.

Piazzale Castel S. Pietro,
(If you are interested in dining in TeodoricoRe, www.teodoricore.com, note that the bar is open Wednesday-Monday, 12:00 p.m.-midnight. The kitchen is open 12:00 p.m.-3:00 p.m. & 7:00 p.m.-10:00 p.m. Closed Tuesday).★★★★★

Torre dei Lambreti,
Via della Costa 1 (just off Piazza Erbe), Verona. Tel: 045.927.3027. Open daily, 11:00 a.m.-7:00 p.m. ★★★★

Terrazza-Bar al Ponte,
Via Ponte Pietra 26, Verona.
Tel: 045.569.608,
www.terrazzabaralponte.eu.
Open daily, 9:00 a.m.-midnight. ★★★

74 **Revel in a Memorable Lunch** at One of the Best Restaurants in Verona

A light and simply-decorated dining hall, a small terrace on the street—it might seem like **Locanda 4 Cuochi** is just another restaurant in a town brimming with fine dining options, but actually it's one of the most delicious places we've come across in Verona. The Locanda's menu is modern and fresh. Its location—just a minute from Piazza Bra—is perfect for a tasty lunch between sightseeing stops. The dishes here are seasonal and often change, but always include a mix of Veneto classics and southern Italian favorites. In the late spring, for example, we enjoyed their deconstructed version of the classic *mozzarella in carrozza*: originally it's a breaded and deep-fried mozzarella eaten as street food in Veneto, but here the mozzarella of superior quality is served fresh with toasted bread filled with a fantastically creamy anchovy salsa. Meat lovers will like the *battuta di limousine con emulsion di uovo*, a raw beef tartar dish from Piedmont, served with an egg and mustard emulsion. The gazpacho with goat cheese crostini is another must on hot summer days, and the various house-made pasta dishes, such as the tagliatelle with a vegetable carbonara, are all good. From the list of *secondi,* go for the *maialino da latte croccante* (suckling pig served with a fresh lemon and sage sauce) or the *coda di bue*, a reimagined version of the classic Roman dish of oxtail. The wine list is excellent, and ranges from inexpensive Soave sold by the glass to 10-year-old bottles of Valpolicella by Quintarelli. You can end with one of their tasty desserts, or with some ice cream from one of the suggestions in tip 83.

Alternatively, head to **Trattoria I Masenini** (not to be confused with

Pescheria I Masenini, which is reviewed in tip 81). Located right in front of Castelvecchio, the imposing stone palace that has become a symbol of Verona, the restaurant is both central enough to do some people watching and remote enough from Piazza Bra to avoid the crowds of tourists. This is a modern and sophisticated eatery, quite popular with locals in the know, and perfect for a serious yet informal meal. Trattoria I Masenini is all about meat, and carnivores will appreciate the main courses here, which include various meats roasted on a spit (T-bone steak, crispy suckling pig and lamb shank, for example), or northern Italian specialties such as beef fillet with Amarone wine sauce and excellent Milanese veal chops. Alternatively, try the pasta dishes, which are also quite good, and include a number of vegetarian options, too.

Locanda 4 Cuochi,
Via Mario Alberto 12, Verona.
Tel: 045.803.0311,
www.locanda4cuochi.it. Open Wednesday-Sunday, 12:30 p.m.-2:30 p.m. & 7:30 p.m.-10:30 p.m.; Tuesday, open for dinner only. Closed Monday.
★★★★

Trattoria I Masenini,
Via Roma 34, Verona.
Tel: 045.806.5169,
www.trattoriaimasenini.it. Open Tuesday-Saturday, 12:40 p.m.-2:00 p.m. & 7:40 p.m.-10:00 p.m.; Monday, open for dinner only. Closed Sunday. ★★★★

75 **Get Some Serious Shopping** Done in Verona

Verona's historical center offers endless tempting options for fashion lovers. Every well-known Italian brand can be found here, and Verona's main street, **Via Mazzini,** offers everything from Caractere, Wolford and Elena Miro to Furla, Polini, Fossil, L'Occitane, Mac, Liu·Jo, Geox, Coccinelle, Motivi, and many other excellent brands. In addition to these popular stores, those in search of a quality little boutique with a personalized collection should stop by **Bottega Giuliana,** which sells brands such as Escada and Sara Roka (expect prices to be on the high end, too). We also love **Quid,** with their collection of chic, urban clothes by young local designers. Those in search of luxury shouldn't miss **Pavin,** a boutique that sells top brands such as Ralph Lauren and Woolrich, **Duca d'Aosta,** which stocks the most on-trend items of the season, and the **Excelsior,** a one-stop-shop for high-end brands. All three shops are located on the aforementioned Via Mazzini. Verona boasts a couple of particularly lovely vintage shops, too, the sort of alternative boutiques that any fashionista will be glad to rummage through. **Cecile** is the best known among the bunch; it's a luxury vintage boutique that only sells known brands of certain prestige. The selection here is very tempting, so don't miss this little gem. For more modern items, head to **Sottosopra33**. There's a younger vibe here, and some very interesting finds. Lastly, smart shoppers who aren't intimidated by markets will love the **flea and vintage market** held on the first Sunday of each month near San Zeno church. Sure, it requires some digging, but there are some interesting items to discover, and at surprising prices! Clothes aren't the only items on sale; you can find décor, collectibles, books and more. Naturally, Verona boasts its fair share of outlet venues, too, to which we have dedicated a separate tip (tip 98).

For quality men's fashion, Verona is one of the best cities to shop in. In fact, there are more serious boutiques for the fashion conscientious gentlemen here than most other Italian cities. **Boggi,** on the main shopping street (Via Mazzini), is a well-known local brand specializing in cool, clean cut suits. **Corso15** is another store that stocks a fine Italian collection, and **Scotch&Soda** is perfect for those interested in a younger vibe and look. **Arnold** boutique is a great choice for quality items; the collection here ranges from modern jeans and beautiful wool jackets to stylish Italian suits and shirts. Teenagers will enjoy **Blue Express,** an alternative style boutique, while the most demanding fashion connoisseurs will appreciate the stylish and pricey attire at **Tailor's & Ties, Tailor's & Cashmere,** and **De Luca Sartorial,** three first-rate boutiques located on the same street near Piazzetta Pescheria.

Bottega Giuliana,
Via Carlo Cattaneo 33, Verona.
Tel: 045.803.1070. Open Tuesday-Saturday, 9:30 a.m.-1:00 p.m. & 3:30 p.m.-7:30 p.m. (In the summer months the shop is closed on Saturday afternoon); Monday, open in the afternoon only. Closed Sunday. ★★★

Quid,
Via Pellicciai 5, Verona.
www.progettoquid.it. Open Tuesday-Friday, 10:30 a.m.-1:30 p.m. & 2:30 p.m.-7:30 p.m.; Saturday 10:30 a.m.-8:00 p.m.; Sunday 10:00 a.m.-1:30 p.m. & 2:30 p.m.-7:30 p.m. Closed Monday. ★★★★

Cecile,
Vicolo Rensi 3 (just off Via Oberdan).
Tel: 045.803.6206, www.cecileboutiques.it. Open Tuesday-Wednesday, 10:30 a.m.-1:30 p.m. & 4:00 p.m.-7:30 p.m.; Thursday-Saturday, 10:30 a.m.-7:30 p.m. Closed Sunday and Monday. ★★★★

Sottosopra Contemporary Vintage,
Via Scrimiari 3. Tel: 045.803.1928, www.sottosopra33-vintage.com. Open Tuesday-Saturday, 10:00 a.m.-12:30 p.m. & 3:30 p.m.-7:30 p.m. Closed Sunday and Monday. ★★★★

Corso15,
Corso Sant'Anastasia 15, Verona.
Tel: 045 8004092, www.corso15.it. Open Tuesday-Sunday, 10:30 a.m.-12:30 p.m. & 3:30 p.m.-7:00 p.m.; Monday, open in the afternoon only. ★★★

Scotch&Soda,
Via Carlo Cattaneo 8, Verona.
Tel: 045.595.505. Open Tuesday-Friday, 10:00 a.m.-1:30 p.m. & 3:30 p.m.-7:30 p.m.; Sunday and Monday, open in the afternoon only. ★★★★

Arnold,
Via Quattro Spade 3,
Verona. Tel: 045.801.4974,
www.arnoldverona.it. Open Tuesday-Sunday, 10:30 a.m.-12:30 p.m. & 3:30 p.m.-7:00 p.m.; Monday, open in the afternoon only. ★★★★

Blue Express,
Via Quattro Spade 7,
Verona. Tel: 0459.273.044,
www.blueexpressfamily.it. Open Tuesday-Friday, 9:30 a.m.-1:00 p.m. & 3:30 p.m.-7:30 p.m.; Saturday 10:00 a.m-7:30 p.m.; Monday and Sunday, open in the afternoon only. ★★★

Tailor's & Ties, Tailor's & Cashmere,
Piazzetta Pescheria 5, Verona.
Tel: 045.801.5217, www.tailors.it. Open Tuesday-Saturday, 9:30 a.m.-1:00 p.m. & 4:00 p.m-8:00 p.m.; Monday, open in the afternoon only. Closed Sunday. ★★★★

76 **Celebrate Summer with a Concert** or an Opera in the Famous Verona Arena

Only in Italy can you see Sting in a venue that hosted gladiatorial contests 2,000 years ago! That venue, of course, is the Verona Arena—a world-famous, first-century AD Roman amphitheater located in the heart of the city. There is something wonderfully unique about stepping into the arena on the evening of your concert to enjoy modern festivities in the most ancient of surroundings. And whether it's a full-cast production of *La Traviata* or a concert by Patti Smith, you're guaranteed to have fun.

Every year the Verona Arena hosts several events and concerts by both big international acts and smaller local artists. Consult the arena's website and buy tickets well in advance, especially if you are interested in one of the elaborate opera productions that take place every summer. Prepare yourself for the uncomfortable seating by bringing a small cushion, and don't forget a fan (Verona's summers can be quite hot) and a pair of binoculars.

To find out more about the various concerts and opera held at the Verona Arena, consult www.arena.it. ★★★★

77 Stay at a Charming and Romantic B&B In Verona

Verona is packed with hotels and B&Bs, but **Casa&Natura Breviglieri,** a little gem of and tranquility situated just minutes from the Piazza Bra, is quite different from the others. Small and intimate, beautifully furnished, and decorated in fresh neutral tones, this is the perfect lodging for travelers who prefer the intimacy of a unique B&B over the anonymity of a hotel. The breakfast here is generous and tasty, and the owners are friendly and attentive. The rooms have been designed according to the principles of bioarchitecture, complete with wooden floors and organic cotton sheets, but the best feature of all is the garden, which is as romantic as it is peaceful. Booking your stay here in advance is advised, especially if travelling in high-season.

Alternatively, if you prefer a B&B located outside the city, in the countryside, look no further than **Agriturismo Delo Coutry Relais.** Surrounded by blooming olive trees and vineyards, just eight kilometers from Verona, this agritusimo makes for an incredible stay. Escape the hustle and bustle of the city to relax at this quaint 16th century rural lodge, which has been perfectly restored by the proud and friendly owners. The rooms are large and have a rustic elegance about them. The communal spaces are every bit as inviting, with stone walls, a fireplace which dates back to the 18th century, and a traditional living room with dark wood beams and rich terracotta floor tiles. Acres of rolling hills surround you, and there are a number of outdoor dining areas from which you can take in the vistas and add to the experience of simple bliss.

Casa & Natura Breviglieri,
Via S. Nazaro 49, Verona.
Cell: 349.2827.781, Tel: 045.591.137,
www.casaenaturabreviglieri.com.
★★★★★

Agriturismo Delo Relais,
Via del Torresin, Novaglie (Verona).
Tel: 0454.858.380, Cell: 333.4753.688,
www.agriturismodelo.it. ★★★★★

78 **Book a Guided Tour of the Prosecco** and Valpolicella Wine Regions

Travelling on your own has many benefits, not least a sense of independence, freedom, and adventure. But travelling in the wine region under your own steam has one glaringly obvious drawback, too—who is the designated driver? Aside from that, it can be nice to sit back and relax, comfortable in the knowledge that your guide is well-informed about the best sights and wineries in the area.

If you are interested in taking an organized tour of the Prosecco and Valpolicella wine regions then **Venice Countryside** is your best option. They offer professional, knowledgeable and friendly guides, and the tours can be customized to your personal expectations. Other possibilities are **Veronaround** and **Pagus;** both offer guided tours of the region, including excursions to Valpolicella, Amarone and Soave wineries, as well as guided tours to Lake Garda and various historic villas. Check all three of their websites, compare the activities, and choose whichever suits you most. If you want to discover the treasures of these wine regions by yourself, use the information in tips 88, 93, 94, and 96 to build the perfect itinerary.

Venice Countryside,
www.Venicecountryside.com. ★★★★

Veronaround,
www.veronaround.it. ★★★

Pagus,
www.valpolicellawinetours.com. ★★★

79 Stay at an Excellent Value Hotel in Verona

What **Hotel Accademia** lacks in style it makes up for in comfort, location and amenities. Centrally positioned in the heart of Verona, just meters from Juliet's house, this hotel offers large rooms with ample bathroom space and comfortable beds. Breakfast is generous and varied, and the staff are refreshingly professional. Despite the busy location, the hotel itself is very peaceful.

If you can't book a room here, try **Hotel Aurora.** Perfectly located—right on Piazza Erbe—this hotel is the ideal base for touring Verona on foot. It offers smallish but comfortable rooms, friendly staff, and all the modern amenities you'll need when you come back from a day of sightseeing.

Hotel Accademia,
Via Scala 12, Verona. Tel: 045.596.222, www.hotelaccademiaverona.it. ★★★★

Hotel Aurora,
Piazza Erbe (at the corner of Piazzetta XIV Novembre 2), Verona.
Tel: 045.594.717, www.hotelaurora.biz.
★★★★

80 Enjoy a Fun *Aperitivo* in Verona

"L'appetito viene mangiando" (appetite comes when you eat), goes the Italian saying that provides the logic of one of the country's most loved dining traditions. The humble *aperitivo*, the famous pre-dinner drink and light snack, is said to prepare or open (*aperto*) one's stomach for the much larger meal to follow. It is no secret that this is one of the best ways to enjoy Italian food, culture and wine. And in Verona, there is no shortage of fabulous little places to sample this popular social tradition.

For a lively ambiance go to Il **Bugiardo,** perfectly located right off Piazza Erbe. This *osteria* and *enoteca* is run by the same family that operates the Bugiardo restaurant in Negrar (in the Valpolicella area, see tip 89), and the same principles of operation apply—hearty food and a lively atmosphere. The *osteria* is quite small, so come early or you'll find yourself fighting off merry locals for an open spot.

For some quality wine go to the **Antica Bottega del Vino.** This venue is more upscale, so expect the food to be slightly expensive, but the ambiance is fantastic and the wine list will please even the most demanding client. When we are feeling particularly indulgent, we combine their delectable tiramisu with a glass of extra-dry Prosecco. This place is hugely popular, so come early and hang out with the locals by the bar, or book a table in advance and enjoy the dinner menu.

If it's cocktails with a beautiful view that you are craving, then move to **TeodoricoRe** (also mentioned in tip 73). Their menu may be slightly limited, but the view alone justifies the trip.

Lastly, for a trendy and hypermodern *aperitivo*, stop at **Via Roma 33 Café**. While this wouldn't be our first choice for a full meal, it certainly hits the spot for an *aperitivo*. Drop in between the hours of 6:00 p.m. and 8:00 p.m. and enjoy their selection of local wines and well-prepared Spritz cocktails. Add €3 and you can enjoy the buffet, too, which is filled with fresh fruit, *bruschette*, cold cuts and more.

Il Bugiardo,
Corso Porta Borsari 17, Verona.
Tel: 045 591869. Open daily, 12:00 p.m.-11:00 p.m. ★★★★★

Antica Bottega del Vino,
Via Scudo di Francia 3, Verona.
Tel: 045.800.4535, www.bottegavini.it. Open daily, 10:00 a.m.-midnight.
★★★★★

TeodoricoRe,
Piazzale Castel S. Pietro 1, Verona.
Tel: 045.834.9903, www.teodoricore.com. Open Wednesday-Monday, 12:00 p.m.-midnight. The kitchen is open 12:00 p.m.-3:00 p.m. & 7:00 p.m.-10:00 p.m. Closed Tuesday. ★★★★

Via Roma 33 Café,
Via Roma 33, Verona. Tel: 045.591.917, www.viaromacafe.it. Open daily, 8:00 a.m.-2:00 a.m. ★★★

81 Dine at One of the Two Best Seafood Restaurants in Verona

Venice may be famous for fish, but Verona, a city of foodies, stands its ground and offers visitors some seriously delicious seafood of its own. **Antica Torretta** is one of Verona's finer restaurants. It's loved by locals and tourists alike, and the chefs here use the finest ingredients—lobster, truffles, caviar, oyster, salmon—to create indulgent and mouthwatering dishes. The location, on a small and secluded square just off the famous Ponte Pietra, is wonderfully romantic and is matched by the accommodating service. Book a table outside, and open with the *millefoglie* of aubergines and buffalo mozzarella cheese, the swordfish tartar, or the thinly sliced raw beef served with an aromatic herb sauce. For your *primo*, the King crab ravioli with shellfish bisque and caramelized red onions are a good choice, as are the homemade pappardelle with a roughly chopped veal ragout. The scallop risotto, served with red pepper cream and lime, is another tasty option. For your *secondo*, try their sea bass fillet, baked in a crust of fresh fennel and potatoes, or the juicy rack of lamb, served with Sichuan pepper sauce and baked artichokes. A selection of local cheeses, delicious tiramisu or rich dark-chocolate cake, together with a good espresso, will be a perfect ending for your meal.

Somewhat lesser known, but in our opinion equally deserving, is **Pescheria I Masenini,** a serious seafood restaurant that hides away from the chaos of the center in Piazzetta Pescheria. Prices aren't cheap (but are similar to Antica Torretta – €15 for an *antipasto* or a *primo,* and around €24 for a *secondo*), but the quality is excellent and the cuisine is original, modern and tempting. Tuck into their red snapper tartar with hot pepper and candied lemon or the red mullet fillets with olives and artichokes for your *antipasti*. For your *primo*, the black ink gnocchi with lobster ragout, the spaghetti with baby eel, and the black linguine with garlic, olive oil, chili pepper, *scampi* and squid are all very good. For your *secondo*, try the delicious amberjack with almonds, honey, spinach and raspberries, the pescheria's mix of deep-fried fish and vegetables, or the spiny lobster and king prawns.

Ristorante Antica Torretta,
Piazza Broilo 1, Verona.
Tel: 045 80.15292,
www.ristoranteanticatorretta.com.
Open daily, 12:00 p.m.-3:00 p.m. & 7:15 p.m.-11:00 p.m. Reservations are recommended. ★★★★

Pescheria I Masenini,
Piazzetta Pescheria 9, Verona.
Tel: 045.929.8015,
www.imasenini.com. Open Tuesday-Saturday, 12:40 p.m.-2:00 p.m., & 7:40 p.m.-10:00 p.m.; Monday, open for dinner only. Closed Sunday. Reservations are recommended. ★★★★

82 **Buy Authentic Handmade Knives** and Kitchenware in Verona

Those who enjoy unique kitchenware will think of Verona as a little bit of heaven. There are quite a few old-fashioned shops in town, all selling distinctive items that will serve you for years and add an immediate sense of style and authenticity to any serious kitchen.

Coltelleria Fazzini Carlo, in Via Roma (half way between Piazza Bra and Castelvecchio) sells some beautiful knives, coffee makers, professional salami slicers and other items that make for one-of-a-kind souvenirs or presents. Fazzini has a second shop in Via Mazzini, which is more exclusive than the one in Via Roma and stocks some stunning items that we would proudly bring as a wedding gift, including exquisite knife sets, tiny silver-gilded salt dispensers, handcrafted wine stands and much more. This historic shop is a real threat to your wallet, so beware!

AnnaMaria, in Via Carlo Cattaneo, has a beautiful collection of tableware and other items by good mid-range and top Italian designers. They also have a little discount showroom in Via Filarmonico 10 (right next to Il Cenacolo restaurant), filled with a mix of interesting and not-so-interesting items, that is worth checking out (we once found there a splendid set of cutlery by Alessi, at half-price).

Last but not least, there's a **Bialetti** shop in Via Mazzini, if you want something cute and modern by the quintessential Italian brand.

Coltelleria Fazzini Carlo,
Via Roma 21 & Via Mazzini, Verona.
Tel: 045.800,6544,
www.fazzinicoltelleria.it. Open Tuesday-Saturday, 9:00 a.m.-12:30 p.m. & 3:00 p.m.-7:30 p.m.; Monday, open in the afternoon only. Closed Sunday.
★★★★★

Annamaria,
Via Carlo Cattaneo 14, Verona.
Tel: 045.590.687. Open Tuesday-Saturday, 9:00 a.m.-12:30 p.m. & 3:00 p.m.-7:30 p.m.; Monday, open in the afternoon only. Closed Sunday. ★★★

83 **Refresh Your Senses** with the Best Ice Cream in Verona

Savoia, in Piazza Bra, has been serving its decadent traditional ice cream for many years and has, deservedly, become known as one of the city's finest *gelaterie*. And it's not just their full-cream *gelato* that has won them renown; their wonderful, albeit slightly heavy, semifreddo desserts are every bit as delicious.

A newer but equally worthy addition to the gelato scene is **Pretto,** which is located in Piazza Erbe. The ice cream here is rich, fresh and made with the finest ingredients. It is also one of the best we've tasted. Try one of their signature flavors, such as *Il Segreto di Lorenzo,* which was created by local chefs especially for the shop. If you dare, add a generous topping of their delicious *panna montata* (whipped cream), made with milk straight from the Dolomites. For something more refreshing, try their coffee *granita*, a real energizing treat!

Savoia,
Via Roma 1b, Verona (right off Piazza Bra). Tel: 045.800.2211, www.gelateriasavoia.it. Open daily, 9:30 a.m.-9:00 p.m. May close down off-season. ★★★

Pretto,
Piazza Erbe, Verona. www.gelatopretto.it. Open Sunday-Thursday, 12:00 p.m.-10:00 p.m.; Friday-Saturday 12:00 p.m.-midnight; A second Pretto shop can be found in Corso Portva Nuova 2 (just off Piazza Bra), and has the same hours of operation. Both shops may close down off-season. ★★★

84 Dine at a Perfectly Located and Elegant Restaurant in Verona

If you've had your fill of family-style *trattorie* and are fantasizing about a fancier (but still accessible) venue, then head to **Maffei.** Refined but not pretentious, this popular restaurant is located in a private cortile off Piazza Erbe and is immediately enchanting, thanks to an easygoing sense of elegance. Prices here are quite reasonable and the food, which includes dishes such as fusili pasta with duck ragout and fresh asparagus and Monte Stravecchio cheese, is quite good.

If you can't find an opening at Maffei, or if you simply prefer a different stylish venue, try **Antico Caffè Dante.** This is a somewhat pricey restaurant that offers diners a particularly charming location, overlooking Piazza Signori. You will be impressed with their modern cuisine and presentation and with the friendly and attentive service. Their desserts, especially the *cupola di ciocolato bianco,* a white chocolate extravaganza, are perfect for sharing at the end of a romantic meal.

Ristorante Maffei,
Piazza Erbe 38. Tel: 045.801.0015, www.ristorantemaffei.it. Open daily, 12:00 p.m-2:30 p.m. & 7:00 p.m.-10:30 p.m. ★★★

Antico Caffè Dante,
Piazza dei Signori 2, Verona. Tel: 045.800.0083, www.caffedante.it. Open daily, 12:00 p.m.-2:30 p.m. & 7:30 p.m.-10:30 p.m. ★★★

Surrounding Venice and Verona

85 Drive a Ferrari!

Luxurious, sporty and flashy—the Ferrari embodies the Italian automobile industry like no other car. Enzo Ferrari, the founder, was a successful race car driver for Alfa Romeo, but he was eager to break new ground and start his own company. After a rocky start, Ferrari gained world fame when his 12-cylinder 125 S race car won the Rome Grand Prix. This was the first of over 5000 victories for Ferrari cars world-wide. The Ferrari racing team is loved by fans, and currently holds the record for the most Grand Prix victories (in the Formula One race), having won 222 times. Formula One aside, this legendary car is an icon of style even for those who aren't particularly interested in cars or races. Coming to the home of Ferrari and sitting behind the wheel of one of these flashy vehicles is a dream for many. And if you are willing to drive about 1.5 hours outside of Venice, then that dream could easily become a reality.

Ferrari has two museums near Modena. The first is more historical and is dedicated to the life of Enzo Ferrari. The second, which we recommend, is located outside Modena, in the small town of **Maranello,** and features several impressive vintage Ferraris that draw many visitors. You can even extend your visit and add a guided tour of certain parts of the Ferrari factory, and of the track where cars are tested. In the museum itself you can drive a simulator, pretending to be a Ferrari driver, but it's outside the museum that the real fun begins. By the exit (in Via Fornace) you will find 3 or 4 tour operators who will let you rent a Ferrari for 10-15 minutes, or even half an hour, and take it out for a spin. Prices charged by the various tour operators are pretty similar, so simply choose the one that interests you most, or the one that offers a model of Ferrari that you are especially keen on driving. (Representatives of the various tour operators will jump on you as soon as you park in the museum parking lot—walk around and take a look before deciding.)

End your visit with some shopping. There's a shop in the museum, of course, where you can buy Ferrari hats, jackets, and other paraphernalia. Alternatively, if you are looking for some cool gifts for kids or are passionate about model cars, visit the **Formula Uno shop** in Via Alfiero 1, about 200 meters down the street from the museum. Their selection of models is immense. If cars are your passion, you should know that in this area you will also find the Ducati museum, as well as the Lamborghini museum. Both Ducati and Lamborghini offer guided tours of their factories, in addition to a guided tour of their museum.

Ferrari Museum,
Via Dino Ferrari 43, Maranello. Tel: 0536.949.713, www.museomaranello.ferrari.com. Open daily, 9:30 a.m.-7:00 p.m. Off-season (November 1-March 31) the museum closes one hour earlier, at 6:00 p.m. ★★★★★

Formula Uno model shop,
Via Alfieri 1. Tel: 0536.941.613, www.shoppingformula1.it. Open Monday-Friday, 9:00 a.m.-6:00 p.m.; Saturday, 9:00 a.m-12:30 p.m. & 2:00 p.m.-6:30 p.m. Closed Sunday. ★★★

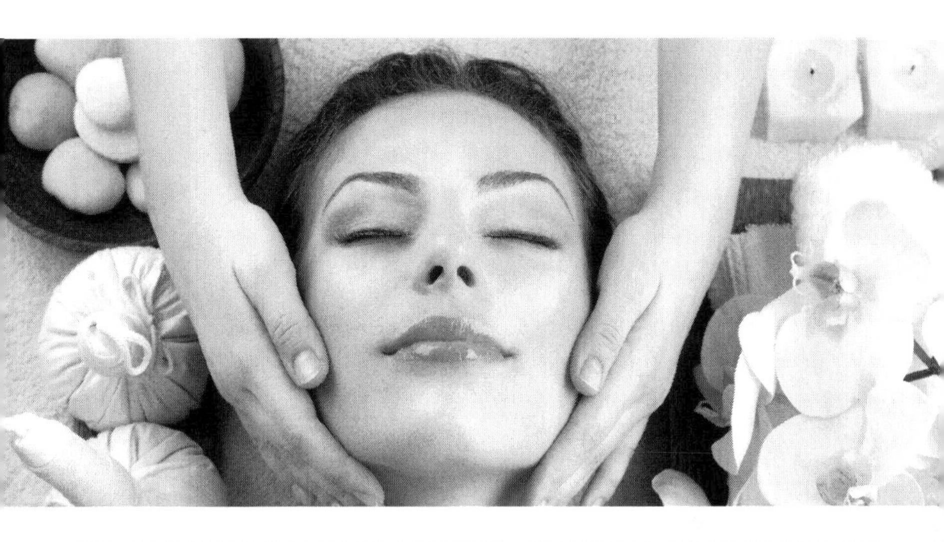

86 **Enjoy a Romantic and Relaxing Dip** at the Thermal Baths of Abano Terme

Abano Terme is a famous spa town just minutes from Padova (Padua) and just over an hour from Venice. The thermal springs attract those seeking the warmth and medicinal properties of the water or the pampering respite of the spas. Those who are familiar with the area know that Abano Terme is just one of many towns built on such springs; the whole Veneto region is famous for its thermal water and is, in fact, the largest thermal field in Europe. The city of **Abano Terme,** however, is the most celebrated city in the region. Here the thermal water, at a balmy 87°C, originates from the Dolomites, and rises up from incredible depths (sometimes as deep as 3,000 feet) to emerge at the surface.

There are several excellent options for places to stay in town. **Hotel Terme Metropole** is a 4-star hotel located at the center of Abano Terme; it's bursting with old-world charm and shows a strong Oriental influence. There are four thermal swimming pools at different temperatures, hot tubs, a sauna, and a thermal grotto. Mud therapy, Ayurveda and traditional massages, such as shiatsu and hot stone massage, are on offer, and the spa is open for non-guests, too. If you want to stay for the night, try to book the rooms that overlook their flowering garden.

For some extra pampering, try the **Abano Grand Hotel,** which is an even more luxurious option. This is a beautifully spacious 5-star venue, favored by many locals, and the perfect antidote for tired bodies in need of some TLC. Guests can book a room for a special weekend, or just come for a day spa and various treatments. Standard detox and pampering packages are available, but they are most famous for their special anti-aging treatments, combining the natural qualities of the water and biothermal clay. A team of doctors are on hand to help you find the best treatments for your specific needs.

Hotel Terme Metropole,
Via Valerio Flacco 99, Abano Terme.
Tel: 049.861.9100,
www.gbhotelsabano.it. ★★★★

Abano Grand Hotel,
Via Valerio Flacco 1, Abano Terme.
Tel: 049.824.8100,
www.gbhotelsabano.it. (The Metropole and the Grand Hotel belong to the same owners and operate under one website). ★★★★★

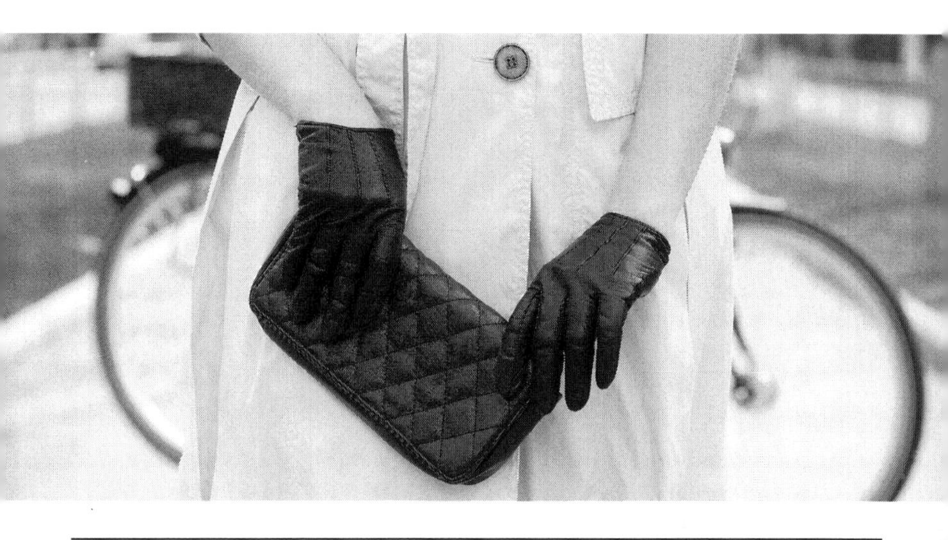

87 **Hit the Outlet Shopping Villages outside Venice and Verona** for Top Italian Fashion at Great Prices

Venice has no shortage of fine boutiques and shops, and you can find many wonderful pieces around the city (see tips 12, 33, 40, 42, for example). But if it's outlet bargains you are looking for, then you are going to have to head out of town. The first and most famous place to visit is **Noventa di Piave.** This large outlet village is just 30 minutes from Venice and has over 200 shops with the best Italian and foreign brands. Discounts of 35% to 70% are available for savvy shoppers on a range of designer brands, including Armani, Zadig & Voltaire, Boggi, Versace, Bluemarine, Guess, Jil Sander, Trussardi, Miss Sixty, Burberry, Calvin Klein, Diesel, Gucci, Sergio Rossi, and many others.

If you are nearer Verona, and are looking for an outlet village in the vicinity, the best options are either **Franciacorta** or the **Mantova Fashion District.** Both outlet villages are about an hour from Verona – Franciacorta is about an hour west of Verona, near Brescia, and the Mantova Fasion District is about one hour South of Verona, near Mantova. Both offer excellent deals on a vast array of mid-range and top brands. Additionally, there is another venue about 15 minutes from Verona called **La Grande Mela,** but unlike the previous two suggestions, this is a regular shopping mall, not an outlet village.

In addition to the aforementioned villages, there are several smaller outlet **shops** in Veneto; unlike the outlet villages, the outlet shops are much smaller and usually stock only one brand. You should also know that these shops are usually located in unappealing industrial areas that aren't always very easy to reach.

If you have your heart set on hunting for bargains in one of these shops, we suggest you skip the tiny outlet shops near Venice and focus on the shops near Vicenza, instead, as they are the more varied, better stocked, and, to be honest, the only ones worth your time. Near Vicenza you will find the **Armani** Outlet (15 minutes from Vicenza, in Montecchio Maggiore), as well as the **Sorelle Ramonda** outlet. The Armani outlet isn't bad, but unless you are already in the area, there is no reason to drive here specifically—there are Armani shops in the larger outlet villages, too. The Sorelle Ramonda outlet shop is very large, almost as large as a village, and has a nice selection of clothes from most leading Italian fashion brands, as well as housewares, shoes, and sportswear. Note that the Sorelle Ramonda outlet is divided into two separate shops: a huge shop that is dedicated to clothes is located at Viale Trieste 45, while a much smaller shop that is dedicated to shoes is located about 500 meters away, in Via Nogara (and isn't really worth your time).

Right outside Vicenza you will also find a **Bottega Veneta** outlet shop, but you should know that it is absolutely tiny, and we recommend coming here only if you are in the area and only if you are visiting during sale season (the famous *saldi* in July and January), when the discounts are serious.

Note that if you are a non-EU citizen, you can further your discount by claiming a VAT (value added tax) refund, saving you an additional 20%. Obtaining the VAT refund is actually much simpler than you might think. In every shop you go into (not just in outlet malls, but generally, in Italy), look for a tax refund sign or sticker, or ask the cashier if they provide tax refunds to non-EU citizens (all large shops, and many small shops, do). Before you pay, notify the cashier that you require a tax refund form, and then fill it in and keep a copy. When you leave Italy, go to the customs officer and show them your forms, together with your passport, and they will validate them. Then go to the tax return office with your validated forms. The money will be given to you directly or credited to your credit card.

Noventa di Piave Designer Outlet, Via Marco Polo 1, Noventa di Piave (VE). Tel: 0421.5741, InfoNoventa@McArthurGlen.com. Open daily, 10:00 a.m.-8:00 p.m. To reach the outlet, take the *autostrada* from Venice and exit at Noventa di Piave. Alternatively, use the outlet's shuttle bus service, which leaves from Venice twice a day, at 10:00 a.m. and at 2:00 p.m. (from the Tronchetto parking lot, in front of the people-mover tram). The shuttle costs €15 for a round-trip ticket. ★★★★

Franciacorta Outlet Village, Rodengo Saiano (BS). www.franciacortaoutlet.it. Open daily, 10:00 a.m.-8:00 p.m. ★★★★

Mantova Fashion District, Via M.Biagi, Località Bagnolo San Vito, Mantova (exit the autostrada at Mantova Sud). Open daily, 10:00 a.m.-8:00 p.m. www.fashiondistrict.it. ★★★★

La Grande Mela, Via Trentino 1, Lugagnano di Sona. www.lagrandemela.it. Open daily, 10:00 a.m.-8:00 p.m. ★★★

Armani outlet, Via Stazione 93, Trissino (near Montecchio Maggiore, 15 minutes from Vicenza). Tel: 0445.492.105. Open daily 10:00 a.m.-7:00 p.m. Off-season hours of operation may vary. ★★★

Sorelle Ramonda (main shop), Viale Trieste 45, Alte di Montecchio Maggiore (right outside Montecchio Maggiore itself, 15 minutes from Vicenza). Tel: 0444.491.777. www.sorelleramonda.com. Open Monday-Saturday, 10:00 a.m.-7:00 p.m. ★★★

Bottega Veneta, Viale della Scienza 9, Vicenza. Tel: 0444.965.665. Open Monday-Saturday, 10:00 a.m.-7:00 p.m. ★★★

88 Explore the Great Wine Routes of Veneto

Veneto is one of Italy's premier wine-producing regions and a pioneer in wine promotion. It was the first region in the country to have a dedicated school for wine growing and oenology, and it was one of the first to have a *strada del vino* (a wine touring route). In fact, this region's fame and reputation are second only to Tuscany. With world-famous wines like Valpolicella, Bardolino, Amarone, and Prosecco, it's not hard to see why wine enthusiasts and curious foodies flock here every year to try the goods. And even if you are not a wine connoisseur, tours of the region will allow you to take a break from the hustle and bustle of Venice in favor of some peaceful exploration of the countryside.

Since this guide is dedicated exclusively to Venice and Verona and their surroundings, reviewing the entire wine scene in Veneto would be beyond the scope of this book. Instead, we have limited ourselves to suggesting only the best, most important, and undoubtedly enjoyable vineyards and tastings in the region. Luckily, all of these recommendations can be found within an hour's drive of Venice or Verona, and can be explored as a quick day trip or as part of a more extensive tour of the region. The first wine we chose to review is Soave; in the following pages you will also find detailed tips about Prosecco (see tip 93 and 94), Valpolicella and Amarone (see tip 89), and wines from the Euganean Hills (see tip 96). Let's begin!

Soave, the crisp, light, straw-colored wine so typical of the Veneto region, is also one of the most popular whites in Italy. Soave wines are made principally with Garganega grapes (up to 30% of Pinot Grigio, Verdicchio and Chardonnay grapes may be used), and they are perfect for an afternoon *aperitivo*. These wines are surprisingly affordable—bottles from top producers cost as little as €7 to €12. Soave is the perfect accompaniment for almost any fish-based summer meal, and goes very well with several classic Venetian seafood dishes.

Begin your tour in the town of Soave, which is located halfway between Venice and Verona. Not all the producers here merit your time and money, but Pieropan and Cantina Adami certainly do.

Pieropan's fascination with wine began when Leonilo Pieropan, a physician, developed an interest in the chemistry of wine, and began experimenting with the family vineyards. Soon wine became his main occupation, and his sons, and then grandsons, continued the family business, which grew to become one of the best wineries in town and has won numerous awards. Their Soave Classico La Rocca DOC is simply one of the best we've tried, and, on an unrelated note, it is worth mentioning that they also make a fantastic Amarone – we would recommend their Amarone della Valpolicella Vigna Garzon DOC 2009 to any visitor and fellow wine lover.

Another producer worth noting is **Cantina Adami.** Their cantina is far less scenic than Pieropan's, but is very accessible, and their wines are worth a try. Tours and tastings can be organized, but are unnecessary, since there are more interesting options in the area (from a touristic point of view). Try their CimAlta Soave, which has been selected as one of the top Italian wines of 2014 by *Decanter* magazine, or their Corte Adami Soave, which is deliciously fresh.

The town of Soave aside, some of the best finds, in our opinion, hide 15 minutes away, in the much smaller town of Monteforte d'Alpone. The surrounding area is a pleasure for the eyes as much as it is for the palate – vineyard-covered hills stretch as far as the eye can see, making this little town one of the most scenic in the region. To enjoy some of the best views, take a drive from Monteforte along Via Palustrelo towards Località Ponsara. Our two favorite stops in Monteforte

are **Azienda Agricola Prà,** run by the talented and knowledgeable Graziano Prà, and the famous **Cantina di Monteforte,** the largest producer in town. A visit to the Prà winery is a special experience (that should be booked in advance). If you are looking for a more intimate and serious encounter, this would be it. A visit to the Monteforte winery is slightly easier, and doesn't require advance booking. You can just stop by and enjoy their excellent wines, such as the Soave DOC Passo Avanti 2011.

Azienda Agricola Pieropan,
Via Camuzzoni 3, Soave.
Tel: 0456.190.171, www.pieropan.it.
The wine shop on-site is open Monday-Friday, 8:00 a.m.-1:00 p.m. & 2:30 p.m.-6:00 p.m.; Saturday, 9:00 a.m.-1:00 p.m. Closed Sunday. Guided tours and tastings can be organized, cost around €15 per person, and must be booked at least a week in advance. ★★★★★

Cantina Corte Adami,
Via Circonvallazione 32, Soave.
Tel: 045.516.105, www.corteadami.it.
The small wine shop is open Monday-Friday, 9:00 a.m.-12:30 p.m. & 2:30 p.m.-6:30 p.m. Saturday and Sunday are by advance booking only. ★★★

Azienda Agricola Prà,
Via della Fontana 31, Monteforte d'Alpone. Tel: 045.761.2125, www.vinipra.it. Wine tours and tastings can be organized by advance booking. ★★★★★

Cantina Sociale di Monteforte d'Alpone,
Via XX Settembre 24, Monteforte d'Alpone. Tel: 045.7610110, www.cantinadimonteforte.it. The wine shop is open Tuesday-Saturday, 8:30 a.m.-12:30 p.m. & 2:30 p.m.-6:30 p.m.; Monday, open in the afternoon only. Closed Sunday. ★★★

89 Discover the World Famous Valpolicella and Amarone Wines

In this tip we have listed a number of fantastic Valpolicella and Amarone producers. We have intentionally included both big, well-known names and some smaller, promising new players in the field. Choosing which wine tours and tastings to pursue depends on your personal taste (and budget, naturally). But before we review our top recommended wine makers, it's important to understand a few key concepts about the Amarone and Valpolicella wines that will help you make the most of your experience.

Amarone di Valpolicella (usually simply referred to as Amarone) is the most prestigious wine produced in Veneto. It is a dominant, full-bodied, complex red, so named because it surprises the palate with a light and pleasing bitter (*amaro* in Italian) undertone. This wine is only produced in very specific areas of Veneto, and enjoys a great reputation. It is made with a mix of Corvina, Rondinella, and other permitted grape varieties. The wine-making process is specific and rigorous, involving a long desiccation period designed to remove much of the water from the grapes in order to reach a precise sugar concentration. This is followed by fermentation (during which all the sugars are fermented into alcohol, creating a very dry and potent wine), and a long aging in French or Slovenian oak barrels.

Valpolicella is a fresh, fruity, and for the most part a very drinkable red wine. It is to Veneto what Chianti is to Tuscany, and quality and style vary greatly between producers. Valpolicella DOC is produced exclusively in 19 towns in the northern part of the province of Verona. There are different categories and types of Valpolicella that take into consideration the various production processes, but the most famous are Valpolicella Classico, Valpolicella Classico Superiore (which is aged longer), and Valpolicella Ripasso (the production process includes mixing the wine with the must of the grapes used to make Amarone wine, and leaving it for 15 to 20 days to absorb some flavor and aroma from the must). In order for a wine to be considered a real Valpolicella, it must not only be produced in a specific geographic location, but it must also be made with specific percentages of authorized grape varieties. Producers who have rebelled against the "fixed recipe" are today revolutionizing the scene and creating new wines that by law can't be called "Valpolicella," but are interesting and delicious nonetheless. This is similar to what happened in Tuscany 30 years ago, when some famous producers broke with tradition and rejected the "fixed recipes" for Chianti, used new and different grape varieties, and created what is known today as the "Super-Tuscans." Another thing to note when buying your wine is the *annata* (year of production). Naturally, this is one of the most influential factors; 2014, for example, was a terrible year for Italian wine, and many producers declined to make any Amarone, citing the poor quality of the harvest. On the other hand, 2008, 2009, and 2011 were excellent years for Valpolicella and Amarone.

Those looking for a tour and tasting that combines enological excellence and contemporary architecture need look no farther than **Zýmē.** As soon as you arrive, the uniqueness of this winery becomes clear, and is reflected in the innovative ways in which Celestino Gaspari, the founder, approaches winemaking. In recent years Zýmē has become one of the best-known producers in the area, which comes as no surprise, given the origins of its founders. (Gaspari is married to Maria Rosa Quintarelli, daughter of Giuseppe Quintarelli, one of Italy's most celebrated wine producers, and worked alongside his father-in-law for many years). But attributing Gaspari's success solely to the Quintarelli influence would be a mistake, as he is today, quite clearly, an excellent wine maker in his own right.

Zýmē offers an interesting variety of wines, from classic Valpolicella and Amarone to complex, experimental wines such as the Harlequin, made with a blend of 15 different grapes. If the price tag for Harlequin seems excessive (it is currently one of the most expensive wines in Italy), know that Harlequin's younger and more affordable brother, Kairos, is an excellent choice, too, and one of our personal favorites. The tour of the state-of-the-art winery, in which every corner is planned and carries historical significance, is a pleasure (far more interesting than many other winery tours, we might add). The tour is followed by a tasting, naturally.

Just a few streets down from Zýmē you will find the friendly **Brunelli Cantina,** which is a great place to pick up a bottle or two if you are in a hurry and don't have time to book any tours or organize any tastings. Specifically, try their Amarone Campo del Titari 2010, which is very

good, and their Valpolicella Classico 2013, which was recently awarded a "best value for the money" prize by *Gambero Rosso* magazine.

Next on our list is a personal favorite: **Allegrini** makes fantastic wines and is, in our opinion, a must-visit. The Allegrinis are hardly novices in the game of wine; their ancestors have been living and working in the Valpolicella area since the 16th century. Today Allegrini is considered to be, alongside big names such as Masi, Tedeschi, Quintarelli and Dal Forno, one of the most important producers in the area. The greatest challenge here would be deciding what to buy. An obvious choice would be their excellent Amarone Classico (2008 and 2009 are particularly worth your time and money), but we suggest that you also try their award-winning La Poja 2008, which is fascinating, rich, and fresh. Guided tours and tastings can be organized, but must be booked in advance through their website.

Pieropan, which we've reviewed in tip 88, also makes a fantastic Amarone that is well worth your time and money (specifically, try 2009, 2010, and 2011).

To discover one of the lesser known yet promising producers in the area, head to **Monte Santoccio.** This smallish winery is expertly and passionately run by Niccola Ferrari, a young wine maker who is slowly building quite a reputation. Monte Santoccio's Amarone and Valpolicella Ripasso are both very good.

Alternatively, make your way to the **Accordini Estate.** For such a small family-run winery, Accordini has accrued an impressive number of reviews and awards. Situated on just four hectares of land near Negrar, not far from Lake Garda, the estate benefits from a rich southeasterly exposure that provides the perfect conditions for the fine wine they produce. We love their fruity and intense Valpolicella Classico and their intense Amarone.

The spicy, full-bodied, ruby red Valpolicella Ripasso Acinatico is also excellent.

Lastly, we cannot end this list without mentioning the two most famous and prestigious Valpolicella makers in Italy—**Quintarelli** and **Dal Forno.** Both of these historic, multiple-award-winning wineries enjoy a large group of fans (Dal Forno's 2008 Valpolicella was even named the best wine in Italy in 2014). Although visiting the estates usually isn't possible, you can still call in advance and set up an appointment if you want to buy a bottle or two (know that prices start at €100 a bottle). The easier option, of course, would be to simply enjoy their wines in one of the better local restaurants in the area that holds a serious stock. Be warned that Quintarelli's Amarone, specifically, is known as one of the priciest wines in Italy (similar to Tuscany's famous Biondi Santi Brunello), and a 1998 Amarone can easily cost over €3,000.

Zýmē,
Via Cà del Pipa, 1, Località Mattorona, San Pietro In Cariano. Tel: 045.770.1108, www.zyme.it. ★★★★★

Brunelli,
Via Cariano 10, San Pietro in Cariano. Tel: 045.770.1118, www.brunelliwine.com. The wine shop is open daily, 9:00 a.m.-7:00 p.m. ★★★

Allegrini - Villa della Torre,
Via della Torre 25, Fumane. Tel: 045.683.2060, www.allegrini.it. Guided tours and tastings can be booked through the website, or by emailing ospitalita@allegrini.it. ★★★★★

Monte Santoccio,
Santoccio 6, Fumane. Cell:349.646.1223, www.montesantoccio.it. Guided tours and tastings are available by advance booking. ★★★★

Accordini,
Loc. Camparol 10, Frazione Cavalo, Fumane. GPS: 45.56660°, 10.86889. Tel: 045.776.0138, www.accordinistefano.it. Guided tours and tastings are available by advance booking. ★★★★

Dal Forno,
(Azienda Agricola Dal Forno Romano), Località Lodoletta, Illasi (VR). Tel: 045.783.4923, www.dalfornoromano.it. ★★★★★

Quintarelli,
Via Cerè 1, Negrar. Tel: 045.750.0016. ★★★★★

90 | **Enjoy an Enticing Meal** in the Valpolicella Hills

Valpolicella is wine country. At every turn in the road a different winery appears, each as knowingly tempting as the last. When they come to Valpolicella, people often have a long list of wine stops to make, but in their haste to sample the region's famous produce they forget something equally important—food. Finding a restaurant can be challenging in these parts: Quantity may not be an issue (there is an ample selection), but quality most certainly is. However, with a little advance planning you can find some particularly delicious local food that will serve to cleanse the palate and energize the senses.

In Negrar (or right outside Negrar, to be exact), our favorite choice has to be **Trattoria Alla Ruota.** Vaulted ceilings, an intimate feel, and a seasonal menu featuring staple dishes such as *tortelli all'Amarone* and handmade pasta with truffles make this a reliable stop. Excellent locally produced cold cuts and prosciutto are all recommended. If you decide to come here don't forget to book a table in advance on the terrace, which has a panoramic view of the valley and Verona (inside seating is available too, but it isn't as pretty).

Another option is **Locanda del Bugiardo,** a favorite among locals. It's not as charming as Trattoria alla Ruota (you are seated by the road, not on a terrace with a view), but the food is well-prepared and tasty, the prices are reasonable, and the portions are generous. This restaurant belongs to the Buglioni winery, so, naturally, you'll find an ample selection of their wines here.

In San Pietro in Cariano, **Locanda Dal Nane** is a top-notch choice. Our favorites dishes include the *guancciale di vitello* (braised beef cheek), which is succulent and tender, the *brasato all'Amarone* (sliced steak served with rich Amarone sauce), and the *tagliere di salumi* (a fine selection of locally sourced prosciutto and other cold cuts).

In Fumane, **Enoteca della Valpolicella** is the best restaurant in town, and is highly recommended. Alternatively, try the very welcoming **Osteria N. 1.** Don't be intimidated by the simple setting; the food here is very good and the menu is strictly regional and seasonal, featuring several dishes that pair beautifully with the area's wines. Try the tortellini with blue cheese, the slow-cooked beef cheek topped with a generous pouring of Amarone sauce, and the *burrata* (cream filled mozzarella).

Trattoria alla Ruota,
Via Proale 6, Mazzano di Negrar.
Tel: 045.752.5605,
www.trattoriaallaruota.it. Open Wednesday-Sunday, 12:30 p.m.-2:30 p.m. & 7:30 p.m.-10:00 p.m. Closed Monday and Tuesday. Reservations are recommended. ★★★★

Locanda Dal Nane,
Via Chiesa 73, San Pietro In Cariano.
Tel: 045.770.2396, www.base.locandadalnane.it. Open Tuesday-Saturday, 12:00 p.m.-2:00 p.m. & 7:30 p.m.-10:00 p.m.; Sunday, open for lunch only. Closed Monday. ★★★

Locanda del Bugiardo,
Via Cariano, 24, Località Cariano, S.Pietro in Cariano. Tel: 0456.801.725, www.buglioni.it/locanda. Open daily, 12:30 p.m.-2:30 p.m. & 7:30 p.m.-10:30 p.m. ★★★

Enoteca della Valpolicella,
Via Osan di Sopra 45, Fumane.
Tel: 045.683.9146,
www.enotecadellavalpolicella.it. Open Tuesday-Saturday, 12:30 p.m.-2:00 p.m. & 7:30 p.m.-10:00 p.m.; Sunday, open for lunch only. Closed Monday. Reservations are recommended. ★★★★

Osteria N. 1,
Via Flaminio Pellegrini 2, Fumane.
Tel: 045.770.1375,
www.osterianumero1.com. Open Thursday-Monday, 12:00 p.m.-2:00 p.m. & 7:00 p.m.-10:00 p.m. Closed Tuesday and Wednesday. Reservations are recommended. ★★★★

91 **Get your Adrenalin Pumping** with a Jeep or Quad tour!

Quad biking isn't something most people necessarily associate with elegant Italy. But trust us—there is no better way to explore the wildness of Veneto's hills than on a quad! Adventure seekers will certainly get their dose of adrenalin on the tours we recommend here. There are a number of travel agencies and guides that operate quad tours in Veneto, and choosing the one for you depends mostly on the area you want to explore. IQuaD and Extreme Adventure are two leading operators, both offering several itineraries in the area. Those who prefer the wild views of the Dolomite foothills (recommended) shouldn't miss IQuaD's Lake Corlo tour, which will take you along some dazzling paths. Tours of the vineyards around Valdobbiadene and the hills of Asolo are also available.

IQuaD,
Cell: 333.1084580 (Corrado),
www.noleggio-iquad.it. ★★★

ExtremeAdventure,
Cell: 345.7176542,
www.extremeadventure.it. ★★★

92 **Visit the Incredible** Villa Pisani in Stra

Just half an hour from Venice (by car) hides one of the most impressive villas in northern Italy. Villa Pisani was owned, as the name suggests, by the Pisani family, an extravagantly wealthy dynasty of Venetian bankers. Constructed in 1721, this mansion was the largest residence built on Venetian territory during that century. Napoleon Bonaparte bought the villa in 1807. His defeat in 1814 brought the Habsburg family to the villa, and it continued to serve as a meeting place and vacation residence for nobles, royalty, governors and military officers. Many of Venice's *Doges* and various foreign statesmen spent their summers here. On a far less pleasant note, in 1934 the villa was chosen as the location for the first meeting between Mussolini and Hitler.

Villa Pisani is located along the Riviera del Brenta, in the town of Stra, and boasts an incredible number of rooms (144, according to a recent count, though not all can be toured), most of which were opulently decorated by the finest artists and craftsmen of the time. The property is an enormous construction by any standard—the baroque edifice marks the center of the estate, and is surrounded by 30 acres of manicured gardens, a dazzling orangery, Versailles-like reflecting pools, and a miniature forest. Inside the villa is a museum with many beautiful examples of 18th and 19th century artwork. Additionally, frequent exhibitions are held on the premises, which are worth exploring in their own right. Our favorite part, however, is the garden, especially the famous maze, a classic medieval circular path with nine concentric repeating patterns and many dead ends surrounding a small tower in the center. According to rumor, the maze is so complicated that even Napoleon couldn't find his way out!

Villa Pisani,
Via Doge Pisani 7, Stra (VE).
Tel: 049.502.074, www.villapisani.beniculturali.it. Opening hours tend to vary throughout the year, so call before your visit or check the website. At the time of this publication, the villa, gardens, and museum are open April 1 - September 30, Tuesday-Sunday, 9:00 a.m.-7:00 p.m. Closed Monday. Additionally, the labyrinth (within the garden) is closed for 45 minutes (lunch break), between 1:30 p.m. and 2:15 p.m.
★★★★★

93 **Traverse the Flowering Hills** of Valdobbiadene to Enjoy the Finest Prosecco

Of the many wines one might enjoy in Venice and its surroundings, few are as famous as Prosecco. Bubbly, fragrant and delicate, Prosecco is the base for several wonderful Italian cocktails (including the Bellini and the Spritz) and has become a regular feature at dinner parties across Europe. Prosecco wine is made in the northern part of the Veneto region, in the province of Treviso, an arable area that has long been associated with the production of fine white wines. This part of Veneto is of such natural beauty, with kilometer upon kilometer of vineyard-covered hills that stretch as far as the eye can see, charming little *borghi,* hills, streams, and striking lakes, that it is astonishing to us that so few tourists make the drive here. Hopefully this tip will manage to tickle the interest of some of our readers, and those who have the extra time and are searching for a different kind of experience in the countryside might consider making a visit.

The heart of the Prosecco area lies in the towns of Conegliano, Carpesica and Valdobbiadene, all of which can be reached in just 50-70 minutes from Venice (by car). Depending on the amount of time at your disposal, you can build a short half-day excursion or enjoy a long and leisurely full day of exploration of this area. From a touristic point of view, the most appealing sections to visit are the roads leading from **Carpesica** to **Valdobbiadene** and from **Carpesica** to **Refrontolo** (passing through **San Pietro di Feletto**). Here you will find not only excellent wineries, but also scenery that is a joy to explore. In high season there is no need to book any tastings in advance (unless you are interested in certain

specific producers); simply drive around and stop at whichever winery you find open. To help you make the most of your trip, we suggest following all or part of the itinerary provided in this tip, which will take you along the most scenic routes and to the most typical wineries and best restaurants. If you have some extra time on your hands, consider enriching your visit with a stop at one or more of the wineries reviewed in tip 94, which is dedicated specifically to the most renowned producers in this area.

Start your tour of the land of Prosecco in Carpesica (Conegliano, which is more industrial and far less appealing, can be skipped). The tiny town of Carpesica boasts two excellent Prosecco makers—**Bellenda** and **Le Vigne di Alice.** The first is known on an international scale; the second is a newer winery run exclusively by women that has recently garnered attention. Tours are theoretically available, but are unnecessary in our opinion; most visitors simply drop by to buy one of their excellent bottles and move on. The choice of Prosecco here is ample, but don't miss Le Vigne di Alice's fantastic Alice Extra-Dry, a delicate, fragrant and fruity Prosecco that we can't get enough of. From Bellenda, try the award-winning Sei Uno, an elegant Spumante prepared following the most traditional techniques.

From here, make your way to Refrontolo (passing through San Pietro a Feletto). There isn't much to see in this tiny village, but it has become a popular local tourist attraction thanks to its picturesque operating mill, perched on the side of a small waterfall and brimming with fairytale charm. If you do stop here, don't forget to sample a glass of Refrontolo Passito DOCG, the village specialty and a wine made famous by Mozart's opera, *Don Giovanni* (the Refrontolo Passito was the preferred tipple of none other than Don Giovanni himself). The best place to enjoy this fragrant red, along with some delicious Prosecco, naturally, is at the **Toffoli**

Winery, just outside the village. The friendly owners at Toffoli offer an ample selection of reasonably priced and award-winning wines; their fruity, crispy and fresh Spumante Extra-Dry Maria Millesimato 2013 is particularly good. Those who prefer a lighter, sweeter taste will enjoy the Prosecco DOCG Spumante Brut.

Then, head to Cison di Valmarino, a little village where you will be able to enjoy a particularly tasty lunch (our favorite spot in town is da Andreetta Restaurant, see below for details). The last part of the tour is also the most scenic: the drive from Cison di Valmarino to Valdobbiadene, passing specifically through Miane and Guia, two delightful little towns that enjoy an incredible position at the very heart of the Prosecco vineyards. There are numerous Prosecco producers in Miane and Guia and all the way up to Valdobbiadene. The choice of where to stop and what to taste depends on your personal preferences. Those who seek a more "rustic" experience, and would like to try wines made by the local farmers, can simply walk into any of the wineries en route; the quality is good for the most part, and prices are very reasonable.

So much wine cannot be enjoyed without food, of course. Luckily, finding a place for lunch or dinner in this area is a simple and pleasurable task. If you are near Carpesica or Vittorio Veneto, the best option is **Al Larin,** a favorite among locals. In the area's dialect, the restaurant's name means "the place of the fire," which makes sense, considering that they specialize in grilled meat dishes (such as their famous 'tomahawk steak') and fine pasta.

If you are in the Guia and Miane area, the restaurant at **Agriturismo La Rondine** is a good option. The food here is much simpler, but it is served on a terrace with a panoramic view, overlooking the endless vineyards. Near Cison di Valmarino you will find the previously mentioned **da Andreetta,** which is, in our opinion, one of the best restaurants in the entire area (and it's just 15 minutes from Miane and from Refrontolo). Da Andreetta is located in the tiny hamlet of Rolle, on the outskirts of Cison di Valmarino, and prides itself on its serious and sophisticated fare, serving delicious homemade pasta and creamy risottos to demanding clients. Be sure to call in advance and book a table on the terrace.

In Refrontolo, we enjoy eating at **Trattoria al Forno.** The owners of this small-town family-style trattoria offer a simple but tasty seasonal menu. The pasta dishes are the restaurant's forte.

In Valdobbiadene, our favorite spot is actually not a restaurant but a bar. **Bar Alpino,** located right off the main piazza, serves a small but delicious selection of *stuzzichini* (nibbles), everything from *antipasti* plates of fine cheeses and cold cuts to elaborate sandwiches. Luca and Patty, the owners, also hold a serious selection of some of the best wines in the area.

Should you be too tired to drive all the way back to Venice, **CastelBrando** (near Cison di Valmarino) is the perfect place to stay. Sleeping in this renovated 500-year-old castle that towers above the valley is quite the experience. How many other hotels offer you the chance to walk up and down ancient corridors decorated with armor and antiques on the way to your room? Prices here are surprisingly reasonable, even in high season, and the hotel is actually an active museum, too; on weekends visitors can enjoy guided tours to the ancient prison, the armory, the count's private wing, and more.

Bellenda & Le Vigne di Alice,
Via Gaetano Giardino 90, Carpesica.
GPS Coordinates: 45° 57120, 12° 17340.
Despite what is written on their website, Bellenda and Le Vigne di Alice actually operate from just one shared wine shop, which is located at the address noted above. Tel: 0438.920.025, www.bellenda.it. Open Monday-Friday, 9:00 a.m.-12:00 p.m. & 2:00 p.m.-6:00 p.m.; Saturday, 9:00 a.m.-12:00 p.m. Closed Sunday. Off-season and in August, call in advance, as the hours of operation may change. ★★★

Toffoli,
Via liberazione 26, Refrontolo.
Tel: 0438.978204, www.preoseccotoffoli.it. Open daily, 9:30 a.m.-12:30 p.m. & 3:00 p.m.-7:00 p.m. Off-season, call in advance to verify their opening hours. ★★★★

Al Larin Da Bepo,
Via dei Soldera 3, Vittorio Veneto.
Tel: 0438.561.102,
www.allarindabepo.com. Open Thursday-Tuesday, 12:00 p.m.-2:00 p.m. & 7:00 p.m.-10:00 p.m. ★★★★

Agriturismo La Rondine,
Strada Grappe 9, Guia di Valdobbiadene (TV).
Cell: 340.336.7745,
www.agriturismolarondine.net.

Ristorante Da Andreetta-Terrazza di Rolle,
Via Enotria 7 (Loc. Rolle), Cison di Valmarino. Tel: 0438.85761, www.andreetta.it. Open Friday-Tuesday, 12:30 p.m.-2:30 p.m. & 7:30 p.m.-9:30 p.m.; Thursday, open for dinner only. Closed Wednesday. ★★★★

Bar Alpino,
Via Mazzolini 14, Valdobbiadene.
Tel: 0423.982.118, www.baralpino.it. Open Monday-Saturday, 10:30 a.m.-2:30 p.m. & 5:00 p.m.-8:30 p.m.; Sunday, 10:30 a.m.-1:30 p.m. & 5:00 p.m.-8:30 p.m. Off-season, closed on Wednesday. ★★★

Trattoria al Forno,
Viale degli Alpini 15, Refrontolo.
Tel: 0438.894.496, www.alforno.it. Open Wednesday-Sunday for lunch only, 12:30 p.m.-3:00 p.m.; Friday-Sunday open for dinner only, 7:30-p.m.-10:45 p.m. Booking in advance is recommended. ★★★

Hotel CastelBrando,
Via Brandolini Brando 29, Cison di Valmarino (TV).
Tel: 0438.9761
www.hotelcastelbrando.com.

94 **Visit Some of the Most Famous** and Prestigious Prosecco Wineries in Italy

A relaxed tour along the central Prosecco route is itself a very pleasant experience. However, if you are in the mood for something on a larger scale, or if you are interested in the area's finest, internationally renowned products, don't miss the wineries reviewed in this tip.

The **Adami family** has been making some of the finest Prosecco in the area for years. Founded by Abele, then expanded by his son, Adriano, and today led by the third generation, Franco and Armando, this is a must-stop for connoisseurs. Try their Bosco di Giga Prosecco, a well-loved classic that can be found in any self-respecting *enoteca*, or the Sul Lievito Prosecco, which is suitable for those who prefer a touch of tradition in their wine. The Col Credas Brut is an innovative and award-winning Prosecco, perfect for a serious dinner party.

Equally worthy is the premium Prosecco by **Nino Franco.** Founded by Antonio Franco in 1919, this is one of the oldest and most established producers in the region. Their classic Valdobbiadene Prosecco DOCG Superiore Brut is delicious, crisp and fragrant, but our favorite bottles are the fruity and very satisfying Vignetto della Riva di San Floriano, and the soft and aromatic Grave di Stecca Brut DOCG.

A newer and more original Prosecco comes from the **de Nardo-Cantina Fasol Menin.** Silvana and Massimmo De Nardo grew up in these hills, surrounded by the Prosecco culture from a young age, but they then gravitated toward a different career in the world of business, and even moved abroad. Only years later did they decide to return to their roots and open an unusual winery that brings together excellent wine and cultural events and gatherings. Consult their website, which is constantly updated, for the full list of events. Their shop is open to the general public, but guided visits and tastings are available for groups only.

Last but not least on our list of recommendations is the exquisite **Villa di Maser** (also known as Villa Barbaro). Located south of Valdobbiadene and about one hour north of Venice, this estate is worthy, not necessarily because of the quality of its wines (which are good, but not exceptional), but because of the beauty of the villa itself and the surrounding gardens. Built by the great Andrea Palladio in the 16th century, the villa's rooms are decorated with priceless frescos and works of art by Paolo Veronese, and the vineyards, surrounded by a vast flowering garden, are enchanting. Tastings and even a light lunch can be booked in advance, and it is always worth consulting the villa's website before your visit, as they often host cultural events and *sagre* (food festivals) on the premises.

If you decide to visit Villa di Maser but want to dine somewhere else, you will be pleased to know that **Osteria Jodo,** a delicious modern restaurant, is nearby.

Adami,
Via Rovede 27, Colbertaldo di Vidor (TV). Tel: 0423.982.110, www.adamispumanti.it. Adami's wine shop is open year-round (except for the month of August), and can be visited without advance booking - Monday-Friday, 8:00 a.m.-12:00 p.m. & 2:00 p.m.-6:00 p.m.; Saturday, 9:00 a.m.-12:00 p.m. Closed Sunday. For guided tours contact the winery directly. ★★★★★

Nino Franco,
Via Garibaldi 147, Valdobbiadene. GPS Coordinates: 45.89743, 11.99090. Tel: 0423.972.051, www.ninofranco.it. The winery doesn't have a wine shop for the general public (though they do sell wine by the carton, if you are interested–6 bottles per carton). Led tastings and tours can be organized, but must be booked in advance through the winery's website, and are subject to availability. ★★★★

De Nardo - Cantina Fasol Menin,
Via Fasol Menin 22, Valdobbiadene. GPS: 45.89252, 11.98761. Tel: 0423.974.262, www.fasolmenin.com. The wine shop is open year-round (though it may close down for two weeks in August), Monday-Friday, 9:30 a.m-12:30 p.m. & 3:00 p.m.-6:00 p.m.; Saturday, usually open in the morning only (call before driving here). To book a tour and review the full list of cultural events organized by the winery, consult their website (available in English, too). ★★★★

Villa di Maser,
Via Barbaro 4, Maser, TV (the villa is actually located in Via Cornuda 7, Maser, but many GPS devices don't recognize this address). Tel: 0423.923.004, www.villadimaser.it. The villa can be visited March-October, on Tuesday, Thursday and Saturday, 10:30 a.m.-6:30 p.m.; Sunday, 11:00 a.m.-6:00 p.m. Closed Monday and Wednesday. Note that in March the villa opens and closes half an hour earlier than in April-October. The villa is also open November-February (except between December 9-January 31), weekends only, 11:00 a.m.-5:00 p.m. Hours of operation tend to vary, be sure to consult the Villa's website before planning your visit here. ★★★★★

Osteria Jodo,
Via Caldretta 152, Maser (TV). Tel: 0423.565.886, www.osteriajodo.com. Open Tuesday-Saturday, 12:30 p.m.-2:30 p.m. & 7:30 p.m.-9:30 p.m.; Sunday, open for lunch only. Closed Monday. Reservations are recommended. ★★★★

95 **Visit One of the Top Events** and Festivities in the Region

Venice is awash with glamorous events—the historic and colorful Carnival (see tip 31), the glamorous and celeb-filled Film Festival (see tip 72), and the family-oriented Il Rendentore (See tip 17) are just a few. But what about the surrounding countryside? Not to be overshadowed by their larger neighbor, the small towns and villages near the city organize their own fun-filled festivities which are well worth exploring if you have the time. Here are a few of our favorites:

The **Human Chess Game in Marostica** takes place in September, once every two years. It is, quite literally, a human chess game in which actors play the roles of king and queen, knight and pawn, to the delight of the cheering crowd.

If you are traveling to Italy in winter to participate in the famous carnival in Venice, know that **Verona** celebrates its own **carnival,** which is slightly smaller but every bit as lively and colorful and includes the crowning of the king of gnocchi (yes!). This festival has also managed to stay more of a local event, and isn't as commercialized as the one in Venice. The highlight of the festivities is a huge, colorful parade, which takes place on the last Friday before Lent, near San Zeno Church.

The **Palio dei 10 Comuni** is one of the largest, most vibrant and most colorful medieval events in Italy. It is perfect for families, naturally, but adults who are young at heart will enjoy it, too. The festival takes place every summer in Montagna (near Padvoa, and about an hour from Venice). Medieval parades and dinners, archery contests, live music and a *palio* (horse race) are just some of the activities that delight the thousands of visitors. Alternatively, visit the **Giostra della Rocca,** a much smaller but equally amusing medieval festival that takes place in Monselice (see tip 96) on the second and the third Sundays of September. This is a family-friendly event, complete with colorful parades, food markets and concerts.

Lastly, on a more gustatory note, **Vinitaly** in Verona is the largest and most important wine event in Italy. It takes place in April and draws a huge crowd of professionals and wine lovers.

In addition to these large events, there are many other smaller festivities to enjoy, everything from local *sagre* (food festivals) and *feste* (village events) to concerts and summer music festivals. Listing all of these small-town events would be impossible in the limited space available in this guide, but we highly recommend that you consult with local tourist offices to find out if there are any special activities planned during your visit. Throughout the summer there are usually several events to choose from.

The Human Chess Game in Marostica,
www.marosticascacchi.it. ★★★★

The Palio dei 10 Comuni,
www.palio10comuni.it. ★★★★

Vinitaly,
www.vinitaly.it. ★★★★

96 **Explore Ancients Villas and Majestic Gardens** along the Euganean Hills

Valpolicella may be famous, Soave is tempting, and the bubbly, vivacious Prosecco needs no introduction. But we have fallen in love with a far more subdued and laid-back part of Veneto—the Colli Euganei (Euganean hills), a beautiful slice of land that offers striking views, delicious wines, serenity and nature. Thanks to the fact that it is often overshadowed by more famous and glamorous neighboring attractions, the area is blissfully calm even in high season.

The Euganean Hills stretch southwest of Padova (Padua) and consist of about 100 hills of volcanic origin that today are covered with lush vineyards and dotted with ancient towns. Just 50 minutes from Venice (by car), this area is the perfect antidote to the stress of visiting crowded Venice. Here you will discover aging baroque villas and romantic gardens, sleepy wineries and chatty locals. Those searching for an alternative wine route will surely be pleased.

Start your day at **Villa Valsanzibio,** in **Galzignano Terme.** This 17th century villa is only open on special occasions, but the adjoining garden, designated as one of the prettiest in Italy, is open daily and is actually far more beautiful than the residence itself. Spend a few hours making your way along hidden paths and admiring the fauna, as well as the many fountains, sculptures and other little jewels this garden holds. If you are lucky enough to pass through in the spring, when the park positively bubbles with color, the villa is a must-visit.

From here, drive 10 minutes to the nearby town of **Monselice** for lunch.

Park your car at Piazza Mazzini, and head straight to **Ristorante La Torre.** Don't be put off by the dated décor; the food here is excellent. Try their homemade pasta, especially the *ravioli ripieni,* which are stuffed with delicate ricotta and wild asparagus. As it melts in your mouth, you will probably agree with us that this is one of the best ravioli plates you've tried. The meat (*carne alla bracce*) is also good, and is prepared right outside, on the grill at the entrance. The wine list rightfully focuses on local products. Try a glass (or bottle) of Monte Archino, a delicious Pinot Grigio produced by Borin winery (see description below).

Before you move on, make a stop at the aforementioned **Borin winery,** located on the outskirts of Monselice. Nothing about the unassuming exterior of this family-run winery suggests that it is a stop worth making, but Gianni, his wife Teresa, and their children Francesco and Giampaolo are actually quite well known for their top-notch yet reasonably priced reds and whites. Don't bother with a guided tour; simply stop by during their hours of operation and choose a bottle or two. Try their much-heralded Colli Euganei Rosso Zuan 2012 or their Cabarnet Sauvignon Mons Sillicis Riserva and the Colli Euganei Manzoni Bianco 2012.

If you are particularly interested in local wine production, make a quick detour and visit **Ca' Lustra Winery,** too. Founded by Franco Zanovello, this is one of the best-known producers in the area, and as such it is one that caters to the best restaurants in Padova, Venice, and their surroundings. Their mineral and complex whites and corpulent reds are all organic. Try the popular Zanovello A Cengia Moscato Secco 2013 or the Sassonero Merlot 2010. Interestingly, right above the winery there is a small and beautiful **amphitheater** overlooking the hills and vineyards. During the summer months (usually on Sundays), various shows and concerts take place there (consult Ca' Lustra's website to discover the full list of events).

Alternatively, don't miss a visit to the stunning **Vignalta** winery, a renowned producer whose tasting room is located in an antique villa (Villa dei Vescovi) overlooking the valley. This will surely be one of the more dramatic tastings on your tour.

End your day with a visit to **Arquà Petrarca,** an ancient hamlet nestled between the hills, and the birth place of the famous Italian poet Francesco Petrarca. Touring the thousand-year-old alleys of this tiny but beautiful *borgo* will be a marvelous way to relax after a wine-filled day.

If you wish to stretch your day just a little bit longer, enjoy an early dinner at Arquà Petrarca, and then drive out to **Lago della Costa** (Lake La Costa, in Località La Costa, 15 minutes from Arquà Petrarca) for a romantic stroll at sunset. This tiny lake makes for a perfect location for an evening break, especially if you can find a secluded spot to sit and relax, watching the last rays of light dancing on the water.

If driving back to Venice at this point seems unfeasible, stay for the night. **Ca' Orlogio** is one of best *agriturismi* in the area, tempting guests with beautifully decorated apartments surrounded by peace and nature. Wine enthusiasts will be happy to know that the owner of this manicured property is also a wine producer herself. Maria Gioia Rosellini was a 26-year-old mother of two when she decided to open this farm in 1995. With time, the business grew and became a well-known local point of reference.

Villa Valsanzibio,
Via Diana 2, Valsanzibio di Galzignano Terme (PD). Tel: 0499.130.042, Cell: 340.082.5844, www.valsanzibiogiardino.it. The gardens are open March-early November, Monday-Saturday, 10:00 a.m.-1:00 p.m. & 2:00 p.m.-sunset. Sunday and festivities, 10:00 a.m.-sunset. Guided tours are available (by advance booking). The villa itself can only be visited with a guided (and quite expensive) tour. ★★★★

Ristorante La Torre,
Piazza Mazzini 14. Tel: 0429.73752, www.ristorantelatorremonselice.it. Open Tuesday-Saturday, 12:30 p.m.-2:00 p.m. & 7:30 p.m.-10:00 p.m. Sunday, open for lunch only. Closed Monday. ★★★

Vini Borin (Borin Winery),
Via dei Colli 5, Monselice (Località Monticelli). Tel: 0429.74384, www.viniborin.it. Open Monday-Saturday, 9:00 a.m.-12:00 p.m. & 2:00 p.m.-6:00 p.m. Saturday, open until 5:00 p.m. Closed Sunday. ★★★

Ca' Lustra Winery,
Via San Pietro 50, Cinto Euganeo. Tel: 0429.94128, www.calustra.it. Open Monday-Saturday, 9:00 a.m-12:30 p.m. & 2:30 p.m.-6:30 p.m. Sunday, 10:00 a.m.-12:30 p.m. & 2:30 p.m.-6:30 p.m. ★★★★

Vignalta winery,
The ***cantina*** is located in Via Scalette 23, Arquà Petrarca. Tel: 0429.777.305, www.vignalta.it. Open Monday-Friday, 9:00 a.m.-12:30 p.m. & 2:30 p.m.-5:30 p.m. Vignalta's tasting rooms are located about 10 minutes away (by car), in Villa dei Vescovi, Via dei Vescovi 4, Luvigliano di Torreglia. Open Tuesday-Sunday, 10:00 a.m.-12:30 p.m. & 3:30 p.m-7:00 p.m. Closed Monday. ★★★★

Ca' Orlogio,
Via Ca' Orologio 7A, Baone (PD). Tel: 0429.50099, www.caorlogio.com. ★★★★

97 Visit an Antique Market in Veneto

Veneto's three most famous antique markets are held intermittently throughout the year. The popular market in Venice's **Campo San Maurizio** (see tip 52) takes place just a few times a year. Verona's equivalent is organized once a month in **Piazza San Zeno** (see tip 75), and the large antique market in **Piazzola sul Brenta** (30 minutes from Venice) is held on the last Sunday of the month. In all three you can find some beautiful and unique souvenirs. If you've missed these events, are still keen to explore and are willing to settle for smaller local markets, then you are in luck. Many towns in the area hold their own little events, and while these are not worth making a special trip to visit, they are fun to explore if you already happen to be in the area and have some free time on your hands. Do note, however, that many of the smaller markets suspend their activities during the summer months of July and August, so a quick check with the tourist office before setting out can be useful.

Padova, a tourist destination in its own right, holds a large market in the main piazza of Prato della Valle (right next to the parking lot at Piazza Yitzhak Rabin) on the third Sunday of the month. **Soave** (half way between Venice and Verona, see tip 88), **Este** and **Montagnana** (near Padova) all have small markets on the third Sunday of the month. **Marostica** (see tip 95) holds its market on the first Sunday of the month and **Monselice's** tiny antiques market takes place on the last Saturday of the month. **Asolo,** a delightful antique *borgo* near Treviso and near Villa di Maser (see tip 94) holds a fun market on the second Sunday of the month (except on July and August). Finally, **Vicenza,** offers its very own popular market on the second Sunday of the month, at Piazza Signori. Vicenza is known for its many Palladio-designed villas, including the world-famous Villa La Rotonda, which inspired Thomas Jefferson's Monticello, and a visit to the town's market after your historical tour can be a fun way to relax.

98 **Explore the Countryside** on a Horseback Ride

Horseback rides may seem like an adventure reserved exclusively for the experienced, but in reality it's an accessible and fun activity for all ages. In Veneto, horseback riding is quite popular, both as a sport and as a leisure activity. Those who have no previous experience can still book a tour that will be adapted to their skill levels and allow them to lazily trot through the splendid countryside. If you have some extra time, you can book a couple of introductory lessons, too, to boost your confidence.

Agriturismo Altobello, in collaboration with **Maneggio Vito Salvia,** offers guided tours for children and adults. Walks in the countryside leave from the *agriturismo* (rural B&B), which is located just 15 minutes from Verona. **B&B Paglia e Fieno,** near Vicenza, offers guided rides for beginners (including children over 14 years old), even those with no previous experience. **Da-Dolomite Adventure,** in collaboration with **Zoldo Farm,** leads rides in the beautiful natural scenery of the Dolomites. **Le Piane** guides beginners (14 years or older) on the scenic routes near Vallada Agordina, at the foot of the majestic Mount Civetta (north of Belluno, about two hours north of Venice). Lastly, **MD Ranch** rides through some beautiful trails near Lake Arsie.

All tours should be booked in advance, specifying your level of experience and any special requirements or restrictions you may have. Note that many ranches require that they be informed of any riders weighing more than 170 pounds, to match you with an adequate horse for your height and weight.

Da-Dolomites Adventure - Zoldo Farm,
Cell: 339.692.9077 (Rick),
www.dolomites-adventure.com. ★★★★

Maneggio Vito Salvia,
Tel: 0459.16810 (Call Vito between 12:00 p.m.-3:00 p.m. and 6:30 p.m.-9:00 p.m.). ★★★

Paglia e Fieno,
Cell: 335.5764.580 (Oriano),
www.bebpagliaefieno.it. ★★★

Le Piane,
Cell: 349.8763363 (Fabio),
www.le-piane.com. ★★★

MD Ranch,
Cell: 348.3050480 (Simona),
www.mdranch.jimdo.com. ★★★★

Index by subject

Hotels, B&Bs and *Agriturismi*

Restaurants and *Trattorie*

Aperitivo Bars (*Bacari*) & Ice Cream Shops

Venice

Verona

Shopping and Outlet Villages

Venice

Verona

Surrounding Venice & Verona

Wine Tastings and Tours

Surrounding Venice & Verona

Artisans & Artists

Venice

Cooking Classes, Attractions and Activities

Venice

Page 5 Petr Jilek / Shutterstock.com; page 8-Laborant/Shutterstock.com; Page 13-Ariela Bankier; page 23-Renata Sedmakova/Shutterstock.com; page 29-StevanZZ/Shutterstock.com; page 31- irynal/ Shutterstock.com; page 37- Sunny studio/Shutterstock.com; page 41- javarman/Shutterstock.com; page 42&43- ©Hotel Palazzo Stern; page 45- ©Giovanni Mozzato-Le chat qui rit; page 46- Ariela Bankier; page 48- Istvan Csak/Shutterstock.com; page 50-Ariela Bankier; page 51- ©Skyline Rooftop Bar; page 52-Ariela Bankier; page 54- ©Skyline Rooftop Bar; page 55 – ©Federico Sutera; page 57- vsl/Shutterstock.com; page 58- arturasker/Shutterstock.com; page 59- francesco de marco/Shutterstock.com; page 60- Ariela Bakier; page 62- ©Ostaria da Rioba; page 64- Chantal de Bruijne/Shutterstock.com; page 65- Malgorzata Kistryn/ Shutterstock.com; page 66- Ariela Bankier; page 67- ChiccoDodiFC/Shutterstock.com; page 68- Nejron Photo/Shutterstock.com; page 70- Masson/Shutterstock.com; page 72&73- Ariela Bankier; page 74- ©CimaRosa (photographer: Milda Bendoraityte); page 75- ©Ca' Gottardi; page 76- © Thomas Mayer; page 78- Ariela Bankier; page 80- Gargano/Shutterstock.com; page 82-Ariela Bankier; page 83- Island of Burano – Photo by ©Luca Granzini; page 84- Kondor83/shutterstock.com; page 86- Mark Sivak/Shutterstock. com; page 88- Pariyes Arunrat/Shutterstock.com; page 89-Ariela Bankier; page 91- Ariela Bankier; page 92- DavidYoung/Shutterstock.com; page 95- ©Il Bragozzo; page 97- David P. Smith/Shutterstock.com; page 99- andras_csontos/Shutterstock.com; page 101&102- ©Marc De Tollenaere; page 103- Milles Studio/ Shutterstock.com; page 104- ©Acquolina cooking school; page 105-Ariela Bankier; page 107- Ariela Bankier; page 108- Nitr/Shutterstock.com; page 109-Ariela Bankier; page 110- ©Ottica Urbani; page 111- Circumnavigation/Shutterstock.com; page 112-Ariela Bankier; page 113&114- ©Mario Bevilacqua; TL_ Studio/Shutterstock.com; page 117- ©RIVA ROSA RESTAURANT BURANO VENICE (Emilia Group SAS); page 118&119- ©Emilia Group SAS; page 120- Stokkete/Shutterstock.com; page 122- Kostiantyn Ablazov/ Shutterstock.com; page 123- Jan Faukner/Shutterstock.com; page 124- marla dawn studio/Shutterstock. com; page 126- Tania Zbrodko/Shutterstock.com; page 127- Angelo Giampiccolo/Shutterstock.com; page 129- © Michele Crosera/Teatro La Fenice; page 131- Ariela Bankier; page 132- Photosiber/Shutterstock. com; page 133- aaltair/Shutterstock.com; page 134- Ariela Bankier; pages 136&137, photos courtesy of ©The BAUERs; page 138- R.L.Hausdorf/Shutterstock.com; page 139- jurra8/Shutterstock.com; page 140- Ariela Bankier; page 141- vichie81/Shutterstock.com; pages 142&143- ©JOLLY ROGER DI LONGO ANDREA; page 144- ©Vineria all'Amarone; page 145- Jarp2/Shutterstock.com; page 146- Maksim Toome/ Shutterstock.com; page 149- photo courtesy of Venissa ©Francesco Galifi; page 150- photo courtesy of Venissa ©Mattia Mionetto; page 151- Pecold/Shutterstock.com; pages 152&153, ©Studio Matusiak; page 155- photo courtesy of ©The BAUERs; page 157- Laborant/Shutterstock.com; page 158- Ariela Bankier; page 159- Lost Mountain Studio/Shutterstock.com; page 161- Hotel Metropole ©Daniele Nalesso; page 162- gianni triggiani/Shutterstock.com; page 163- Ariela Bankier; page 164- Honza Hruby/Shutterstock. com; page 165- jurra8/Shutterstock.com; page 166- Ariela Bankier; page 168- Abate Zanetti furnace ©Diego Lazzarini; page 169- Banet/Shutterstock.com; page 170-Ariela Bankier; page 171- Martin Charles Hatch/Shutterstock.com; page 172- Ariela Bankier; page 175- Renata Sedmakova/Shutterstock.com; page 176&177- Ariela Bankier; page 178- S.Bachstroem/Shutterstock.com; page 179- HLPhoto/shutterstock.com; page 181- Progetto Quid ©Federico Sorrentino; page 182- ChiccoDodiFC/Shutterstock.com; page 183&184 - ©Agriturismo Delo Relais; page 185- FooTToo/shutterstock.com; page 186- Banauke/Shutterstock.com; page 187- ©Antica Bottega del Vino; page 189- svry/Shutterstock.com; page 190- Miguel Puga/Shutterstock. com; page 192- Paolo Bona/Shutterstock.com; page 193- Nick_Nick/Shutterstock.com; page 194- ChiccoDodiFC/Shutterstock.com; page 195 - ©Musei Ferrari; page 197- Subbotina Anna/Shutterstock.com; page 199- Daria Minaeva/Shutterstock.com; page 200- Nejron Photo/Shutterstock.com; page 202- Lukasz Szwaj/Shutterstock.com; page 203- Angelo Giampiccolo/Shutterstock.com; page 205- Shchipkova Elena/ Shutterstock.com; page 207- Zyme ©Stefano Gasparato; page 209- kuvona/Shutterstock.com; page 210- Shebeko/Shutterstock.com; page 213- ©Hotel Castelbrando.it; page 214-Ariela Bankier; page 216- ©Hotel Castelbrando.it; page 217- Dasha Petrenko/Shutterstock.com; page 219- Ariela Bankier; page 221- Paolo Bona/shutterstock.com; page 223- Ariela Bankier; page 225- Cathleen A Clapper/Shutterstock.com.

NOTES